EAST ASIAN ECONOMIC REGIONALISM

East Asian Economic Regionalism

Feasibilities and Challenges

Edited by

AHN, CHOONG YONG

Korea Institute of International Economic Policy,
KIEP, Korea

BALDWIN, RICHARD E.

Graduate Institute of International Studies,
Geneva, Switzerland

and

CHEONG, INKYO

Inha University,
Korea

Springer

A C.I.P. Catalogue record for this book is available from the Library of Congress.

ISBN-10 0-387-24330-5 (HB)
ISBN-10 0-387-24331-3 (e-book)
ISBN-13 978-0-387-24330-6 (HB)
ISBN-13 978-0-387-24331-3 (e-book)

Published by Springer,
P.O. Box 17, 3300 AA Dordrecht, The Netherlands.

www.springeronline.com

Printed on acid-free paper

Printed in the Netherlands.

Contents

Preface

CHOONG YONG AHN, RICHARD E. BALDWIN, AND INKYO CHEONG

East Asia largely ignored the proliferation of regional trade blocs and the subsequent regional integration phenomenon, despite the global wave of free trade agreements (FTAs) in the 1990s. Until recently, East Asian economies had not developed any meaningful economic cooperation schemes covering the whole region. However, in recent years, the growing interdependence in East Asia through trade and financial cooperation heightened the need for East Asian economies to engage in regional economic cooperation and integration. The Asian financial crisis triggered a rising sense of East Asian identity, and in November 1999, the ASEAN+3 (China, Japan, and Korea) Summit released the Joint Statement on East Asian Cooperation that outlined a wide range of possible areas for regional cooperation.[1]

In addition to the existing ASEAN Free Trade Agreement (AFTA), the three major Northeast Asian countries – China, Japan and Korea – recently joined the FTA bandwagon. Furthermore, the 1997 Asian Financial Crisis brought about consensus among East Asian countries for regional economic cooperation to avoid a recurrence of another regional financial crisis. The framework for financial cooperation was consolidated in May 2000 by the ASEAN+3 Chiang Mai Initiative (CMI), which involves a regional currency swap and support mechanisms.

The possibility of an East Asian FTA has been actively discussed at the ASEAN+3 Summits. The report by the East Asian Vision Group (EAVG)[2] presents a vision of an East Asia Community of Peace, Prosperity and Progress (3Ps). It also presents 22 matters of key recommendations under six divisions, which include economy, finance, politic/national security, environment/energy, and society/culture/education, and 57 matters of concrete measures. More specifically, it contains policy recommendations concerning the transformation of the ASEAN+3 Summit to an East Asian Summit, East Asian FTA (EAFTA), East Asian investment region, East Asian agreement to borrow or East Asian Monetary Fund, the organization of East Asian environmental co-operation, East Asian educational fund and so forth.

In view of East Asian economic cooperation and integration, the most attractive scheme might be the introduction of EAFTA and its institutional cooperation. Many East Asian countries are exploring the benefits in subregional or bilateral FTAs. Perhaps, EAFTA may be set as the goal of these countries regarding regional

[1] The areas for cooperation were diverse, including trade, investment, financial cooperation, technology transfers, e-commerce, agriculture, small and medium-sized businesses, tourism and the development of the Mekong river basin.

[2] The Vision Report was reported to the ASEAN+3 Summit held in Brunei Darussalam in November 2001.

economic cooperation. Also, EAFTA will be the first step in East Asian economic integration. Even though it is difficult to promote EAFTA in the near future due to differences in economic environment, political structures and conflicts over regional hegemony, it is worth investigating in the mid-to-long term basis.

This book attempts to discuss emerging economic integration efforts in East Asia with special reference to an East Asian FTA. Although economic integration is desirable economically, positions and approaches of each regional economy toward East Asian economic integration may be different depending on the circumstances of the countries concerned. This book consists of three parts; Part I contains positions of ASEAN countries towards East Asian economic integration. Part II those of China, Japan and Korea. Finally Part III provides economic assessment of EAFTA and evaluates East Asian economic integration.

Editors' Biographical Notes

Dr. Choong Yong AHN is currently the president of the Korea Institute for International Economic Policy (KIEP). At present, he also serves as the Chair of the APEC Economic Committee and is a member of the Presidential Economic Advisory Council. From 1974 until taking up his post at KIEP in January 2002, Dr. Ahn was a professor in the Department of Economics at Chung-Ang University in Seoul. Since receiving his Ph.D. from Ohio State University in 1972, Dr. Ahn has published empirical and theoretical articles on open development economics, including industrial, financial and trade aspects. He has also served as a consultant to the World Bank and as UNIDO Chief Technical Advisor to the Economic Planning Unit of Malaysia and Chairman of the Board at Chohung Bank in Korea. Dr. Ahn's received the Okita Research Award from the National Institute for Research Advancement in Japan for the book "Gendai Higashi Asia Geizairon (Modern East Asia Economy)," published by Iwanami Shoten in 2000.

Dr. Richard Edward BALDWIN is Professor of International Economics at the Graduate Institute of International Studies, Geneva as well as Co-Managing Editor of the journal Economic Policy. He has published in the areas of international trade, regionalism, European integration, economic geography, political economy and growth. He is a Research Associate at the NBER and CEPR. In 1990-1991 he was Senior Staff Economist for the President's Council of Economic Advisors in the Bush Administration, and has consulted for the EU, OECD, World Bank, EFTA, USAID and UNCTAD. Before coming to Geneva in May 1991, he was a professor at Columbia University Business School, having done his PhD in economics at MIT with Paul Krugman, an MSc at LSE with Alasdair Smith, and an first degree at the University of Wisconsin-Madison with Andre Sapir.

Dr. Inkyo CHEONG is Professor of Economics at Inha University, Incheon, Korea. He also serves as Director of Center for FTA Studies at the university. Before joining Inha University, he has been Research Fellow for eight years in Korean Institute for International Economic Policy (KIEP), Seoul, Korea. He has been instrumental in establishing the groundwork for and has been actively involved in negotiating of Korea's first FTA with Chile. He participated at all the official negations for the FTA with Chile. He has lead FTA studies on behalf of the government of Korea, in forms of internal evaluations as well as joint studies for the bilateral FTAs with Japan, Singapore, ASEAN, Mexico, the US, India etc. He advises governmental agencies and private sectors on FTA policies, as well as is working on several researches on FTA policies and regional economic cooperation in East Asia.

Contributors

Choong Yong AHN
President, Korea Institute for International Economic Policy (KIEP)
E-mail: cyahn@kiep.go.kr

John Lawrence AVILA
Program Director, Institute of Political Economy. University of Asia and the Pacific, Manila, Philippines
E-mail: javila@uap.edu.ph

Richard E. BALDWIN
Professor, Graduate Institute of International Economics, Geneva, Switzerland
E-mail: baldwin@hei.unige.ch

Termsak CHALERMPALANUPAP
Special Assistant to the Secretary-General of ASEAN
E-mail: termsak@aseansec.org

Inkyo CHEONG
Professor, Department of Economics. Inha University, Incheon, Korea
E-mail: inkyo@inha.ac.kr

Guoqiang LONG
Fellow and Deputy Director-General, Department of Foreign Economic Relations. The Development Research Center. Beijing, PRC
E-mail: longgq@drc.gov.cn

Kazuhiro IGAWA
Professor, Department of Economics. Kobe University, Kobe, Japan
E-mail: igawa@rieb.kobe-u.ac.jp

Bonggil KIM
Professor, Department of Economics. Toyama University, Toyama, Japan
E-mail: bgkim@eco.toyama-u.ac.jp

Sung-Hoon PARK
Professor, Graduate School of International Studies. Korea University, Seoul, Korea
E-mail: shpark@korea.ac.kr

Mohd Haflah PIEI
Director, International Division. Melaka State Economic Action Council, Melaka, Malaysia
E-mail: haflah@melaka.gov.my
Deddy SALEH
Director, Center for Research and Development of Foreign Trade. Ministry of

Industry and Trade, Jakarta, Indonesia
E-mail: deddy@saleh.to

Liping ZHANG
Economist, Department of Foreign Economic Relations. The Development Research Center. Beijing, PRC
E-mail: zhanglp@drc.gov.cn

List of Tables

List of Figures

Introduction and Overview

CHOONG YONG AHN

Economic regionalism has become a worldwide phenomenon. However, East Asia, Northeast Asia in particular, lags behind other major regions such as the EU and North America in terms of economic integration. The Asian financial crisis triggered a sense of East Asian regional identity. The natural response for East Asian countries toward recently rising regionalism would be the acceleration of the ongoing market-driven economic integration as well as institutional economic integration. Then the question is whether East Asia can reach an East Asian FTA (EAFTA), which is the first step of institutional economic integration.

Since 1998, political leaders of the ASEAN+3 (China, Japan and Korea) have established an annual summit, discussing economic cooperation measures in the region. The ASEAN+3 process, which started in 1997, can be an igniting source for an EAFTA. The region discusses the transformation of the ASEAN+3 summit meeting into an East Asian summit for a more enhanced institutional approach in East Asian cooperation. Then, within this framework, the idea of an EAFTA is likely to gain more momentum among member countries.

There are many obstacles, however: differences in their political systems and level of economic development as well as historical remnants and so on. But in spite of these impediments, East Asia will overcome these and pursue economic integration in order to respond to the global trend of regionalism. The EU was enlarged, encompassing ten Central and Eastern European countries and a Free Trade Area of the Americas (FTAA), which covers both North and South America, will be realized. Given the prospects of the advent of the two major blocs, East Asia recognizes the need for deeper economic integration, including an EAFTA. Then, the question is how to reach an EAFTA. All potential member countries of an EAFTA have different ideas and directions to pursue a regional free trade agreement. Another question is whether there is any way to narrow the gap between the countries in respect to their perception of an EAFTA? How can we maximize the synergy gains in creating the EAFTA?

Part I discusses the positions of Northeast Asian countries - China, Japan and Korea – on an EAFTA. Authors from China, Japan and Korea are supportive of the establishment of an EAFTA. Although they deliver different views on how to achieve it, they all agree that China, Japan and Korea, which represent 90% of the East Asian GDP, must play a leading role in forming an EAFTA.

The paper by Guoqiang LONG and Liping ZHANG from China provides an overview of the evolution of China's trade and industrial structure, a discussion of why China is now pursuing preferential trade arrangements in the region, and the prospects of an EAFTA from the perspective of China. After discussing China's both industrial and trade structure and its investment and trade relations with East Asian economies, they analyze the factors that influence changes in China's regional economic cooperation policies.

The Chinese position is quite clear. Long and Zhang advocate the merits of an ASEAN-China FTA and then ASEAN + 3 approach. But apart from this dual path through a series of bilateral FTAs, other paths can be considered, depending on the positions of the countries concerned. Kazuhiro IGAWA and Bonggil KIM in Chapter 2 and Inkyo CHEONG in Chapter 3 present prospects on how to achieve an EAFTA from the viewpoints of Japan and Korea respectively.

Igawa and Kim emphasize the path through a series of bilateral FTAs in East Asia for an EAFTA. According to them, a Korea-Japan FTA and an ASEAN-China FTA are regarded as the most important FTAs in East Asia. They go as far as to say, that there are three types of players in East Asia, Japan-Korea, ASEAN4 (Thailand, Malaysia, Indonesia, Philippines) and China. They see a Korea-Japan FTA as strategically important for Japan.

Benefits of FTAs are that the trade creation effects are larger than trade diversion effects. In a competitive market of decreasing returns, a small member country will get a larger share of the benefits than a large member country, depending on the gains from international trade arguments. Based on this reasoning, they evaluate that an FTA between China and ASEAN is not beneficial enough for China. Other benefits of FTAs come from the formation of a larger market. Monopolistic competition with increasing returns provides member countries with the benefits of scale and diversity of final products (and also of intermediate inputs), according to new (imperfect competition) trade theory. An FTA between Japan and Korea would be an example of such a case.

One interesting point they suggest is that an FTA between ASEAN and Japan (or Korea) is not beneficial enough for Japan (or Korea) in terms of market size. Also they are not supportive of FTAs with China, taking into account Chinese institutional and political risks (uncertainties).

They propose one possible strategic approach to East Asian regionalism by forming a Japan-Korea FTA first, and then concluding bilateral FTAs with ASEAN and China, taking into account the static and dynamic benefits. In conclusion, they evaluate a Japan-Korea to be the most important FTA in the region.

However, a Korea-Japan-China (CJK) FTA can be an effective starting point for economic integration in East Asia. Inkyo CHEONG in Chapter 3 suggests that the formation of a CJK FTA will be the most critical foundation for an EAFTA, regarding economic and political considerations. Although he highlights the importance of a CJK FTA, he advocates prior establishment of a Korea-Japan FTA, since Japan and China are not ready for a bilateral FTA. His paper examines the background of the recent embrace of trade agreements by China, Japan, and Korea. Discussions of a Japan-ASEAN FTA are under way, following the talks of an FTA between ASEAN and China blossomed in late 2000. China and Japan are competitively promoting bilateral FTAs with ASEAN. As discussions of an FTA with ASEAN heat up in China and Japan, Korea has also begun reviewing the economic feasibility of an FTA with ASEAN. If China, Japan, and Korea competitively pursue bilateral FTAs with ASEAN, this may result in some important issues, including spaghetti bowl effects, a hub-and-spoke dilemma, or struggles for regional leadership. Cheong argues that an East Asian FTA is most desirable in the long run. An East Asian FTA is expected to go through a long-term process because of inherent economic, political, and social obstacles. However, East Asia, which already lags behind other regions in terms of regionalism, should not passively wait for the East Asian FTA.

Positions of ASEAN countries are given in Part II. Some experts from ASEAN pointed out possible side effects due to regional economic integration might result in trade diversion and building an exclusive bloc against the world market. Nevertheless East Asia could improve regional competitiveness through an EAFTA. There is no doubt that the success of the EAFTA will produce economic development and improve the welfare of the region. To overcome the difficulties in the process, they agree to the necessity of accelerating economic reforms, gearing them into models of an open economy, and developing an innovative model, not just following existing integration models.

Termsak CHALERMPALANUPAP in Chapter 4 traces the genesis of the idea of an EAFTA to Malaysian Prime Minister Mahathir Mohamad's idea of an East Asia Economic Group (EAEG), which transformed into an East Asia Economic Caucus (EAEC) within APEC in the early 1990s. According to him, the EAEC was superseded by the emergence of the ASEAN+3 process in which ASEAN actively and increasingly engages China, Japan and Korea in a wide range of cooperation areas. And the Malaysian Prime Minister took the pride of hosting the inaugural meeting of the ASEAN+3 Summit in 1997. At the ASEAN+3 level, some concrete cooperation activities have been undertaken. The paper shows some details of the cooperation in development, trade and finance, and provides the progress of ASEAN-China FTA. Meanwhile, ASEAN is moving on with its AFTA and other liberalization schemes. The priority in ASEAN is twofold: First, four newer members, Cambodia, Laos, Myanmar and Vietnam, needs to be integrated into the ASEAN economic mainstream. Second, ASEAN needs to intensify cooperation and engagement with China, Japan and Korea bilaterally as well as multilaterally in the ASEAN+3 process.

Because of these priorities coupled with some fear of marginalization if the ASEAN+3 process is replaced by a new regional grouping in East Asia, most ASEAN members prefer a gradual evolution and step-by-step approach to all big ideas for East Asia - including the proposed EAFTA.

Deddy SALEH from Indonesia in Chapter 5 describes the dilemma that Indonesia has in pursuing FTAs. While Indonesia is well aware of the significance of FTAs as a global trend, the internal situation is not yet ready for fully embracing the open economic system. This dilemma is probably being shared by all East Asia except a few countries such as Singapore. From the South Asian countries' perspective, it is more desirable to have an FTA with Korea or Japan rather than with China, but currently China is the most active player in pursuing a free trade agreement with ASEAN. Saleh is skeptical about the success of ASEAN-China FTA because competing countries can rarely achieve great benefits from an FTA. However, according to an economic theory, competing countries gain more than complementary countries due to larger trade creation. His skepticism may be based on political considerations rather than on economic theory.

Mohd Haflah PIEI from Malaysia explains three modalities of the proposed EAFTA in Chapter 6. Since China, Japan and Korea have shallow experience in the area of free trade agreement, it would be difficult to realize a comprehensive FTA among all East Asian countries. A more realistic scenario would be a series of several individual FTAs between AFTA and the three Northeast Asian countries and then reaching an FTA of the entire East Asian countries in the long run. He presented three scenarios for introducing an EAFTA. One of them is the ultimate merging of the two FTA blocs (Japan-Korea FTA and ASEAN-China FTA) into one large regional bloc (EAFTA). Another option Piei suggests in his paper is AFTA's individual negotiations with the three countries in Northeast Asia, respectively. Currently, China, Japan and Korea are trying to establish separate bilateral FTAs with AFTA. Then the next issue is how to achieve an EAFTA after the three FTAs in East Asia.

John Lawrence AVILA from Philippines presents possible benefits from an EAFTA in his paper. His paper in Chapter 7 provides a brief overview on East Asian regionalism and then, underlines the central role of ASEAN in the process of regional economic integration in East Asia. Discussing the wide coverage of economic cooperation measures in recent FTAs, he suggests that East Asia can introduce a very comprehensive FTA, contributing to the development of the multilateral trade system of the WTO and regional cooperation mechanisms such as APEC. Yet it is not sufficient to persuade people and governments of the member countries involved on the necessity of a regional trade arrangement. The paper concludes with an evaluation of the prospects of the EAFTA.

Part III provides the numerical estimation of economic impacts of various FTAs in East Asia, and evaluation of an EAFTA from the viewpoints of non-East Asian countries. In Chapter 8, Inkyo CHEONG estimates the economic impacts of possible FTAs in East Asia, using an economic model. It is estimated that capital accumulation effects rather than trade liberalization effects under an FTA with Japan would generate greater benefits. Under Northeast Asian free trade arrangement, Korea is expected to gain relatively more economic benefits compared to China or Japan. According to the estimation, China is found to be a more suitable FTA partner to both Japan and Korea. In other words, both Japan and Korea will gain more benefits by forming an FTA with China rather than concluding a bilateral FTA with each other. An East Asian FTA will bring more economic benefits to all member countries compared to a China-Japan-Korea FTA.

Richard E. BALDWIN's paper argues that East Asia regionalism will shift from talk to action – resulting in a rapid spread of preferential arrangements – provided that at least one major FTA gets signed. He predicts that the Korea-Japan FTA currently under negotiation may well be the trigger. The arguments supporting this assertion are based both on historical analogy and political economic reasoning. In the Americas and Europe, the 1990s witnessed waves of regionalism trigger by single idiosyncratic events of preferential liberalization - the US-Mexico FTA in North America and the European Union's Single Market programme. The paper argues that the 'domino theory' is the political economic logic behind the waves of regionalism. To put another way, trade and investment diversion created by a preferential trade arrangement among a nation's trade partner tends to stimulate extra political pressure within the nation to redress the discrimination. Since signing a new FTA is the easiest way to redress the discrimination, one FTA tends to encourage others. Moreover, the paper argues that the 'force for inclusion' and the cost of exclusion gets stronger as more FTAs are signed, so the spread of FTAs can be quite rapid.

Baldwin's paper also argues that such regionalism is likely to foster multilateral liberalization in Asia as well. Again his argument is based on both history and logic. Historically, three of the greatest proponents of multilateralism - the US, Canada and Western Europe - have simultaneously pursued preferential arrangements. Moreover nations, like the Andean nations, which failed in their preferential liberalizations, have also typically failed to open up multilaterally. The paper argues that this is due to fact that liberalization tends to strengthen pro-trade forces and weakens anti-trade ones.

Finally the paper points out a number of pitfalls that East Asian regionalism might encounter. First, there is a danger that Asian regionalism might take the form of 'hub-and-spoke' bilateralism. That is, a string of bilateral FTAs with big market economies such as Japan. This tends to favor production in the centre, or hub economy, at the expense of the 'spokes'. To avoid this, the FTAs should be 'multilateralised' either by a network of bilateral FTAs among the spokes, or by adopting an institutional arrangement like that of the European Free Trade Association (the group of non-EU nations in Western Europe). The paper also argues that preferential liberalization between large and small nations pose the risk of industrial delocation. To counter this, the paper suggest asymmetric phase out of tariffs. That is, in implementing an FTA, both partners should go to zero tariffs in a reasonable period (say, 10 years) but large nations should maintain lower barriers during the transition period.

The paper by Sung-Hoon PARK discusses the evaluation of EU on East Asian regionalism. His paper argues that regionalism should be compatible with the multilateral trading system in order to make sure that the former does not have potential conflicts with the latter. Park points out that the idea of the EAEG and EAEC faced strong resistance from the US. So, it would be hard for those countries to neglect the US interests in promoting deeper regional integration, since East Asian countries have depended on the US economy as a major export market.

He also emphasizes the US' strong political security concerns in East Asia. The EU acknowledges the unique and predominant role of the US in East Asia, and therefore focuses more strongly on the economic relationship than political and security cooperation. In case East Asian countries succeed in establishing a region-wide FTA, the EU will be more concerned with developing economically strong relations with East Asia. He presents some evidences for his argument with reports such as the EU's New Asia Strategy and the Asia-Europe Vision Group (AEVG). He predicts that an Asia-Europe FTA proposed by the EAVG in 1996 would be possible in the long run.

Over the past two decades, regionalism has changed dramatically to involve more countries on a global scale. The biggest policy shift toward regionalism has occurred in East Asia, where until recently China, Japan, and Korea had fully abstained from regional trade arrangements. Ahn and Cheong (2004) and Schott (2004) offered several factors to explain newly emerging interest in regionalism in East Asia: the rapid integration of China into the regional economy to create new opportunities for trade and investment, the Asian Financial Crisis of 1997-1998, and Korea-Japan FTA negotiations.

Given the diversity of Asian economics and differential motivations of key players in shaping East Asian regionalism, it might be difficult for countries in East Asia to reach a regional trade pact in the near future. At present, economies in East Asia are in full agreement that lowering international trade barriers expands trade among partner countries and encourages economies of scale of production together with inter- and inter- industry specialization. In this context, countries in East Asia and China, Japan, and Korea in particular, should maximize the potential benefits of FTAs while minimizing negative effects of preferential regional trade arrangements. FTA partners in East Asia should commit to harmonizing and lowering trade barriers so that there is complementarity in regional and multilateral liberalization and reform efforts. Like the EU and FTA movement, East Asia economies should also work together towards building an "East Asian Economic Community" consistent with WTO principles in the years to come. Obviously, regional political leadership in making the current ASEAN+3 framework to a more viable institutional setup appears to be critical to a long march toward "East Asian Economic Community" as an important building block toward a viable WTO.

REFERENCES

Ahn, C. Y. 2001. "A Search for Robust East Asian Development Models after the Financial Crisis: Mutual Learning from East Asian Experiences," *Journal of Asian Economics*, 12(3), North-Holland.

Ahn, C. Y. and I. Cheong. 2004. "East Asian Economic Cooperation and Integration: Korea's Perspectives." Korea Institute for International Economic Policy. *Mimeo*.

Cheong. I. 2002. "East Asian Economic Integration: Recent Development of FTAs and Policy Implications." KIEP Research Paper. Seoul: KIEP.

Eichengreen, Barry. 2003. "What to Do with the Chiang Mai Initiative," *Asian Economic Papers*, 2(1), pp.1-49.

Schott, J. J. 2004. "Free Trade Agreements: Boon or Bane of the World Trading System?" in *Free Trade Agreements: US Strategies and Priorities*. J. J. Schott. Institute for International Economics, Washington D.C., p. 6.

Wanandi, Jusof. 2000. "East Asian Institution Building," remarks made at the 2000 annual meeting of the Trilateral Commission in Tokyo. [www.trilateral.org]

Part I: Northeast Asian Views on an EAFTA

CHAPTER 1

CHINA'S APPROACH TO AN INSTITUTIONAL REGIONAL ARRANGEMENT

GUOQIANG LONG and LIPING ZHANG

CHAPTER 2

EAST ASIAN FREE TRADE AGREEMENT: STRATEGIC ASPECTS FOR JAPAN

KAZUHIRO IGAWA and BONGGIL KIM

CHAPTER 3

EVALUATION OF RECENT PROGRESS OF FTAS IN EAST ASIA – A KOREAN PERSPECTIVE

INKYO CHEONG

CHAPTER 1

CHINA'S APPROACH TO AN INSTITUTIONAL REGIONAL ARRANGEMENT

GUOQIANG LONG and LIPING ZHANG

1. INTRODUCTION

In the first year for the new century, two historic economic events made China the focus of global economic observers. The first event was China's accession to the World Trade Organization (WTO) on November 2001 after 15 years of negotiations. Within one month, the world again was impressed by an announcement during the "10+1" summit in 2001 that ASEAN and China would establish a Free Trade Area (FTA) before 2010.

China had been known as an advocate of open regionalism. After joining the Asia Pacific Economic Cooperation (APEC) in 1991, China has carried out trade and investment liberalization under a framework of open regionalism. The establishment of an FTA with ASEAN is an important event not only to China itself, but also to the East Asian region. Does the ASEAN-China FTA indicate a shift of China's regional economic policy from open regionalism to FTAs? What will be the implications for the prospects of East Asian regional economic cooperation?

This paper will analyze reasons for the evolvement of China's regional policy and probe into the prospects of an East Asian FTA from the perspective of China. The section following the introduction will review the evolution of China's industrial and trade structure; and analyze China's investment and trade relations with East Asian economies. The third section will analyze the factors that influence the shift in China's regional economic cooperation policies. The fourth section will analyze the factors impacting the prospects for an East Asian FTA and the last section will be the conclusion.

2. EVOLUTION OF CHINA'S INDUSTRIAL STRUCTURE AND TRADE STRUCTURE

2.1. Development of China's Industrial Structure

Since the reform and opening policies were launched in 1979, China's industrial structure has experienced remarkable changes, which have been reflected in the following three aspects:

C. Y. Ahn et al (eds.), East Asian Economic Regionalism, 1-19.

Firstly, the proportion of the primary industry in GDP has continuously shrunk, with the exception of a few years. The proportion of the primary sector was 31.2% in 1979, and by the year 2000, this figure had almost halved to 15.9%.

Secondly, the proportion of the secondary industry tended to decline in the 1980s, but shifted upwards in the 1990s. No matter what its tendency, the secondary industry has always been of the first importance in the national economy. In the year 2000, the proportion of the secondary industry exceeded 50%.

Thirdly, as far as the tertiary industry is concerned, its proportion in GDP has continued to increase, with the exception of 1992 to 1995, to reach 33.2% in 2000. Its proportion has surpassed that of the primary industry since 1986. (See Figure 1 and Table 1.)

Comparing those economies with similar levels of development across the world, the proportion of the secondary industry in China is 10-20% higher, while the proportion of the tertiary industry is 10-20% lower. Such an industrial structure reveals that China is in the process of industrialization.

Figure1. Structure of China's GDP

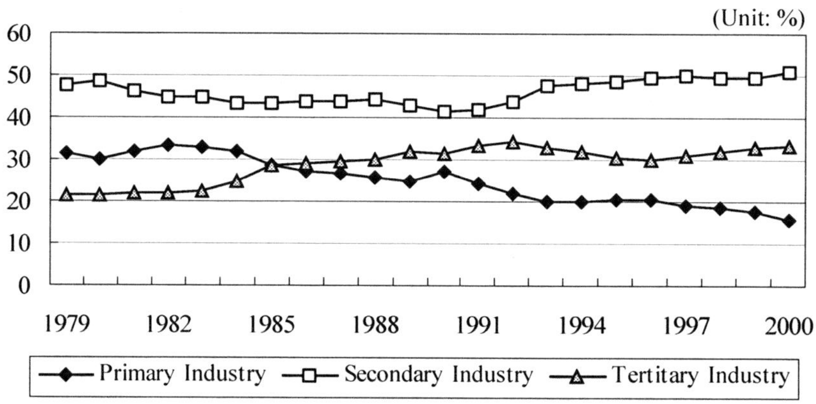

Table 1. Structure of China's GDP

(Unit: %)

Year	Primary Industry	Secondary Industry	Tertiary Industry
1979	31.2	47.4	21.4
1986	27.1	44	28.9
1990	27.1	41.6	31.3
1992	21.8	43.9	34.3
1995	20.5	48.8	30.7
1998	18.6	49.3	32.1
2000	15.9	50.9	33.2

Note: Calculations are based on the prices of the respective years.

Manufacturing has been the most important sector in the economy, accounting for 86% of the value added in the secondary industry in 2000 (Figure 2). The rapid growth of China's manufacturing industry may be attributed to several factors that include domestic and foreign direct investments, the development of township enterprises, foreign trade, and technological progress as well as institutional renovation. Foreign direct investment (FDI) has played an important role in the development of the manufacturing industry in China. The FDI in China has cumulated more than US$390 billion as of the year 2001, about 60% of which was invested in manufacturing sectors. Most FDI projects are export-oriented and this has greatly spurred on China's export of manufactured products. From 1980 to 2000, the export of manufactured products has increased at an average rate of 16.5% annually, nearly 2 percentage points higher than the average growth rate of exports as a whole over the same period. Foreign invested enterprises provided 51% of total exports in 2001.

Figure 2. 1979-2000 Changes of Internal Structure of the Secondary

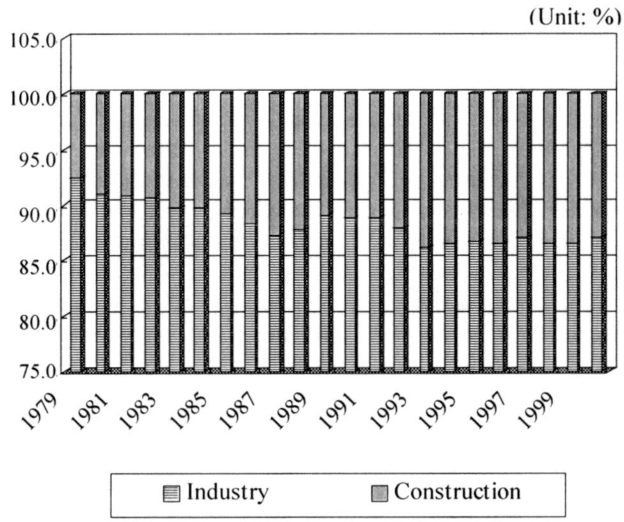

2.2. Development of China's Foreign Trade

2.2.1. Rapid growth of China's foreign trade

China has pursued an opening-up policy and devoted major efforts to developing foreign trade since 1979. Accordingly, China's achievements in the field of foreign trade have drawn the attention of the world. The volume of foreign trade increased by 24-fold during 1978 to 2001. The average annual growth rate of imports and exports was as high as 14.96% during the period from 1978 to 2001, in which exports rose by 15.46% annually on average and imports by 14.47% (see Figure 3). China's ranking in terms of foreign trade in the global trade system also improved from 32nd in 1978 to 6th in 2001. The rapid growth of foreign trade has greatly contributed to accelerating the development of the Chinese economy.

Figure 3. Development of Foreign Trade by China (1979-2001)

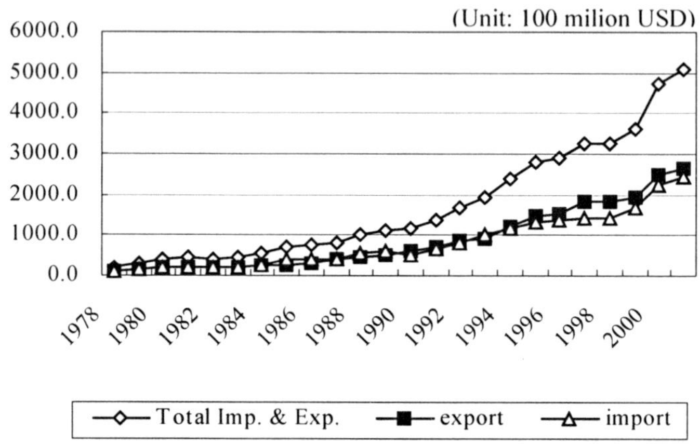

The basic reason for the rapid growth of foreign trade was processing trade export, of which 73.3% was conducted by foreign invested enterprises. Since the late 1980s, China has benefited from industrial restructuring and relocating activities of neighboring economies from which huge numbers of labor-intensive activities have moved into China. Most of the foreign investment enterprises have been export-oriented, and after moving to China, they continue to export their products to their traditional market, mainly the U.S., while importing inputs from their original sources. This trade pattern, known as processing trade has played an important role in the development of China's foreign trade. Processing trade exports have grown by 27.9% annually during 1985-2000, which is 17.5 percentage points higher than ordinary exports. As a result, the share of processing exports in total exports increased from 12.5% in 1985 to 55.2% in 2000. And meanwhile, the share of processing imports increased from 9.7% to 41.1%. The contribution of processing exports to total export is as high as 60.5% for the 1985-2000 period.

2.2.2. Changes of China's export mix

Since 1980, exports of Chinese manufactured products have enjoyed continuous and rapid growth, while exports of primary products have declined. Table 2 shows that the proportion of manufactured products to total exports rose from 49.7% in 1980 to 89.8% in 2000, to exceed the export of primary products by a big margin. In the year 2000 primary products accounted for a mere 10.2% of total exports.

As far as the export of manufactured products is concerned, product upgrading has become an evident phenomenon. The export of machinery and transportation equipment increased faster than any other category. As a result, the share of machinery and transportation equipment increased from 9.4% in 1980 to 36.9% in 2000. The shares of chemicals and relevant products, textiles and other light industrial goods, rubber, minerals, and metallurgical goods as well as miscellaneous and unclassified manufactured products generally tended to decrease. And the most serious decrease (25.4%) was found in the export of products of the material industry, such as textiles, rubber, mineral products, and metallurgical goods as well as manufactured products based on them. The increase in the share of machinery and transportation equipment, which are capital and technology-intensive products, in total exports, reflects a continuous upgrading of China's export mix.

Table 2. Changes in China's Export Mix

(Unit: %)

	Primary Products	Manufactured Products	Chemicals	Textiles, other light industry goods, rubber, minerals, metallurgical goods as well as manufactured products based on them	Machinery and transporting equipment	Miscellaneous and unclassified manufactured products
1980	50.3	49.7	12.4	44.4	9.4	33.8
1983	43.3	56.7	9.9	34.6	9.7	45.8
1985	50.6	49.4	10.0	33.2	5.7	51.0
1986	36.4	63.6	8.8	29.9	5.6	55.7
1990	25.6	74.4	8.1	27.2	12.1	52.6
1995	14.4	85.6	7.1	25.3	24.7	42.9
1996	14.5	85.5	6.9	22.1	27.3	43.7
1997	13.1	86.9	6.4	21.7	27.5	44.4
1998	11.2	88.8	6.3	19.9	30.8	43.0
1999	10.2	89.8	5.9	19.0	33.6	41.4
2000	10.2	89.8	5.4	19.0	36.9	38.7

Source: China Statistics Yearbook, various years

2.2.3. Changes in China's import mix

The change of China's import mix is much less marked than that of exports. The proportion of manufactured products in imports generally stabilized at around 80% in spite of some fluctuations after 1985. Machinery and transporting equipment have always held the biggest share in the import of manufactured products, and the proportion generally remained between 37% and 43% in the 1990s. As processing trade exports grew to account for more than half of total exports, more and more manufacture goods had to be imported as inputs for processing.

The share of manufactured products in the import mix was seriously influenced by the domestic business cycles, which was the main cause of the fluctuations in the import mix. Whenever there was an investment boom, which has been the main locomotive in the Chinese economy, the import of machinery and transportation equipment jumped, pushing up their shares in the import mix. From the data shown in Table 3, we can easily see that the shares of machinery and transportation equipment jumped sharply in 1985, 1993, and 1998 as result of the domestic investment boom.

Table 3. Changes in China's Import Mix

(Unit: %)

	Primary Products	Manufactured Products	Chemicals	Textiles, other light industry goods, rubber, minerals, metallurgical goods as well as manufactured products based on them	Machinery and transporting equipment	Miscellaneous and unclassified manufactured products
1980	34.8	65.2	14.5	20.8	25.6	4.4
1985	12.5	87.5	10.6	28.2	38.4	10.3
1990	18.5	81.5	12.5	16.7	31.6	20.8
1993	13.7	86.3	9.3	27.4	43.3	6.2
1995	18.5	81.5	13.1	21.8	39.9	6.8
1996	18.3	81.7	13.0	22.6	39.4	6.6
1997	20.1	79.9	13.6	22.6	37.1	6.6
1998	16.4	83.6	14.4	22.2	40.5	6.6
1999	16.2	83.8	14.5	20.7	41.9	6.7
2000	20.8	79.2	13.4	18.6	40.8	6.4

Source: China Statistics Yearbook, various years.

2.2.4. Changes in the modes of foreign trade

In China, ordinary trade and processing trade are the two main modes of foreign trade and account for more than 82% of total foreign trade, and 97% of exports. Other trade modes, including compensation dealing[1] and barter trade,[2] etc. hold relatively smaller shares in terms of trade volume. The ratio between ordinary trade and processing trade has undergone significant changes over the past two decades in spite of their stable proportion as a whole in total imports and exports. In the 1980s and first half of the 1990s, the proportion of ordinary trade in foreign trade tended to decline sharply and in 1996 the figure hit a low of 35.3%, dropping by 58.2

[1] Compensation trade is trade in which Chinese companies either receives or import by foreign export credit machinery or technology from foreign companies, and then sell their products to those foreign companies as payment for the machinery or technology or the loan.

[2] Barter trade is trade in which Chinese companies trade goods directly with foreign counterparts without using currency.

percentage points compared with 93.5% in 1981. In contrast, the proportion of processing trade rose by a big margin over the same period and exceeded that of ordinary trade after 1993. By 1998 processing trade had increased by 48 percentage points from 1981 to account for more than 53.4% of China's foreign trade volume. Afterward, the proportion of processing trade began to decline and in 2001 the proportion of processing trade in foreign trade was 47.3% (see Table 4). The main reason for the sharp fall in the share of processing trade in total trade volume is the increase of the local content ratio of processing exports. The ratio of processing imports to total imports dropped more than 10 percentage points from 48.9% in 1998 to 38.6% in 2001, while the ratio of processing exports to total exports dropped only 1.4 percentage points from 56.8% to 55.4%.

Table 4. Changes in the Modes of China's Foreign Trade

(Unit: %)

Year	Ordinary Trade	Processing Trade			Total
		Overall	Processing with components provided by foreign clients	Processing with imported materials	
1981	93.5	5.6	4.4	1.2	99.2
1986	81.7	16.7	10.8	5.9	98.4
1993	41.5	41.2	14.8	26.4	82.7
1996	35.3	50.6	14.5	36.1	85.8
1997	36.0	52.2	15.5	36.7	88.2
1998	36.4	53.4	15.6	37.8	89.8
1999	40.5	51.1	16.5	34.7	91.7
2000	43.3	48.5	14.6	34.0	91.8
2001	44.2	47.3	13.9	33.4	91.6

Source: China Custom Statistics Yearbook, various years.

China's policies on processing trade and FDI have greatly promoted the development of processing trade. In the past, the Chinese domestic market was highly protected by high tariff and non-tariff barriers. These trade barriers distorted the prices of imported goods and encumbered the development of processing trade, although China had comparative advantages for processing trade in terms of a cheap and well-trained labor force, cheap land and complete industrial system. Since the initial stage of reform and opening measures, the Chinese government has adopted preferential policies to encourage the development of processing trade as it could satisfactorily solve the problem of the foreign exchange shortage, provide more employment opportunities, introduce advanced production technologies and management expertise, increase exports and consequently promote China's economic development and industrialization. The basic policy is to offer exemptions from tariffs and value-added taxes (VAT) on imported inputs for re-export processing activities. This means that about 40% of China's imports are exempted from tariffs and VATs. Meanwhile, China also has provided preferential treatments such as exemptions from tariffs and VATs on imported machinery, income tax cuts, and so on to foreign invested enterprises (FIEs). China had been the second biggest receiver of FDI in the world from 1993 to 2001 and will rank first in 2002. As a very big share of the FIEs in China are export-oriented and aiming to take advantage of cheaper production factors in China. The boom of FDI has also contributed greatly to the development of processing trade. The share of FDI in processing trade jumped from 28.8% in 1990 to 73.3% in 2001. Consequently, the processing trade in China grew rapidly before the mid-1990s by taking advantage of the adjustment in the international division of labor. In 1995 the Chinese government launched measures to straighten out the foreign trade order, crack down on smuggling and strengthen the supervision of processing trade, which affected the development of processing trade to some extent. As a result, the growth rate of processing trade slowed down.

2.3. Economic Links between China and Other East Asian Economies

2.3.1. Investment relationship with other east asian economies

China and other East Asian economies (OEAE) have formed a close link in terms of investment. China is a receiver of foreign direct investment rather than a source in the East Asia region. East Asia as a whole has been the most important source of foreign investment for China. Around 74% and 69% of foreign direct investment (FDI) absorbed by China came from this region in 1999 and 2000, respectively.

Hong Kong has been the biggest source of FDI to China. The proportion of FDI to China flowing in from Hong Kong is 40.58% and 38.07% in 1999 and 2000, respectively. ASEAN ranked second in terms of investment in China in 1999 with its share of 8.16%, much lower than that of Hong Kong. In 2000, ASEAN ranked third with its share dropping dramatically to 6.99%, lower than that of Japan (7.16%). In ASEAN, Singapore has been the biggest FDI source for China, and the reduced proportion of FDI contributed by the country served as the main reason for the decreasing share of FDI from ASEAN. In 2000, the share dropped to 5.34% from 8.16% in the previous year.

Taiwan is a very important source of FDI for Mainland China. It is thought that the official data of FDI from Taiwan was under-valued because a very big proportion of Taiwan's FDI to the Mainland is directed through a third location, such as Hong Kong, Virgin Islands, etc., to escape the restrictions imposed by the Taiwanese authorities. The official data indicates that cumulated FDI from Taiwan is about US$30 billion. According to some estimates, the real figure of Taiwanese investment in the Mainland is two to three times higher than the official figure. A large portion of the Taiwanese investments is in the information industry, which makes the Mainland one of the most important exporters of IT products in the world.

2.3.2. Trade relationship with other east asian economies

China has maintained close trade links with OEAEs. In 2000, more than 59% of

China's imports and exports were realized in East Asia (see Table 6). Japan and Hong Kong were the largest trade partners of China. The trade between China and Japan accounted for 17.53% of China's foreign trade in 2000, while the trade between Mainland China and Hong Kong accounted for 11.37% of China's foreign trade. As far as exports were concerned, exports to Hong Kong ranked first with a proportion of 17.86% in 2000. However, imports from Hong Kong held a very small share of total imports, lower than both the shares of Taiwan (around 11%) and Korea (around 10%). ASEAN as a whole ranked third in East Asia in terms of the proportion in China's foreign trade, but each individual country in ASEAN held a very limited share; Singapore, China's largest trade partner in ASEAN, accounted for less than 2.4%.

Table 5. Proportion of Investment from East Asian Countries/Regions in Total Foreign Investment attracted by China

(Unit: %)

Country/Region	1999		2000	
	FDI	Foreign Investment in Other Forms	FDI	Foreign Investment in Other Forms
Japan	**7.37**	**4.25**	**7.16**	**1.68**
Korea	**3.16**	**0.26**	**3.66**	**0.13**
ASEAN	**8.16**	**0.002**	**6.99**	**0.005**
Singapore	6.55	0.001	5.34	0.005
Malaysia	0.59	0.001	0.50	——
Indonesia	0.32	——	0.36	——
Thailand	0.37	——	0.50	0.0002
Philippine	0.29	——	0.27	——
Vietnam	0.001	——	0.001	——
Burma	0.03	——	0.01	——
Cambodia	0.01	——	0.005	——
Laos	——	——	——	——
Brunei	0.0004	——	——	——
Hong Kong	**40.58**	**48.83**	**38.07**	**14.23**
Macao	**0.77**	**1.37**	**0.85**	**0.41**
Taiwan	**6.45**	**7.51**	**5.64**	**2.78**
Total	**74.64**	**62.23**	**69.36**	**19.23**

Source: MOFTEC

In view of the fact that trade with East Asian economies accounted for more than 50% of China's imports and exports, the economic development and the trend of foreign exchange rates in that area can exert a very important influence on China's foreign trade. As the East Asian economies have shaken off the negative influence of the financial crisis which broke out in 1997 with their economies recovering at a relatively fast pace, the trade between China and these countries enjoyed rapid growth in 2000, compared to 1999. However the growth rate of the trade between China and Japan was at a relatively low level due to Japan's failure to recover from its economic difficulties.

The FDI from other East Asian economies to China played a very important role in enhancing the trade relationship between China and the OEAEs. After the OEAEs moved their processing enterprises to China, the companies in the upper levels of their production chain became suppliers of inputs to these enterprises in China.

Because the traditional market of these enterprises was the US, China's exports to the US have increased sharply while the shares of the OEAE in the US market dropped, accordingly. The total market share of East Asia in the US has remained almost the same over the past twenty years. The triangle relationship among China, OEAEs and the US has changed as a result of FDI from OEAEs to China: China became an important exporter to the US market by importing huge volume inputs from OEAEs. As a result, most OEAEs run huge trade surpluses with China.

Table 6. Proportion of Import and Export between China and East Asian Countries/Regions in China's Foreign Trade

(Unit: %)

	1999			2000		
Country / Region	Import & Export	Export	Import	Import & Export	Export	Import
Japan	18.35	16.63	20.38	17.53	16.72	18.44
Korea	6.94	4.01	10.40	7.27	4.53	10.31
ASEAN	7.522	6.254	9.01	8.33	6.96	9.853
Singapore	2.37	2.31	2.45	2.28	2.31	2.25
Malaysia	1.46	0.86	2.18	1.70	1.03	2.43
Indonesia	1.34	0.91	1.84	1.57	1.23	1.96
Thailand	1.17	0.74	1.68	1.40	0.90	1.95
Philippine	0.63	0.71	0.55	0.66	0.59	0.75
Vietnam	0.34	0.44	0.21	0.52	0.62	0.41
Burma	0.14	0.21	0.06	0.13	0.20	0.06
Cambodia	0.04	0.05	0.03	0.05	0.07	0.03
Laos	0.01	0.01	0.01	0.01	0.01	0.003
Brunei	0.002	0.004	——	0.02	0.01	0.03
Hong Kong	12.13	18.91	4.16	11.37	17.86	4.19
Taiwan	6.51	2.03	11.78	6.44	2.02	11.33
Macao	0.20	0.33	0.06	0.17	0.28	0.04
Total	59.172	54.394	64.79	59.45	55.33	64.023

Source: China Custom Statistics Yearbook, various years.

3. CHINA'S REGIONAL ECONOMIC POLICY

China had not been a member of any regional economic organization until it took part in APEC in 1991. In the following ten years, China's officially advocates open regionalism. Soon after becoming a WTO member in 2001, Chinese premier Zhu Rongji and ASEAN leaders jointly announced that the two sides agreed to establish a Free Trade Area before 2010. This is a sign that China is gradually accepting the concept of institutional regional arrangements, although it is not giving up its principles of open regionalism. What is the reason behind the policy shift?

3.1. APEC and China's Open Regionalism

In 1991 China joined APEC, which was the first regional organization in which China took part. The Asia-Pacific region played an essential role in China's foreign economic relations. Around 80% of foreign trade and 90% of foreign investment absorbed by China came from the Asia-Pacific region.

Although APEC played a limited role in promoting trade and investment in the region due to the fact that APEC covers an excessively wide region, pursues open regionalism and embraces the voluntary principle of favorable arrangements among the members, China's APEC membership has promoted its trade and investment liberalization. After joining APEC, China unilaterally reduced its tariff rates and has gradually lifted its non-tariff barriers. From 1992 to 1997, China voluntarily and extensively cut down tariff rates, resulting in a decrease in its arithmetic average tariff rate from 43.2% to 17% and weighted average tariff rate falling from 32.7% to 13.3%. At an informal meeting attended by APEC leaders in Vancouver in November 1997, the Chinese government promised to reduce the average rate of custom duties of industrial products to 10% by 2005. Moreover, in the unilateral action plan of APEC, China also promised to examine all non-tariff measures, gradually lift non-tariff barriers and increase the transparency of non-tariff measures by 2000. In addition, China also made efforts to open its service and trade sectors, increase the transparency of the polices in the field of investment, reinforce protection of intellectual property rights and render more business conveniences to foreign investment.

Table 7. China's tariff cuts in APEC (1991 –2001)

(Unit: %)

Year	Average Tariff
1991	44.1
1992	43.2
1993	39.9
1994	35.9
1996	23.0
1997	17.0
2000	16.4
2001	15.3

3.2. Institutional Regional Arrangement: Development of China's Regional EconomicPolicy

In the new century, China has become more and more active in establishing an institutional regional arrangement (IRA). In April 2000 China joined the Bangkok Agreement, which was the first RTA with substantive preferential arrangements for China. The leaders of the Shanghai Organization agreed to extend the coverage of the organization to economic cooperation. China began to negotiate with ASEAN to set up a free trade area before 2010 and a framework agreement was signed this year. China's senior economic officials are working with their Hong Kong counterparts, the special administration district of China, on establishing a "closer economic relationship" under the framework of the WTO. Also, a joint research team, appointed by each central government of China, Japan and Korea, has been working on economic cooperation among the three biggest economies in East Asia. It is believed that this research project will eventually bring about an official negotiation for a free trade area among the three economies.

Although China still emphasizes open regionalism in the international community, its active attitude toward institutional regional arrangements is drawing global attention. China's regional economic policy shifted from pure open regionalism to a dual track mode: both open regionalism and institutional regional arrangements. This is considered a big development in China's regional economic policy. What caused the decision-makers to initiate this development?

Besides the closer economic relationship with neighboring economies, which is the basic reason, there are various factors encouraging Chinese policy makers to pay attention to institutional regional arrangements:

3.2.1. Asian financial crisis

The Asian Financial Crisis in 1997 made the Chinese leaders realize the importance of regional economic cooperation. The crisis broke out in Thailand and spread quickly to other East Asian economies. During the Crisis, China promptly reacted by providing loans to some of the crisis-hit countries. However, the sluggish rescue efforts of the international community, especially from developed countries, did not prevent the crisis from spreading over the region. The crisis caused everyone, including the Chinese, to realize the need for an institutional cooperation mechanism. During the development boom, most of the countrics in this rcgion paid less attention to regional cooperation. While there were regional trade blocs in Europe and North America, most East Asian economies still stressed the importance of their main export markets rather than cooperation within the region. A valuable legacy of the Asian Financial Crisis is that policy makers in the region realized the importance of regional cooperation, especially institutional arrangements.

3.2.2. Global tide of regional economic cooperation

Propelled by the European Union and North America Free Trade Area (NAFTA), regional economic integration began to lead the development trend across the world in the 1990s. The GATT/WTO had received notification of 156 Regional Trade Agreements (RTA) as of September 2001. Most WTO members participated in at least one RTA, some of them even joined as many as ten RTAs. As a result, internal trade within RTAs has accounted for more than 50% of the total global trade volume.

RTAs nowadays present the following new features that have attracted widespread attention.

(1) Bilateral RTAs have exceeded RTAs with a 'spoke-hub' structure[3] and multilateral agreements in terms of number. Among the RTAs signed before 1990, there was only one bilateral agreement, while among those signed after 1990, the share of bilateral agreements accounted for nearly 50%.

(2) More and more RTAs have been signed between countries with different levels of economic development, for example, RTAs between Canada and Chile, between Japan and Mexico, and between Australia and Papua New Guinea, etc.

(3) More and more RTAs have been signed between non-neighboring countries. For instance, RTAs between Thailand and Australia, between Turkey and Latvia, between Hungary and Lithuania, between the U.S. and Israel, between Japan and Mexico, and between Singapore and Chile, etc.

(4) Free Trade Agreements (FTA) make up a big share of RTAs. As of September 2001, GATT/WTO had received effective notices from 156 RTAs, 110 of which were about establishing FTAs or receiving new members into FTAs.

The rapid development of RTAs has exerted an increasingly larger influence on the economies inside and outside RTAs. For instance, since the establishment of NAFTA, the trade volume inside the zone has increased at an average growth rate of 12% annually, among which, the exports of Mexico to the U.S. and Canada rose by nearly 20% annually. Economies outside RTAs have been negatively impacted by the trade diversion effects. For example, China was replaced by Mexico as the biggest supplier of textiles and garments to the U.S. market. This provided a big impetus for Chinese policy makers to think about their strategies on regional integration.

3.2.3. Changes of China's external economic environment

Since the early 1990's, China's external economic environment has gradually changed. Firstly, there have been increasing economic and political frictions with the US. After the Cold War, the international situation changed from a bipolar situation to uni-polar situation. Both political and economic relations between China and the US, the biggest market for Chinese exports, became less smooth than during the Cold War. It is hazardous for China to depend too much on the US market, which, as a final market, receives about 40% of China's exports. The Chinese government

[3] An existing RTA signs an RTA with a neighboring country or region. The original RTA is considered the hub and the latter RTA is a spoke.

launched a so-called "market diversification strategy" in the early 1990s; however, its effects have not yet been evident. A regional trade arrangement will enable China to increase its trade relations with neighboring economies and thus diversify its export markets.

Secondly, China's exports are facing increasing challenges in the overseas markets. The anti-dumping cases that China has suffered are the most in the world. Also, China's exports have encountered more and more technology barriers of trade (TBT). Moreover, China has begun to have trade disputes with neighboring countries, such as Japan and Korea, which are having a negative influence on bilateral relations.

Thirdly, Chinese leaders want to defuse the so-called "China's threat" by sharing economic development with neighboring economies. The Theory of the China Threat emerged in Western countries in the early 1990s. The earlier school of the China Threat claimed that the collapse of China threatened the world. With its rapid economic development and exports, there is little danger of China collapsing. However, there has been another type of China Threat theory, which claims that China is a challenge to the existing powers and neighboring countries. China is seen by some observers as one of the biggest long-term threats to U.S. security and economic preeminence.[4,5] The China Threat theory also has some influence in developing economies that view China as a rival in competing for exports and FDI.[6,7]

Such slander has far-reaching negative influences for China's future development and relations with other countries. The best way to defuse the negative impact is to share the economic development potential with other countries. And a regional economic arrangement would be an effective way to do so.

3.2.4. China's WTO accession

China entered the WTO on December 11, 2001 under conditions in line with the long-term goals of Western countries. China has made extensive commitments, which include:

- cutting down the average tariff to 10% by 2005;
- introducing a tariff rate quota (TRQ) system for bulk agriculture products,

[4] Bruce Einhorn in Shanghai, with Ben Elgin, Cliff Edwards, and Linda Himelstein in San Mateo, Calif., and Otis Port in New York, "Is it a threat to Silicon Valley?," *Business Week*, Number 3805; p. 80, October 28, 2002.

[5] Evan Thomas and John Barry; with Melinda Liu in Beijing, Roy Gutman traveling with Powell, Martha Brant traveling with Bush, Bill Turque in Washington and Ana Figueroa in Honolulu, "The Conflict to Come," *Newsweek*, April 23, 2001, U.S. Edition

[6] Kalinga Seneviratne "ECONOMY-SOUTHEAST ASIA: MOVING AWAY FROM EXPORT RELIANCE," *Business and Industry, Global Information Network*, April 5, 2001, RDS-ACC-NO: 02851498

[7] In his article "Mexico's China Obsession," which appeared in the Atlantic edition of *Newsweek* on November 4, 2002, Scott Johnson says "The People's Republic has already forced many Asian nations to rethink their export strategies. Now a Latin American economy that's fueled by trade, too, feels the pinch."

with a very low tariff for those within the quota;
- eliminating non-tariff barriers such as import quota and license;
- granting trade rights to foreign enterprises;
- opening service markets to foreign investment.

In addition, China promised to abide by all WTO rules, such as TRIPS, TRIMs and so on, and to reform its domestic system to comply with international practices. Moreover, China allows its trade partners to adopt some unusual mechanisms including special safeguard measures to place restrictions on China's exports.

Although there are high adjustment costs in the short run, China will benefit from its WTO accession in the long run. Industrial restructuring and increased international competition will increase economic efficiency. Moreover, joining the WTO also serves as a major external impetus for the reform of the domestic system.

The WTO accession also makes it possible for China to establish a free trade arrangement with other economies. Before the accession, the level of trade protection in China was relatively high. It was impossible for China to set up any free trade bloc under such high trade protection. The WTO accession will increase China's international competitiveness and make it more confident to promote further trade liberalization.

4. PROSPECTS FOR REGIONAL COOPERATION IN EAST ASIA

4.1. Increasing Trade Relations is the Foundation of Economic Cooperation in East Asia

Among East Asian economies, the proportion of trade within the area has been above 35% since 1980 and has continued its upward tendency until 1997 when the financial crisis broke out in Asia. Table 8 shows that the proportion of trade within East Asia is lower than that in European Union (EU) but higher than in the North America Free Trade Agreement (NAFTA), which indicates that there exist close trade links among the East Asia economies.

Table 8. Proportions of Trade Inside Different Regions

(Unit: %)

	1980	1985	1990	1995	1997
EU	57.9	58.6	64.6	61.1	59.9
NAFTA	32.9	38	36.9	41.6	44.1
East Asia	35.3	37.2	41.5	49.1	48.7

Resource: Chang Jae Lee, "A New Approach Toward Enhanced Northeast Asian Economic Cooperation".

4.2. Major Barriers for an Institutional Trade Arrangement in East Asia

4.2.1. Growth of trade of East Asia economies depends on external markets

Apart from China and Indonesia, most economies in East Asia are in a deficit position in foreign trade transactions with Japan, the only developed country in the area, while they enjoy a trade surplus in transactions with the US. The main reason lies in the fact that East Asia economies need to import capital goods and input in order to develop their processing industries and the products they produce are mostly exported to the US and Europe. Consequently, the degree of openness of the market inside the area is not high enough and the ultimate market is outside the area despite the fact that the proportion of trade inside East Asia remains at a high level. Such a situation goes against the development of economic and trade cooperation inside East Asia.

4.2.2. Competition among East Asia economies

Export-oriented is the common characteristic of East Asian economies. Although there is a vertical division between developing economies and developed or newly industrialized economies because of investment from the latter to the former, the competition among economies with similar advantages is more serious than in other regions. Developing economies share the same advantages and similar industrial structures; thus their labor- intensive products compete in the third markets. There is also more competition than complementarity among developed economies and newly industrialized economies. There are some sensitive sectors for further trade liberalization. For example, East Asia is the biggest supplier of iron and steel in the world. The iron and steel industry faces the problem of over capacity. The extent to which the relationship among such sensitive sectors can be coordinated will directly affect the process of regional economic integration.

4.2.3. Agriculture sector will be a major obstacle for regional trade integration

Japan and Korea, as the two developed economies in East Asia, play an important role in regional trade liberalization. Because of historic reasons, farmers have a strong voice in domestic political affairs in the two countries. Although the protection of agriculture has decreased since the Uruguay Round, the agricultural sector is still well protected in both countries. It can be expected that farmers in both countries will oppose any agreement on a free trade area including the agricultural sector. Therefore, the agricultural sector will be a major obstacle for an East Asian free trade arrangement.

4.2.4. Political obstacles exist

Firstly, the attitude toward responsibilities in World War II frequently leads to fluctuation in Japan's relations with its East Asian neighbors. The instability of political relations will negatively affect other countries in making their decisions to negotiate a free trade agreement with Japan. Secondly, there are some tensions on the Korean Peninsula and across the Taiwan Strait, which will also impact the process for a free trade agreement in this region. Thirdly, the attitude of the U.S., which has a strong influence on the region, will be an uncertain factor. Finally, the worries of the people in ASEAN that an East Asian FTA may decrease its influence in East Asia will also delay the process of establishing a free trade bloc in East Asia.

4.3. Prospects for Economic Cooperation in East Asia

In regard to the issue of economic cooperation in East Asia, many institutions and scholars have put forward a variety of recommendations.

4.3.1. Advice of the World Bank

The World Bank brought forward four possible schemes for economic cooperation in East Asia (see Table 9); the first and second schemes are open group type arrangements while the third and fourth schemes are discriminatory and closed group type schemes.

The World Bank believes that the second scheme is the optimal choice for the following reasons:

• First of all, this scheme involves a high proportion of trade within East Asia to maximize the benefits received by the area;

• Secondly, the integration arrangement suggested by this scheme will reduce the effects of trade diversion and the countries/regions outside the area can also benefit, which will encourage more countries to join the regional group.

Table 9. World Bank's view on East Asia economic cooperation

(Unit: %)

Size of Group	Non-discriminatory type	Discriminatory type
Small	① realize liberalization by implementing most-favored-nation status unilaterally or in a limited scope	③ Trade zone in a limited scope, for example, an FTA involving only a few countries
Large	② realize liberalization by implementing most-favored-nation status extensively and all members benefit from liberalization	④ Trade zone in a wide scope, for example, an FTA involving all countries /regions in the area

Source: World Bank working paper

4.3.2. Blueprint of economic cooperation in Northeast Asia put forward by Korean scholars

After the Asian Financial Crisis, Korean scholars brought forward a blueprint for strengthening economic cooperation in Northeast Asia, which involved different fields including institutional construction, trade and investment, and covered only three countries, namely, China, Japan and Korea. The blueprint proposed to set up a Northeast Asia Committee of Economic Cooperation, Northeast Asia Free Trade Zone and the signing of a Northeast Asia Investment and Cooperation Agreement.

The fundamental features of this blueprint are reflected in the following three aspects:

Firstly, this blueprint consults APEC with respect to the operating and organizing structure and adopts a loose and informal cooperation mode which is similar to a forum in nature. However, the structure is more efficient as it concentrates the discussion on issues of common interest among the three countries.

In view of the fact that a vertical division of labor exists among China, Japan and Korea, unification of trade rules rather than market access should be taken as the point of departure to realize trade liberalization. And a reduction of tariffs should be the next step in order to expand market access.

In regard to investment liberalization, besides increasing unilateral investment inside the area, the three countries should, at the same time, work with each other in order to augment investment from countries outside the area. Finally, a production network of transnational companies should be established, an open Northeast Asian investment zone should be set up, and a cooperative framework of sharing production resources should be constructed.

4.3.3. Idea of establishing an AMF proposed by Japanese scholars

Unlike their Korean counterparts, Japanese scholars consider the issue of regional economic integration in view of East Asia as a whole, and pay more attention to cooperation in the financial field, guided by the idea of establishing an Asian Monetary Fund (AMF). Japanese scholars believe that under the new situation Asian countries should consider strategically rearranging the monetary system in the area and reinforce cooperation in the financial field in order to enhance their ability to withstand the impact of financial risks and avoid being exploited by international capital and attacked by another financial crisis.

The main purpose of the establishment of the AMF would be to raise funds from members as well as from the capital market, which would be mainly used to keep the region from financial crises and offer financing support to its members. The AMF will encourage the use of local currencies in business transactions and advocate the establishment of an Asian Clearing System in a bid to shake off the restraints imposed on the economic development in this area by the exchange rate system of pegging currencies to the U.S. dollar. Moreover, Japanese scholars argue that Japan should play a bigger role in the AMF to facilitate the recovery of those countries suffering from financial crisis.

4.3.4. Opinion of Chinese scholars

Views on East Asian cooperation are quite diversified among Chinese scholars. Most Chinese scholars still emphasize the importance of open regionalism and argue that conditions for a regional trade arrangement in the area have not been in place so far in view of the following facts:

A pattern of vertical division of labor exists in the area due to the large gaps between economies in terms of economic development level;

Most economies in the area adopt export-oriented strategies of development and heavily depend on overseas markets. This situation will continue to exist for some time;

Developed countries in the area only undertake limited responsibility for regional economic cooperation;

There are huge differences between countries/regions in the area in terms of social system, nationality and culture.

The authors of the paper have advocated that China actively take part in regional integration. The factors mentioned above make an East Asia FTA (EAFTA) the long-term goal. Before EAFTA is reached, there must be some sub-regional arrangement, such as "10+1", "China+Japan+Korea," and some bilateral FTAs. When most of the economies in the region have taken part in one or more FTAs, it will be much easier to formulate the EAFTA. To accelerate the process of regional integration in East Asia, the following points should be noted:

Firstly, economies in the area may actively engage in bilateral and multilateral dialogue in different scopes regarding various products and cooperative projects in the investment field and to explore the possibility of reinforcing cooperation through an institutional arrangement.

Secondly, some specific fields may be emphasized, such as regional financial cooperation, technological cooperation, and energy development cooperation, etc.

Finally, developed economies should make more contributions, considering the large gaps between the economies in the area in terms of economic development level and market scale.

5. CONCLUSION

With the deepening of market-oriented reforms and greater openness, China experienced rapid economic development and trade development. Meanwhile, its industrial and trade structures have greatly evolved and economic relations with its neighboring economies in East Asia have been enhanced.

China's regional economic policy has evolved from open regionalism to an institutional regional arrangement as well as open regionalism. This policy evolution has led to some big acts by China recently in regional cooperation, such as negotiating a free trade area with ASEAN. This policy evolution also will be a positive factor promoting the establishment of an East Asia Free Trade Area (EAFTA).

There are still some obstacles for EAFTA. A realistic approach is to promote cooperation in specific sectors on the base of bilateral or multilateral negotiations and to promote sub-regional integration. More contributions by developed economies will also be a positive factor and should be encouraged.

CHAPTER 2

EAST ASIAN FREE TRADE AGREEMENT: STRATEGIC ASPECTS FOR JAPAN

KAZUHIRO IGAWA and BONGGIL KIM

1. INTRODUCTION

Although the globalization of economic activities is the main trend, regionalism in the form of regional economic integration also began to develop around the end of the 20th century and has grown more rapidly in the 21st century. The scale and scope of activities of an economic unit has been changed by developments in telecommunication and transportation technologies, as well as in production and distribution technologies. Information technology has improved the network-system of mutual exchanges of those technologies. An optimum economic border is different from a national border, and the integration of national borders will become necessary when an economic space of one nation is not sufficiently large. Economic effects of regional economic integration depend on the level of technologies and the size of markets, above all.

Traditional textbooks of international economics have explained international trade and investment and international financial payments based on existing national borders. However recent developments in the globalization of economic activities have increased the number of issues that can be explained more appropriately in the context of regions or multiple nations than in the context of existing national borders. Multinational firms or international financial firms make decisions about the extent of their activities regardless of existing national borders. They draw their optimal maps. Overlapping those many maps, the world will have a de facto new border map. However existing national borders are determined by a long history and are still effective in many aspects—political, social and cultural. Therefore, it is important to discuss the issue of regional economic integration from the viewpoint of the optimum map of regional integration. This point of view is the foundation of this paper.

Regional economic integration includes both financial and real aspects. The financial aspects are discussed in the context of optimum currency area arguments pioneered by R. A. Mundell (1961), while the real aspects are discussed in

C. Y. Ahn et al (eds.), East Asian Economic Regionalism, 21-36.

arguments on free trade agreements (FTAs) or customs unions. Of course those two aspects cannot be separated and both real and financial investigations are necessary for practical arguments on regional economic integration. Both an optimum currency area and an optimum FTA area (map) could be investigated with comparisons between scale merits of integration and costs of adjustments for integration. However the two optimum areas (maps) may not coincide with each other. In this paper, we focus on East Asian (ASEAN, China, Korea, and Japan) FTA arguments only. We have discussed the idea of an East Asian currency area in a different paper (B. Kim and K. Igawa (2001)), which pointed out that the macroeconomic indices of East Asian countries show a high potential for the development of a single currency area in the region.

FTA arguments often discuss the problem of the distribution of costs and benefits. Countries excluded from an FTA might suffer from trade diversion effects and some groups within an FTA member country might have to bear losses. Therefore, there always exist game strategies among players (countries and interest groups). We will make clear the strategic aspects of an East Asian FTA, especially the aspects of Japan, which we assume. The strategic FTA policy of the Ministry of Foreign Affairs of Japan was revealed in major Japanese newspapers on October 13, 2002. Although the strategy is more comprehensive and general, it does not seem to differ greatly from the strategy we assume here.[1]

In the following sections, we discuss the optimum FTA map of the world (section 2), and FTA players in East Asia (section 3). Section 4 examines the strategies of Japan for an East Asia FTA.

2. FTA MAP

Traditional theories of customs unions and FTAs depend on the pioneering works of J. Viner (1950), which provide a clear view of the trade creation effects of benefits and trade diversion effects of losses. There, costs and benefits comparisons are made between the economic situations before and after integration. The effects of integration of countries with given borders are analyzed, and an optimum size of integration is not taken into consideration. However recent arguments are more conscious of the size of integration and of whether the direction of FTA movements is towards global trade liberalization or fortress construction. P. Krugman (1991) showed by simulation that world welfare is minimal with a three-bloc division map of the world, and J. Bhagwati (1993) promoted investigations about the global versus regional liberalization aspects of FTAs. More than 100 FTAs exist and the number will increase rapidly, with these FTAs overlapping each other. A substantial economic border map will be changed by the development of these overlapping FTAs, or FTA networks. We are now in the position to investigate an optimum free trade area in the world.

[1] Summarizing the reports: the priority of Japanese government is on economic cooperation with East Asian countries, and thus Japan will advance the schedule of FTA between Korea, and between ASEAN, and then will negotiate with China. Japan's FTA with NAFTA and with EU will be long-run subjects.

Arguments of costs and benefits in economic integration have changed the emphasis from static trade creation and diversion effects to dynamic effects of accumulation or concentration of economic activities. The traditional trade theories of D. Ricardo, E. Heckscher and B. Ohlin focus on gains from trade and how such gains are distributed; but the analysis is static. With opening international trade (or trade creation by FTAs), a larger share of gains from trade are distributed to smaller countries, whose terms of trade change by a larger scale, compared to larger countries whose terms of trade change by a smaller scale. However, relative adjustment costs will be larger in a small country facing large changes in terms of trade than in a large country facing small changes in terms of trade. In an increasing return economy, gains from trade come from cost decreasing effects, through mass production and consumption, and from increasing consumption menu effects, through product diversification. This new trade theory was developed by Helpman-Krugman (1985), using a monopolistic competition model by Dexit-Stiglits (1977). With increasing return to scale, the increase in market size and thus production size make possible diversified final and intermediate products. These effects increase the economic welfare of participants in the larger market. These increasing return benefits will be found in capital (technology) intensive industries of manufacturing products, and communication and distribution network services. Advanced countries are more aggressive in FTA formation because they have more increasing return industries. The economies of scale and scope usually have dynamic effects of endogenous development.

If a regional economic integration has accumulation effects or concentration effects of endogenous development, member countries will get enough net benefits by forming an FTA. This idea is not new and can be found in Adam Smith's *The Wealth of Nations* (1776). How and why nations become wealthy depends on the division of labor, which determines a nation's productivity, and the division of labor is determined by the extent of the market. The nation can open its markets to exploit the advantages of labor specialization. This implies that knowledge and technologies, which support works of market mechanisms, and the division of labor in production and distribution determine appropriate productivities and market sizes. This idea is applicable to the problem of an optimum integration of markets and concentration (and accumulation) of economic activities in the world. One of the interesting recent applications is in M. Fujita, P. Krugman and A. J. Venables (2001). A concentration and accumulation of economic activities produces core and periphery relations in the world, where core areas develop faster than peripheral areas. The size of concentration (or accumulation) and relations between the core and periphery, both depend on the level of available knowledge and technology. The technologies of telecommunications, transportation, production and distribution, and also knowledge (know-how) of management are important determinants of scale economies, economies of scope, and network economies.

An optimum FTA map asks how many and what size of economic concentration areas should exist in the world to maximize an economic welfare. The objective function could be the welfare level, world production or consumption, or those of a specific region or country. There are more than 100 FTAs in the world, but NAFTA and the EU are exceptionally large and powerful. Of course there are many effective

FTAs but they are rather restricted to a specific local area or have no strong external effects. There also exist large regional cooperation areas, but they are not effective as free trade areas. APEC, for example, covers a large area but the member's are not strongly concentrated enough to form one FTA. APEC has no unique core and no explicit organizational ability. The two large FTAs are dominant in the present situation of the FTA map of the world. Then the optimum FTA map asks whether the recent situation of "NAFTA and the EU plus small FTA network" is optimal or not. In our opinion, the present map is not efficient enough and there should be one more large FTA concentration in East Asia.

It is easily found that NAFTA and the EU are not absorbing all their peripheral areas and are not fully using up the capacity of those areas. NAFTA is planning to extend its membership to include Central and South America. However, Central and South American countries are not yet prepared to join NAFTA in terms of their economic systems and political environment. The problems of geographical environment and distance are also not yet completely resolved by the present level of technologies and knowledge (know-how). Similarly, the EU is planning to include East Europe and the former Soviet Russia into its union, but the level of technological-knowledge is not yet high enough to make this possible. The system for putting forth a collective view (opinion) is not fully advanced enough to expand the EU. NAFTA. The EU should develop and concentrate within present members, and gradually utilize the potential capacities of their peripheries. In the following sections, we discuss the possibility of the formation of a third large FTA in the East Asian region.

3. FTA PLAYERS IN EAST ASIA

Two concentration cores of FTAs, NAFTA and the EU, do not cover the entire world, and East Asia does not understand the incentive to form one more economic concentration in East Asia region. If East Asia does not have FTAs, East Asian countries must act as players in the NAFTA-EU FTA system. Geographically East Asian countries are located far away from the center core of NAFTA or the EU; thus, East Asian countries face the risk of being treated as a periphery of NAFTA and/or the EU. In this case, East Asian countries will not gain enough benefits from economic concentration in spite of their large potential. On the other hand, when East Asian countries have their own concentration of FTAs, they will be able to form a large enough market and to make full use of their potential, with the existing technology and knowledge. It is well known that the stream of economic development in the region started with Japanese development, and next moved to the Asian NIES, then to ASEAN, and has now moved on to China. This development stream was driven by the technology transfers and foreign direct investment (FDI) first of Japanese firms and then the firms of the Asian NIES. Now ASEAN has started to become more active in regional FDI and FDI into China. Technologies and knowledge are transferred along with FDI in East Asia. After the Asian currency crisis, most East Asian countries have recovered. Their potentials for economic developments, inherited from the era of the East Asian miracle are not lost.

East Asian countries are engines of economic growth of the world, again.

There is a story that a natural concentration is advancing among East Asian countries without an effective FTA, and an East Asian FTA might prompt offensive strategies from NAFTA and EU members. East Asian countries have largely depended on the US and EU as export markets, and these markets are still important. It was true in the past, that an economic strategy of East Asian countries, which might be called as an equidistant foreign policy or a multilateral trade policy, provided advantages to access global export markets. Many FDI inflows of capital-intensive industries and export-oriented products have become feasible with the support of multinational (global or trans-national) firms that based their main business activities in NAFTA or the EU. Loose connections in APEC and in ASEM, have increased opportunities for international trade and investment and have widened policy strategies for East Asian countries.

However economic situations have changed. Increased dependency on intra-regional trade and investment among East Asian countries has given greater importance to East Asian regional markets (see Table 1 and 2).[2] In competing with NAFTA (or EU)-based firms, East Asian firms are seeking to form a larger domestic market, where main business activities can enjoy economies of scale and scope. The change has been strengthened by the Asian currency crisis. The natural concentration story of East Asian countries is being reexamined in the context of uncertainties and risks like currency crises. To ensure the concentration formation, it is better to adopt policy strategies to facilitate an FTA in East Asia.

Table 1. Intra-regional, Extra-regional trade in East Asian countries

(Unit: Millions of US$, %)

			Value		Share		Growth rate	
			1999	2000	1999	2000	1999	2000
Total	Export	Intra-regional	349,606	437,626	35.8	37.2	8.0	25.2
		Extra-regional	626,496	739,802	64.2	62.8	5.6	18.1
		Total	976,102	1,177,428	100.0	100.0	6.4	20.6
	Import	Intra-regional	337,565	433,070	39.3	40.0	8.8	28.3
		Extra-regional	521,288	650,689	60.7	60.0	9.8	24.8
		Total	858,853	1,083,759	100.0	100.0	9.4	26.2
IT Products	Export	Intra-regional	131,085	177,998	39.0	41.2	23.3	35.8
		Extra-regional	205,397	254,199	61.0	58.8	13.3	23.8
		Total	336,482	432,197	100.0	100.0	17.0	28.4
	Import	Intra-regional	122,086	171,595	46.4	49.1	18.4	40.6
		Extra-regional	140,811	177,932	53.6	50.9	13.1	26.4
		Total	262,897	349,527	100.0	100.0	15.5	33.0

Source: JETRO, *JETRO White Paper on International Trade*, 2001.

[2] Intra-regional export and import shares of East Asian countries are about 40%, and their growth rate is high. The figure is not much less than the one of EU (50%). Intra-regional shares of FDI into East Asia are very high (more than 60% for China and about 50% for ASEAN 4).

The US, which has opposed an East Asian FTA in the past, has now adopted a more moderate stance. ASEAN is making an effort to accomplish an ASEAN FTA, including the new ASEAN 4 members. China has called for an FTA with ASEAN and this has led to a call for strengthening cooperation among the ASEAN+3 countries. The recent world trend of FTA formation has pushed East Asian countries to establish a larger FTA in Asia.

Table 2. FDI Inflows in East Asian Countries

(Unit: Millions of US$, %)

		Asian (Japan)	Total	Shares (Japan)
Korea	1990	257 (236)	803	32.0 (29.4)
	1996	1202 (255)	3203	37.5 (7.6)
China	1990	4,440 (457)	6,596	67.3 (6.9)
	1996	44,111(5,131)	73,276	60.2 (7.0)
Thailand	1990	4,827(2,757)	8,182	59.0 (33.7)
	1996	9,122(6,156)	13,050	69.9(47.2)
Malaysia	1990	973 (657)	2,303	42.3(28.5)
	1996	4,006(1,831)	6,780	59.1(27.0)
Indonesia	1990	4,221(2,241)	8,750	48.2(25.6)
	1996	16,147(7,655)	29,931	53.9(25.6)
Philippines	1990	494 (271)	851	58.1(31.8)
	1996	384 (58)	967	39.7 (6.0)

Note: 1) Asian members include Japan, Korea, China, Hong Kong, Indonesia, Malaysia, Philippines, Singapore, and Thailand.
2) Contract Base

Source: JETRO, *White Paper on Foreign Direct Investment*, 1999.

There is another reason to call for a larger FTA in East Asia. East Asia has many countries with similar economic structures that compete with each other in a common export market. Although bilateral FTAs might be a necessary step for forming a larger FTA, bilateral FTAs will have beggar-thy-neighbor effects on third countries in East Asia. A large FTA, alongside NAFTA and the EU, will be accepted as an intermediate situation toward a global free trade system. East Asian countries are now in the position of having to make a big push for the formation of an East Asian FTA.

However, forming an East Asian FTA is not an easy task, and is accompanied by many hurdles to clear. Although East Asian countries are diverse in economic, political, and cultural aspects, we can divide them into three types (or subgroups) of players. One type includes Japan and Korea. These countries are at a higher level of economic development and the products in which they have the greatest comparative advantage are capital-intensive manufacturing products and technology-based products. It is possible to include Taiwan in this group, but this involves complexities in the strategic game of an East Asia FTA because of the political relations between Taiwan and China. This is not to ignore the importance of Taiwan, but excluding Taiwan simplifies the East Asian FTA strategies, without changing the main story of the East Asia FTA. Japan was the first Asian country to join the group of advanced countries. Japan succeeded in catching up with the U.S. in its textile industry, then in the electrical appliances and automobile industries. Korea underwent similar catching up processes following Japan, and has become an OECD member. The similarities between Japan and Korea might stem from the pre-war history of unification of the two and from their political relations with the US after World War II. Geographical location in the Asia-Pacific is also a reason for their similarities. Protecting their domestic market from foreign competitors and promoting the export of manufacturing products have been their main foreign trade policies. Both for Japan and Korea, recent competition with large foreign companies calls for a large domestic market and the recent threat of China catching up calls for FDI into China. Both Japan and Korea are players with advanced technology in the manufacturing industries and who want to have a large domestic market. An FTA including ASEAN and China will provide both countries with a strong strategic advantage against the larger US and/or EU companies.

Although encompassing many different member countries, ASEAN is another type of player for an East Asian FTA. The diversity of East Asian countries is condensed into the diversity of ASEAN. Singapore is one of the financial centers of the world and per-capita income is high, despite the country's small population and land area. Malaysia and Thailand are developed in the labor-intensive manufacturing industries and are aiming an industrial reform with more capital-intensive industries. Indonesia and the Philippines have some difficulties in terms of political stability, but are aiming to gain a comparative advantage in labor-intensive manufacturing industries. Indonesia has a large population and is rich in natural resources. The quality of labor in the Philippines is high. Brunei is exceptionally rich because of its oil production but it should find other industries in which it can be competitive in the future. The new ASEAN 4 countries are transitional economies and have different development levels from the other ASEAN countries; for them, learning the system of the market economy is a priority matter. For Vietnam, Cambodia, Laos and Myanmar, it is necessary to change their latecomer disadvantages into latecomer advantages. It is very difficult to find a typical ASEAN player. However for an East Asian FTA, ASEAN members will have a united strategy as an ASEAN FTA unit. Therefore we treat ASEAN as one player here, assuming Thailand, Malaysia, Indonesia, and the Philippines (ASEAN 4) are the dominant decision-makers of the ASEAN 10. The ASEAN 4 countries are in a position in which they must graduate from the labor-intensive industries at an early stage and must catch up in the capital-intensive industries without enough accumulated experience. This is necessary for the new ASEAN 4 as China catches up in the labor-intensive industries. The situation is harsh for ASEAN because FDI inflows are shifting from ASEAN into China (see Table 3),[3] and this means a decrease in the transfers of technology from the developed countries to ASEAN. It is important for ASEAN to have policy strategies for an East Asian FTA, in the face of the large potential of China's development.

The third player is China. China also has its own complicated problems of

[3] China is the biggest FDI absorber, and ratio of ASEAN4 to China has reduced from 42.5% in 1996 to 16.7% in 2000.

Taiwan and Hong Kong, and there are disparities between China's coastal areas and inland provinces in terms of development levels. China is also a transitional economy with government-owned firms, which are not efficient in many cases. Despite the political difficulties and uncertainties in its transitional economy, the central government retains a firm grip on the Chinese economy. The policies of the government are key for the economic environment not only of East Asia but also of the world. The development of China has large effects on other countries, especially on neighboring countries. Its potential ability has produced rumors of the menace of Chinese power in the future. China has an economic potential comparable to the US economy, which started its development in the 19th century and became the world's top economy in the 20th century. The development stage of China is an important factor in determining the international division of labor. Neighboring countries must take into account China's stage of development in forming their development strategies. In the past, there was a time when China was strong as a unified nation, but it was too big to be one economic unit and there were many sub-regions with many concentration cores. However, recent developments in technology and information knowledge and transportation have made it possible for China to form one economic core.

Table 3. FDI inflow in East Asian Countries

(Unit: Balance of payments base: Millions of US$)

	1996	1997	1998	1999	2000
Japan	200	3,200	3,268	12,308	8,227
China	40,180	44,237	43,751	38,753	38,399
ANIES	25,.22	29,428	26,726	44,043	85,035
Korea	2,326	2,844	5,412	9,333	9,283
Taiwan	1,864	2,248	222	2,926	4,928
Hong	10,460	11,368	14,776	24,587	64,433
Kong	10,372	12,967	6,316	7,197	6,390
Singapore					
ASEAN4	17,343	16,307	11,946	7,573	6,387
Thailand	2,336	3,895	7,315	6,213	3,366
Malaysia	7,296	6,513	2,700	3,532	5,542
Indonesia	6,194	4,677	-356	-2,745	-4,550
Philippines	1,517	1,222	2,287	573	2,029
Total	82,745	93,171	85,691	102,677	138,048

Source: UNCTAD, *World Investment Report 2001*.

It might be easy to understand the development of China by comparing and overlapping the history of its development with that of the United States. The U.S. was a land-rich country and immigrant workers from Europe, starting on the east coast, and capital fund investments, also from European countries, supported its economic development. Agricultural products in the southern area and mining products in the eastern area drove the early stage of U.S. development. The wave of development moved from the Midwest area and then to the west area. In the meantime the north became a developed industrial region. The U.S. depended on

European funds and technologies for its development and also on European markets, but gradually increased its dependency on its own domestic market. After two World Wars, during which European countries suffered severe blows, the U.S. became the supreme ruler of the world.

China is a labor-abundant country whose economic development has been stimulated by FDI of funds and technologies in its southeastern coastal areas. The development wave is now being directed to the inland areas in the north and west. The coastal area has become a development center with manufacturing products, many of which are exported to the U.S. and EU, and also to Japan. The recent economic stagnation of Japan, the U.S. and EU after 2001 has changed the situation of China's development from depending on foreign markets into more dependence on its own domestic market. It is not possible for a large country to continue an export-oriented development strategy and the large potential of the domestic market should be developed. The very recent development of China depends on domestic investment and this is financed by FDI inflows (see Table 4).[4] If FDI inflow into China with advanced technologies continues and if China constructs an efficient domestic economic system and market, it will be one of the largest economies in the world. The problems of how to make those government-owned firms efficient or how to privatize those firms might be critical for this change. Economic growth without productivity growth will impose limits on China's growth and economic development. In the near future, China will be in an important position to change its growth policy of input quantity growth to one of productivity growth. An East Asia FTA will give China a greater chance of maintaining high growth rates with higher productivity growth.

Table 4. FDI into China

(Unit: Millions of US$)

	1999		2000		2001.1~6	
	Contract value	Realized value	Contract value	Realized value	Contract value	Realized value
Hong Kong	13,329	16,363	16,961	15,499	9,667	7,469
U. S.	6,016	2,659	8,000	4,383	3,711	2,050
Japan	2,591	2,973	3,681	2,915	2,937	1,879
Taiwan	3,374	2,599	4,041	2,296	3,339	1,299
Singapore	2,258	2,642	2,030	2,172	802	945
Korea	1,484	1,275	2,385	1,489	1,555	973
United Kingdom	1,085	1,044	834	1,164	641	489
Germany	939	1,373	2,900	1,041	509	684
France	470	884	634	853	268	351
Others	9,677	8,507	20,913	8,902	10,030	4,569
Total	41,223	40,319	62,379	40,714	33,459	20,708

Source: JETRO, *JETRO White Paper on Foreign Direct Investment,* 2002.

[4] China is accepting large FDI from East Asia (Japan, Taiwan, Singapore, and Korea), US, and Europe (UK, Germany, and France).

From the above arguments in this section, it will be understood that each player has its own problems. Depending on the economic environment, the three types of players will move with their own strategies in forming an East Asia FTA. In the following section, we discuss a possible process of FTA negotiations among the three types of players. The focus will be on the strategic aspects from the perspective of Japan, in the sense that possible scenarios in which Japan leads in the formation of an East Asia FTA are considered.

4. THE PROCESS FOR AN EAST ASIA FTA: THE STRATEGY OF JAPAN

Our arguments for an East Asia FTA in this section start by investigating the possibilities of a bilateral FTA between the three types of players if there is no Japan-Korea FTA. It will be shown that a bilateral FTA with practical effects will be difficult to form, although a superficial FTA might be concluded. Then we discuss the necessity and possibility of a Japan-Korea FTA as a strategy for both Japan and Korea. The final arguments show a possible process for an East Asia FTA when a Japan-Korea FTA exists.

4.1. The Case when There is No Japan-Korea FTA

Let us examine the costs and benefits of forming a bilateral FTA between the three types of players. First, China proposed forming an FTA with ASEAN. This comes from political reasons rather than economic reasons because gains from an FTA between China and ASEAN are not large for China. China is relatively larger than ASEAN and static gains of trade creation will go to the smaller members of ASEAN. Dynamic gains of concentration and scale/space economies will not be large with the unification of the two markets, although potential gains in the future will be large. The FDI that flows into China might be diverted into ASEAN. ASEAN might get larger benefits by specializing in relatively more capital-intensive products and inviting FDI, which might have gone to China without an ASEAN-China FTA. These expected gains for ASEAN should be discounted with the risks of China, which is still in transition and has large economic disparities among its various regions. On the other hand, ASEAN might have to pay greater costs in adjusting from labor-intensive products into more capital-intensive products. The costs will be high for new ASEAN members who must compete with China in labor-intensive products. Both China and ASEAN have internal problems to clear, and thus while an FTA between the two parties may be possible, it may not be an effective FTA.

The benefits of a bilateral FTA between ASEAN and Japan, or ASEAN and Korea, will also be limited. The size of the ASEAN market is not large enough, and Japan and Korea are also unable to provide a large export market for ASEAN. Japan and Korea seek a division of labor in which they specialize in more capital-intensive products while ASEAN countries specialize in labor-intensive products. However ASEAN will be interested in specializing in more capital-intensive products, considering the competition from China and from the development of the new

ASEAN 4. For Japan and Korea, both ASEAN and China are important partners of international trade and investment. ASEAN is interested in attracting FDI and in obtaining technology from Japan and Korea. However Japan and Korea, in the economic environment of global competition, are more interested in directing FDI into China. Therefore, Japan and Korea may not be so enthusiastic about forming an FTA with ASEAN, unless it is a step towards a larger FTA including China. ASEAN has received many proposals for an FTA (most recently from the U.S. at an APEC meeting in Mexico). It is not easy to make a strategic choice among the various FTA scenarios, including an ASEAN-Japan FTA or ASEAN-Korea FTA. Of course a bilateral FTA between one of the ASEAN member countries and Japan or Korea could be formed, but it will take time to have a substantial FTA including ASEAN as a whole.

Currently, the situation is not right for a bilateral FTA between China and Japan, or between China and Korea. The capital funds and technology levels of Japan or Korea are not sufficiently large to make the best use of China's potential. Therefore, it is still necessary for the U.S. and EU to participate. As FTA partners, Japan and Korea do not have large enough markets to absorb larger shares of exports from China. Both countries also have a limited capacity to provide China with a large number of machines for manufacturing products. The limitations also come from risks, stemming from China's economic development and transition into a market economy. Japan or Korea alone do not have enough negotiating power against China and will hesitate to conclude a treaty voluntarily in the near future.

A gradual progress of bilateral FTAs among the three player countries will cover the East Asian region but it will take time for an FTA net to cover all of East Asia without a big push and large incentive policy cooperation among East Asian countries. The priority, at this stage, should be put on preparations for an East Asian FTA for each type of player. ASEAN must make efforts to complete an ASEAN FTA, appropriately treating the four new members. Without an efficient ASEAN FTA, it will be difficult for ASEAN as a whole to engage in FTAs with other countries. China should reduce the uncertainties produced by domestic regional disparities and other problems including its transition into a market economy and problems with Hong Kong and Taiwan. It is not easy for a partner to conclude an FTA treaty with China when there are so many uncertain factors. The other players Japan and Korea should form an FTA between themselves. The benefits and strategic aspects of a Japan-Korea FTA (J-K FTA) will be discussed in the following section.

4.2. An FTA between Japan and Korea

As already mentioned, both Japan and Korea have similar experiences of government-led development and manufacturing sector export-led growth. In both countries, household sector savings are high and investments of big manufacturing firms are financed through the domestic banking systems. The government distributes funds for basic or key producers, and there are not many benefits for consumers. After, the explosion of the recent Japanese bubble in the early 1990s, the Japanese economy is at a lower equilibrium (deflation) level of GDP. For Korean firms, after the Asian currency crisis, Korea's small domestic market has become more disadvantaged in terms of international competition. Both Japan and Korea are interested in a Japan-Korea FTA as there is momentum for economic reform in light of the recession from the bursting of the bubble and the damage from the Asian currency crisis. It has become evident that a traditional system of KEIRETSU (organizational system of grouping in enterprises) or ZAIBATSU (combine, a giant family concern) is not efficient. Competition in a global market is the best way for firms to gain competitiveness. Competition in a free and large market with a J-K FTA might help both countries in their economic restructuring. The changes in the economic environment have caused Japan and Korea to transform their negative views on FTAs into the recent positive actions towards concluding an FTA.

There are arguments against the J-K FTA because of the similarity in the economic structures of the two countries and the large adjustment costs. However, most of the arguments depend on the traditional economic assumption of non-increasing returns. As already mentioned, new international trade theory, of monopolistic competition with increasing returns, has pointed out many gains in the case of trade between similar partners. The new theory of the special economy stresses the concentration effects and a J-K FTA will provide a large enough market to yield concentration effects. Firms that manufacture similar products compete with each other and extend their production capacities to obtain economies of scale and scope. With severe competition, only efficient firms will survive. Firms might survive by product differentiation, by concentration in a final or intermediate product, or by outsourcing their parts. The industrial structure after a J-K FTA will be more complex with a horizontal and vertical network relation of firms and with a diversified division of labor in production processes. The protection of agricultural products and marine products is a politically important issue both for Japan and Korea. However, specialization depending on comparative advantages will be accepted if appropriate compensation mechanisms are provided. The weight of the total value of those products in GDP is small so it should not be too difficult to find a political solution with the international pressure to form FTAs.

It is easy to understand that economic competitiveness scenarios with a J-K FTA are better than scenarios without an FTA for both Japanese and Korean firms. One of the factors which determine the international competitiveness of firms is the size of the domestic market, and thus without an FTA, firms in Japan or Korea cannot gain the advantage of scale relative to firms in NAFTA or the EU. The process of structural reforms in the financial and manufacturing sectors with an FTA will result in the survival of a few competitive firms (banks and companies). With a J-K FTA, the joint domestic market is relatively larger. Mutual investments, cooperation between firms or M&As, and a competitive economic environment will produce firms with more competitiveness in the global market. From this point of view, it should be pointed out that a J-K FTA, which entails investment liberalization, deregulation of M&As, and competitive cooperation among firms, will bring more benefits than mere trade liberalization or tariff reduction.

A J-K FTA is also important as a step towards strategic policy cooperation. Joint strategies of Japanese and Korean firms against firms of the EU and U.S. will be more effective than individual strategies. While Japanese and Korean firms now compete with each other in the export markets of the EU or NAFTA, cooperative strategies between those firms will generate more profitable opportunities. By forming an export coalition, Japanese and Korean firms will find it easier to change the protective policies of the EU and NAFTA countries. Japan and Korea now worry about increasing imports from China; a coalition of Japan and Korea will have greater power in negotiations on import protections. A more important strategy might be in negotiating for FDI into China. Competition between Japanese and Korean firms with regards to FDI into China will reduce the benefits for firms of both countries and give China an advantageous position. However, the benefits will increase if Japan and Korea cooperate to devise negotiating strategies against China. Through a J-K FTA, Japan and Korea can strengthen their bargaining power against outsiders.

4.3. East Asia FTA with J-K FTA

If an FTA between Japan and Korea is concluded, the process for an East Asia FTA will be more promising. The market size of a J-K FTA is not as large as the markets of the EU and NAFTA, but is attractive enough for other East Asian members to join.

With a J-K FTA, ASEAN member countries will have more incentive to conclude a bilateral FTA with Japan or Korea because of a larger export market and FDI by firms with more competitiveness in Japan or Korea. Singapore concluded a bilateral FTA with Japan, and the ASEAN 4 of Thailand, Malaysia, Indonesia, and the Philippines will follow this in the future. The new ASEAN 4 should wait for the accomplishment of an ASEAN FTA to have an effective FTA with Japan or Korea. These bilateral FTA networks will cover ASEAN, Japan, and Korea, and will bring about an environment suitable for an FTA between ASEAN as a whole and Japan or Korea, and then for an FTA between the three parties.

An FTA with China holds risks of uncertainty for the partner country, but the risks could be mitigated and shared if the partner is a group of countries. The partner should be large enough to be comparable to China's potential. Together, Japan and Korea through the J-K FTA could be a good candidate. Under a J-K FTA, the market size is not small and the possible international division of labor between China and Japan-Korea could be diverse. Japan-Korea could provide larger capital funds and appropriate technologies; together, the two countries can also share the risks associated with China and ensure greater negotiating power against China. For China, the benefits of forming an FTA with Japan-Korea will not be small, with a larger J-K FTA export market and inflows of efficient FDI firms from Japan-Korea

China has proposed an FTA to ASEAN, which it will advance in steps. However, as already mentioned, gains from the FTA might not be large for China while costs might be large for ASEAN. Now if ASEAN joins a J-K FTA, China will have a strong incentive to join the J-K FTA to avoid losses from not joining. The same is true for ASEAN so it will have a strong incentive to join a J-K FTA if China joins in. Therefore, an East Asia FTA will be realized through a consensus of the three main players in East Asia.

As a strategy for promoting an East Asian FTA, the first important step is an FTA between Japan and Korea. Then, the next step is to extend the FTA network with bilateral negotiations. With a larger network including a J-K FTA, the possibility of an East Asia FTA will be higher. This scenario is urgent for Japan and Korea, where domestic space for economic concentration is limited and there is an urgent need to extend the space for further concentration. Without an East Asia FTA, Korean and Japanese firms might not be competitive in the global market and then might face the problem of international M&As. Recent international M&As show the strong power of firms in the US and EU (see Tables 5 and 6).[5] East Asian firms might be absorbed by U.S. or EU firms.

Table 5. Cross-border M&As (Sale by countries)

(Unit: Millions of US$)

	1997	1998	1999	2000	2001.1~6
World	340,546	616,602	841,677	1,220,854	361,060
U. S.	87,634	221,221	251,791	335,119	111,772
EU	126,203	237,463	400,525	607,635	147,898
Japan	699	5,108	17,156	16,815	14,446
China	2,143	1,273	2,613	4,550	943
ANIES	14,059	9,212	23,880	17,217	11,527
Korea	900	4,810	11,839	7,383	2,155
Taiwan	894	66	1,867	937	1,448
Hong Kong	10,839	3,735	5,047	6,847	4,471
Singapore	1,426	601	5,127	2,051	3,453
ASEAN4	6,645	8,065	7,826	5,126	2,751

Source: JETRO , *JETRO White Paper on Foreign Direct Investment,* 2002.

Table 6. Cross-border M&As (Purchase by countries)

(Unit: Millions of US$)

	1997	1998	1999	2000	2001.1~6
World	340,546	616,602	841,677	1,220,854	361,060
U. S.	87,842	124,813	161,156	142,697	50,028
EU	154,363	332,400	562,708	881,935	234,254
Japan	5,463	9,630	15,107	21,186	14,716
China	7,810	2,866	437	776	755
ANIES	11,257	10,910	8,188	20,949	2,259
Korea	2,336	118	39	1,421	35
Taiwan	551	645	669	1,286	311
Hong Kong	3,954	8,948	3,652	8,309	1,311
Singapore	4,416	1,199	3,828	9,930	603
ASEAN4	3,265	1,147	1,167	3,443	847

Source: JETRO, *JETRO White Paper on Foreign Direct Investment,* 2002.

China and ASEAN do not fully utilize their economic potentials and it could take

[5] It should be noted that sales of Korea and ASEAN4 are larger than purchase, and this is true for China after 1999. Japan is not a big player of M&A.

time for them to promote an East Asia FTA. China and ASEAN need to establish a cooperative economic relationship, not only with Japan and Korea, but also with the US and EU. For now, it might be a better strategy for China and ASEAN, to get the benefit of competitive assistance from Japan, Korea, the US, and EU. Although, as already mentioned, it will be better for all East Asian players to have a large economic concentration in East Asia. An East Asia FTA will enable the region to realize its large economic potential.

REFERENCES

Aoki, K. and K. Umata. 1999. *Economics of regional integration*. Keiso-shobou. (in Japanese)

Bhagwati, J. 1993. "Regionalism and Multilateralism: An Overview." Jaime de Melo and Arvind Panagariya. Eds. *New Dimension in Regional Integration*. Cambridge: Cambridge University Press.

Cheong, I. 1999. "Economic Integration in Northeast Asia: Search for a Feasible Approach." *Conference paper*. (October 24)

______. 2002. "The Economic Impact and Strategic Importance of the Korea-Japan Free Trade Agreement (FTA)." *Journal of Economics & Business Administration*. Kobe University.

Dixit, A.K. and D. Stiglitz. 1977. "Monopolistic competition and optimum product diversity." *American Economic Review* 76 (3).

Fujita, M., P. Krugman and A. J. Venables. 2001. *The Spatial Economy*. Cambridge: MIT Press.

Helpman, E. and P. Krugman. 1985. *Market Structure and Foreign Trade*. Cambridge: MIT Press.

Igawa, K. and B. Kim. 2000. "A Note on Possibilities about Japan-Korea Free Trade Area: A Strategic Approach." *Kobe Economic & Business Review* 44th.

KIEP (Korea Institute for International Economic Policy). 2001. "Economic Effects and Policy Implication of Korea-Japan FTA." December 4

Kim, B. and K. Igawa. 2001. "Monetary Cooperation in East Asian Countries: A Possibility from Macro Economic Indexes and Intra-Regional Trade Dependency." *Kobe Economics & Business Review* 45th.

______. 2002. "Japan-Korea Free Trade Area and Their Structural Reforms." *Kobe Economics & Business Review* 46th.

Korea Institute for Industrial Economics and Trade. 1999. "Korea-Japan Free Trade Agreement: Corresponding Strategies and Effects on Industries." (in Korean)

Krugman, P. 1991. "Is Bilateralism Bad?" In Elhanan Helpman and Assaf Razin eds. *International Trade Policy*. Cambridge: MIT press

Lee, H, D. Roland-Holst, and D. van der Mensbrugghe. 2002. "Emergence of China and the Implications for Regional Trade Initiatives in the Asian Pacific." *Journal of Economics & Business Administration* (Kobe University). (in Japanese)

De Melo, J. and A. Panagaria eds. 1993. *New Dimensions in Regional integration*. Cambridge University Press.

Mundell, R. A. 1961. "A Theory of Optimum Currency Area." *American Economic Review* 51.

Oda, M. and J. Goto. 2001. "Regional Economic Integration." M. Ohyama ed. *The Horizon of International Economic Theory*. Toyo-Keizai-Sinposya.

Viner, J. 1950. *The Customs Union Issue*. New York: Carnegie Endowment for International Peace.

World Bank. 1997. *World Development Indicators 1997*. The World Bank.

Yamazawa, I. 2002. "Regional Economic Cooperation in East Asia and Strategies of Japan." In *IT Era and International Economic System*. Yuhikaku. (in Japanese)

CHAPTER 3

EVALUATION OF RECENT PROGRESS OF FTAS IN EAST ASIA – A KOREAN PERSPECTIVE

INKYO CHEONG

1. INTRODUCTION

Recently East Asian countries have begun to scrutinize a new vision of East Asian economic cooperation and to consider various ways to execute such a vision. Despite the fact that the world economy is focusing on strengthening economic links through the formation of RTAs, there have been few discussions on similar cooperative efforts in East Asia. However, with a combined market of US$6.2 trillion, a population of almost 2 billion, and a trade volume of US$2.6 trillion in 2001, the region's high industrial output, deposits of natural resources and further advances in economic development, sets the stage for the possibility of economic cooperation as well as greater economic benefits from regional economic integration such as an East Asian free trade agreement. Recent efforts by China, Japan, and the U.S. to forge closer economic relations with East Asian countries also hint at East Asia's economic potential.

Discussions on an East Asian FTA (EAFTA) were first officially initiated at the ASEAN+3 meeting in Brunei in November 2001. Discussions of an ASEAN-Japan FTA have progressed rapidly since talks of an FTA between ASEAN and China blossomed in late 2000. Japan is hastening discussions on an FTA with ASEAN for fear of losing its leadership position to China in the area of regional economic cooperation. On his January 2002 visit to Southeast Asia, Japan's Prime Minister Koizumi Junichiro proposed the establishment of the ASEAN-Japan FTA Study Group. Meanwhile, as discussions of an FTA with ASEAN heated up in China and Japan, Korea has also begun reviewing the rationality of an FTA with ASEAN.

If China, Japan, and Korea competitively pursue bilateral FTAs with ASEAN, this may result in several important issues such as the spaghetti bowl effects, a hub-and-spoke dilemma, regional leadership struggle, political instability, etc. Therefore, this paper tries to show that an East Asian FTA covering the whole region is economically desirable. This paper also stresses that East Asian countries should introduce a region-wide FTA, rather than multiple bilateral or sub-regional FTAs. An East Asian FTA can be realized in the long term because of economic, political, and social obstacles. East Asian countries, which already lag behind countries in other

C. Y. Ahn et al (eds.), East Asian Economic Regionalism, 37-56.

regions in terms of regionalism, should not passively wait for the East Asian FTA, which is likely to take some time to be established. Rather, the current momentum of increasing discussions and interest in FTAs should be progressively promoted in order to realize the East Asian FTA. That is, a strategic approach is needed to develop the bilateral and sub-regional FTAs, currently under discussion, into an East Asian FTA.

2. RECENT DEVELOPMENTS TOWARDS AN EAST ASIAN FTA

The growing interest in FTAs in East Asia could be attributed to the proliferation of regionalism, the East Asian financial crisis, East Asia's awareness to boost its economic cooperation, China's WTO accession and the expansion of East Asian personal networks through various forms of meetings.

Since the launch of the WTO in 1995, it has been reported that more than 96 new RTAs have formed, indicating that countries are pursuing RTAs as a strategic trade policy rather than as an insurance policy against the failure of the multilateral system. If regionalism is established in other regions, non-member countries suffer from the disadvantages of trade diversion. Thus, even countries with little previous experience in RTAs are actively participating in smaller RTAs to prepare for regionalism as well as to gain experience for globalization through economic integration.

Generally, it was thought that physical distance affected trade levels due to increasing transportation costs. Although international trade related costs are falling with the development of transportation technology, physical distance is still an important factor in determining the scale of intra-regional trade. Also cultural factors play a vital role. Considering the physical and cultural aspects, it is highly possible that East Asia's intra-regional trade will expand once an institutional framework like the FTA is introduced.

The main regional trade agreement in East Asia is the ASEAN Free Trade Area (AFTA). Initially composed of six member countries including Malaysia, Indonesia, Thailand, the Philippines, Singapore and Brunei, AFTA was formed as a result of the fourth ASEAN Summit meeting in 1992. With Vietnam joining in 1995, Myanmar and Laos in 1997 and Cambodia in 1999, AFTA developed into a regional trade agreement overseeing the entire Southeast Asian region. Recently, these countries have been discussing bilateral FTAs with China, Japan, India and CER (the FTA between Australia and New Zealand), and it is known that the U.S. is considering an FTA with ASEAN countries.[1]

Until recently, the Northeast Asian countries - China, Japan, and Korea - have not participated in any regional trade agreements. After the financial crisis, however, these countries began to show a great interest in establishing FTAs. In 1998, Korea announced its plan to proceed with an FTA with Chile and also began a joint study with Japan. The Korea-Chile FTA negotiations were launched in December 1999

[1] The U.S. announced a new trade initiative with ASEAN, implying the possibility of bilateral FTAs with some ASEAN countries. See "Fact Sheet: Enterprise for ASEAN Initiative" at www.whitehouse.gov.

and concluded in October 2002. In addition to the FTA with Chile, Korea has been participating in joint research on the economic effects of bilateral FTAs with Japan, New Zealand and Thailand. The results of the joint research on the FTA with Japan, which started in 1999, were announced at international symposiums in Seoul and Tokyo respectively held in May and September 2000. Thereafter, by forming the Japan-Korea FTA Business Forum, the private sector of the two countries discussed the promotion direction for the FTA. Leaders at the Japan-Korea summit held in March 20002 agreed to form a government-led joint study group to give impetus to the discussions on the FTA. It is reported that the Korean government will establish its ground plan for the FTA with Japan based on the group's study results.

Table 1. Progress of Regionalism in East Asia

FTAs	Progress				
	Discussion	Joint Study	Negotiations	Conclusion	Implementation
AFTA					V
AFTA-China			V		
AFTA-Japan		V			
AFTA-Korea		V			
AFTA-India	V				
AFTA-U.S.	V				
China-Japan-Korea	V				
East Asian FTA	V				
Japan-Chile		V			
Japan-Canada	V				
Japan-Mexico			V		
Japan-Taiwan	V				
Japan-Singapore					V
Korea-Chile				V	
Korea-Japan			V		
Korea-Mexico		V			
Korea-New Zealand		V			
Korea-Singapore			V		
Korea-Thailand		V			

Source: Cheong (2003)

The Singapore ASEAN-China summit in November 2000 showed the most dramatic change in the FTA policies of Northeast Asian countries when Chinese Premier Zhu Rongji proposed the possibility of an FTA with ASEAN.[2] China is also actively promoting a bilateral FTA with ASEAN. China proposed tariff reductions on 600 agricultural items for ASEAN countries, and announced its wish to conclude an FTA with ASEAN by 2004 at the Phnom Penh ASEAN-China summit. Meanwhile, Japan also made it clear that it plans to promote an FTA with ASEAN within the next ten years. On November 6, 2002, the New Straight Times, the most acknowledged English newspaper in Southeast Asia, published an editorial stating "Japan, playing catch up with China, seeks a piece of the Free Trade Area Pie." In other words, instead of playing a leading role in promoting East Asian Regionalism, Japan was reacting passively to China's FTA policy.

Suggestions for a China-Japan-Korea FTA are mostly raised by private industries. For example, during the 15th Korea-Japan business conference held in Tokyo on October 29, 1998, Korean presenters proposed that the government of Korea examine the possibility of concluding a free trade agreement encompassing China, Japan, and Korea. Later, Korean business circles and economic organizations requested that the government promote a CJK FTA. At the China-Korea Economic Symposium (March 2002), held by the Chosun Daily of Korea and People's Daily of China, in Beijing, Korean businessmen emphasized the promotion of a China-Korea FTA and a CJK FTA[3].

One of most important development towards an East Asian FTA is China's entry into the WTO and China's progressive approach to regionalism. According to Cao (2002), the goal of an FTA might differ country by country; however, common backgrounds can be a policy response against the expansion of regionalism and the complements of the shortcomings of the multilateral trading system. He also points out that a country could secure benefits in terms of trade and investment by concluding an FTA, and raise the ability to cope with shock from any possible economic crisis.

It is highly possible that China will be more progressive in considering bilateral and subregional FTAs in Northeast Asia after 2005. China announced plans to establish an FTA with ASEAN within 10 years; however the date could be advanced. China might launch an earlier FTA with the original six member countries (ASEAN-6) with a mid to long term goal of launching an FTA with all ten ASEAN countries. The biggest advantage for China regarding the FTA policy is that once China's leaders promote an FTA within a certain region, the government can make rapid progress under its socialistic system of centralized decision-making. This contrasts with Japan and Korea where FTA negotiations could be obstructed by members in vulnerable industries and diverse interest groups. When China realizes the economic necessity of an FTA and decides that the internal and external conditions are ready, China will promote FTAs with its neighboring countries, in

[2] During the ASEAN+3 Summits, each country of Northeast Asia holds a bilateral summit with ASEAN.
[3] In a survey conducted by the Federation of Korean Industries (FKI, 2001) targeting its member companies, Korean companies answered that the U.S. (36.8%) and China (29.3%) would be the two most desirable partners for bilateral FTAs.

addition to ASEAN. The proposal for a study on an FTA of China, Japan and Korea can be an important momentum for China's FTA policy.

Japan did not pay serious attention to the formation of preferential trading blocs until 1998, emphasizing its consistent and endless efforts to maintain free trade under the multilateral trading system. The Ministry of Foreign Affairs (MOFA) also held a negative position toward regionalism in 1998. MOFA (1998) emphasized the problems of regional trading blocs and underlined the importance of strengthening the multilateral trading system. However, as Korea and Chile announced their plan to proceed with an FTA, Japan began to show an interest in entering an FTA with Korea. Japan established its first FTA with Singapore January 2002, and is under negotiation with Mexico.

As East Asian countries have experienced disadvantages from the effects of regionalism in other regions, countries in East Asia have begun to consider establishing its own regional trade bloc recently. East Asian countries finally began to reconsider economic integration, realizing that they would be at disadvantage compared to North America and Europe. The 1997 financial crisis led East Asian countries to realize the need to strengthen economic cooperation. A relationship between East Asia's financial crisis and regionalism can be found in studies by Bergsten (2000), Eichengreen (2002), Yamazawa (2001) and Yip (2001). Yamazawa (2001) asserted that the turning point in East Asian regionalism was the Asian financial crisis. "Through the experience of that awful time, policy makers in this region acknowledged that they were not equipped to prevent and manage such a crisis. They were irked by their helplessness and undue dependence on the international financial institutions in Washington, and they began to toy with the idea of resolving their problems for themselves within Asia."[4] Yip (2001) stated, "on the monetary side, the single greatest push for East Asian regionalism was the financial crisis of 1997-1999. Many East Asians felt that they were both let down by the West during the crisis. In their view, western banks and other financial institutions had created and exacerbated the crisis by pulling out their funds from the region."

Eichengreen (2002) says, "The Chiang Mai Initiative is indicative for a historic shift in Asia's approach to regional integration. That crisis fostered the belief that Asian countries need to band together in order to create a framework for economic, financial, and political stability in which the contagious spread of crises is minimized and they are insulated from destabilizing impulses emanating from outside." Thailand's currency crisis in early July 1997 quickly spread to other Asian countries such as Indonesia, the Philippines, Malaysia and Korea. The past decades of rapid economic growth had placed East Asian countries in a position of increased interdependence and competition. A currency crisis in one country has adverse impacts on the economies of other countries and can cause currency devaluation. As a result, a vicious cycle is created where a crisis escalates and deepens from a

[4] Bustelo (2002) denies that East Asia's financial crisis provided an opportunity to establish East Asia's regionalism by stating, "The short- and medium-term effects of the financial crisis might involve a backlash against regional and trans-Pacific economic integration".

national level to a regional level. Also, some East Asian countries took a negative view on the role of the IMF and the U.S. saying that they worsened the crisis by imposing conditions on their aid. Regarding this, Yip (2001) stated that "East Asian countries have decided that they do not want to be beholden to the West should a crisis recur in the future."

In order to prevent the spread of crisis from one country to another, East Asian countries felt the need to reinforce regional economic cooperation. At present, there has been more action in the area of financial cooperation rather than trade cooperation through the creation of an economic cooperative body. Bilateral Swap Agreements (BSAs) are underway in East Asian countries through the Chiang Mai Initiative (CMI). A purpose of CMI is to promptly provide liquidity to regional countries showing signs of a currency crisis by equipping and strengthening liquidity support facility. Currently liquidity support is comprised of two components. One is a monetary swap agreement, introduced by the previous five ASEAN countries (Thailand, Malaysia, Philippines, Singapore, and Indonesia) in 1997, which has expanded to 10 ASEAN countries with a $1 billion fund. It came into effect on November 17th, 2000. Another component includes a network to support liquidity among ASEAN+3, by concluding bilateral monetary swap agreements (BSAs). Currently, BSAs are underway. As of June 2002, a total of eight BSAs were concluded with a fund of $23 billion with six BSAs in progress.

Bergsten (2000) suggested, "Another motivation for Asian regional initiatives is the failure of the existing international economic institutions to provide East Asia with a role consistent with its economic progress." In other words, East Asian countries have been neglected by international organizations like the IMF and IBRD. For example, although Japan's economy of scale is half the scale of the U.S. and Europe, its quota in these organizations is only 1/3 and 1/5 the quotas of the U.S. and Europe, respectively. Korea, which ranks 11th in terms of economy of scale, has a very small quota, while China, ranked 2nd in purchasing power was relegated to 11th place in the size of its quota. Disturbed by their small quotas, countries in East Asia began considering East Asian regionalism as a means of elevating their status in the international community.

The development of personal networks has been an important factor in accelerating recent talks on East Asian regionalism. While discussing economic cooperation between East Asia and Europe through ASEM, East Asian countries began to consider the need to reposition themselves at the regional level against the single entity of Europe. The ASEAN+3 Summit first took place in 1997 when Malaysia's Prime Minister Mahathir unofficially invited the political leaders of China, Japan and Korea to ASEAN's 30th anniversary. This event sparked an acceleration of discussions on intra-regional economic cooperation and consolidation in East Asia. From the first to fourth Summit meetings, the main agenda was on overcoming the financial crisis and strengthening intra-regional economic cooperation. At the third ASEAN+3 Summit in the Philippines in 1999, the "Joint Agreement on East Asian Cooperation" was announced as the basic principle of a long-term cooperation plan. The areas for cooperation were diverse, including trade, investment, technology transfers, e-commerce, agriculture, small and medium-sized businesses, tourism, and the development of the Mekong river basin.

After the financial crisis, East Asian countries realized the limit of export oriented developmental policy, which mainly targeted the U.S. market. Being heavily dependent on a major export market such as the U.S. made East Asia vulnerable to the negative effects stemming from a stagnating world economy. In order to prevent exposure to such risks, East Asian countries should strive to restructure and create their own demand by curbing dependence on non-Asian regions for exports, creating domestic demand or making intra-regional demand the driving force for stable economic growth. Besides domestic efforts like improving the economic system, intra-regional trade liberalization through an FTA can be an effective scheme. Regarding this aspect, Munakata (2001a) pointed out that the East Asian regional market should be integrated to stimulate regional demand. While East Asian countries are concerned about the "hollowing out" of industries triggered by China's industrialization, they hope to make the most of China's economic growth. Moreover, as the stagnation of the world economy triggered a drop in East Asia's exports to other regions, the incentive for East Asian countries to expand exports to China grew.

The possibility of an East Asian FTA has been actively discussed at ASEAN+3 meetings. An East Asian FTA was proposed by the East Asian Vision Group (EAVG)[5] in a report to the ASEAN+3 Summit in 2001, and the issue is expected to be at the top of the agenda at future ASEAN+3 Summit meetings. The East Asian Study Group (EASG), which was assigned to follow up the proposals by the EAVG, also proposed mid to long-term cooperative measures and additional subjects for study in its final report at the ASEAN+3 Summit at Phnom Penh in 2002. Some of the measures proposed in the report are the transformation of the ASEAN+3 Summit to the East Asia Summit, the establishment of an East Asia Investment Area, and an East Asian FTA. Through the official studies by EAVG and EASG, the members of ASEAN+3 began to realize the need for an FTA as a means of promoting economic integration in the region in the long-term, to cope with the economic integration in North America and Europe, and to promote the introduction of institutional measures for trade and investment liberalization in the region. This report recommends that the ASEAN+3 Economic Ministers undertake a feasibility study to examine the impacts, problems, and implications of an East Asian FTA.

Promoting an East Asian FTA may be difficult since there are tricky issues at hand, such as the economic gap between member countries and the struggle for leadership over the region. It may be feasible that East Asian countries promote an East Asian FTA while resolving these issues in the long-term. However, there is a slight chance that rapid progress may be made in East Asian regionalism as East Asia feels the need to strengthen economic cooperation in the face of the continuous global expansion of regionalism and the integration of the world economy

[5] East Asian Vision Group was composed of twenty-six representatives from thirteen member countries (two representatives per country), and was assigned to produce a report for East Asian economic cooperation. The Vision Report was reported to the ASEAN+3 Summit held in Brunei Darussalam in November 2001. The report recommends that East Asia should pursue economic integration through the liberalization of trade and investment, developmental and technological cooperation, and information technology (IT) development.

concentrated in North America and Europe. This point has already been discussed at the ASEAN+3 Summit, and based on enough progress, leaders may discuss the possibility of an East Asian FTA in the future ASEAN+3 meeting. In November 2001, at the fifth Summit in Brunei, the participants examined the establishment of an East Asian FTA as suggested in the EAVG report. This was regarded to be especially meaningful to the three Northeast Asian countries, since it will initiate economic cooperation in East Asia as well as in Northeast Asia.

Since China's proposal to pursue an FTA with ASEAN during the Singapore ASEAN+3 Summit meeting in November 2000, interest is mounting over whether China can become a leader in economic integration. Regarding FTAs, China and Japan show different approaches. As seen in its FTA with Singapore, Japan emphasizes the concept of the "New Age Agreement" or "Economic Partnership Agreement" which promotes financial cooperation, IT cooperation, and limited human resource mobilization while excluding the agricultural sector from the liberalization package. Meanwhile, the current ASEAN-China FTA under discussion shows China's intent to include even the agricultural sector, under the "Early Harvest" package for ASEAN countries, so that they can benefit economically even before the conclusion of an agreement. These examples show the difference in the approaches of China and Japan. One country excluded the agricultural sector due to the weakness of its own agricultural sector, implying that the form it pursues will likely be used in future FTAs.

In contrast, the other country decided to promote FTAs while supporting struggling regional countries. As long as Japan maintains its current position, it will be difficult for Japan to become a leader in economic integration. Recently the Japanese government has been reflecting about FTAs, since ASEAN stresses the liberalization of its agricultural sector during the discussion of the ASEAN-Japan FTA, it will be difficult for Japan to exclude agriculture from the liberalization as it was able to do for the FTA with Singapore.

The three Northeast Asian countries of China, Japan and Korea are now showing a more aggressive attitude toward establishing an East Asian FTA. China has already completed a joint study with ASEAN for a bilateral FTA, and is now discussing the FTA at the government level. Japan has also formed a joint study group with ASEAN.[6] At the Phnom Penh ASEAN-China Summit, ASEAN and China signed the Framework Agreement on ASEAN- China Economic Cooperation, which will serve as the fulcrum for establishing the free-trade area by 2010 for the older ASEAN members and 2015 for the newer members with flexibility on sensitive commodities. As China and Japan strengthen economic cooperation with ASEAN, Korea will inevitably re-evaluate an FTA with ASEAN.[7] Korea concluded an internal examination on the feasibility of an FTA with ASEAN, and it is known that it would propose official discussion on an ASEAN-Korea FTA in 2003 based on the

[6] Munakata (2002) analyzes that "the November 2001 agreement between China and ASEAN to negotiate a free trade agreement sent a shock wave throughout Japan. Some speculated that Japan might try to block this initiative, which could deal a blow to Japan's regional leadership."

[7] During the ASEAN-Korea Summit in November 2001, Singaporean Prime Minister Goh Chok Tong suggested an FTA between ASEAN and Korea.

result of this study.

3. WHY EAST ASIAN REGIONALISM LAGS BEHIND EUROPE'S AND AMERICA'S

The world is tripolar in terms of economics, but only bipolar in terms of regional institutions/initiatives. Along with North America and the EU, East Asia has developed into one of the world's three economic pillars. The Asian development model was greatly praised and the East Asian development was referred to as a "miracle" before the financial crisis.[8] However, struggles over hegemony and the lack of a leading country have hindered the development of an economic bloc in East Asia.

East Asia is the only remaining region without a regional economic bloc like the EU or NAFTA. Although regarded as one of the three major economic pillars, East Asia has the lowest level of economic cooperation compared to the EU and North America. Therefore, countries in East Asia need to strengthen regional economic cooperation.

Table 2. Status of East Asia's Economy (2001)

(Unit: %)

	Population	GDP	Trade	FDI (2000)
Northeast Asia	24.1	20.1	12.7	7.7
ASEAN	8.7	1.9	5.7	1.8
East Asia	32.8	22.0	18.4	9.5
EU	6.2	23.7	17.0	43.9
NAFTA	6.9	40.0	22.0	24.0

Source: IMF (2002), *Direction of Trade Statistics: Yearbook.*
DRI (2002), *The World Economic Outlook*, 1st Quarter.
UNCTAD (2002), *World Investment Report.*

In the meantime, there have been some unsuccessful attempts to establish regionalism in East Asia. Some cases in point are when Malaysian Prime Minister Mahathir proposed the establishment of an EAEG and when Japan attempted to create an Asian Monetary Fund in 1997, with both ending in failure. Yip (2001) showed that East Asia's regional economic integration will be difficult to achieve due to the differing economic stance of each country and the opposition of non-Asian countries. Malaysia's proposal to create an EAEG including ASEAN member countries, China, Japan and Korea was perceived as an alliance of East Asian countries to confront North American and European economic integration amidst delays in the conclusion of the Uruguay Round. However, the proposal broke down due to a lukewarm response from East Asian countries and opposition from the U.S. Although Malaysia modified its proposal to merely holding periodic

[8] According to the World Bank (1993), East Asian countries grew at an annual rate of 7.4%, Africa 1.8% and Latin American countries 1.7% in the 1980s. East Asian economies kept a sustained and high economic growth at the beginning of the 1990s.

conferences to discuss regional economic issues and coordinating economic policies, it ultimately collapsed under the strong objection of non-Asian countries. Japan suggested establishing an Asian Monetary Fund with US$100 billion, which East Asian countries could finance and manage independent of the IMF. But again, the plan was not realized owing to the wariness of several Southeast Asian countries toward Japan and the objections of Western countries.

There are currently two FTAs among East Asian countries: an AFTA of Southeast Asia and a Japan-Singapore FTA. Japan and Korea have been conducting a feasibility study on the economic impact of a bilateral FTA since 1999. China and Japan are in the process of negotiating bilateral FTAs with ASEAN. An East Asian FTA, which is an FTA including all regions in East Asia, is under discussion. During the ASEAN+3 Summit in 1999, the Philippines proposed unifying East Asia into one market by concluding an FTA.

According to Bustelo (2002), economic integration or regionalism has been occurring informally in East Asia for decades; however, except for ASEAN, East Asia still seems far from establishing a formal regionalism like that of Western Europe. The major characteristic of such an informal regional agreement is that there are no spillover effects from economic issues to other technical dimensions. Bustelo believes that such a dimensional limit can even be applied to ASEAN regionalism. However, his opinion is based on East Asian regionalism prior to the financial crisis so it may no longer be relevant to the ongoing debate on the official development of an East Asian FTA.

Possible reasons for the stagnation of East Asian regionalism include the high dependency on trade with the U.S., different political systems, certain aspects of the industrial structure, high economic growth before the crisis, historical factors and the lack of an initiating country.

First, a trade structure that is heavily dependent on the U.S. has led to greater East Asian interest in economic cooperation with the superpower and less interest in promoting similar cooperation within the region.[9] More than 20% of the total exports of most East Asian countries are to the U.S., while Japan and Malaysia's export dependency rates on the U.S. are about 30%. As a result, East Asian countries have not felt a serious need to establish an East Asian regional trade bloc.

Under the Cold War ideology of the 1970s and 1980s when the East Asian economy began to develop full-scale, the U.S. refrained from provoking trade frictions and absorbed exports from developing East Asian countries despite its severe trade deficit. Consequently, East Asian countries looked towards the U.S., which provided large open markets with relatively fewer trade barriers. The U.S., for its part, did not want the formation of a separate trade bloc in East Asia, emphasizing the fact that the U.S. was the biggest importer of East Asian goods.

Despite the great global interest in FTAs in the 1980s, developing countries in East Asia did not feel the need for such agreements since their economies were growing rapidly and they were being praised as the 'miracle of East Asia.' The East

[9] This fact is reflected in trade flows. Eichengreen (2002) shows that East Asia's intra-regional trade ratios are low by the standard of the EU.

Asian region could record higher economic growth rates, and "thus did not feel any need to secure markets through discriminatory economic integration agreements." (Munakata 2001b, p. 2) Developing countries in East Asia achieved an increase in exports and economic growth from a favorable loose international trade environment with the Generalized System of Preferences (GSP) provided by advanced countries.

Except for Japan, developing countries in East Asia had similar export structures. It was thought that the East Asian market was not large and thus expansion of intra-regional trade was unlikely. Therefore, expanding exports to lucrative non-Asian third markets like the U.S. was considered a shortcut to economic growth.

Moreover, problems in industrial structures also hindered the development of East Asian regionalism. Even with the establishment of an FTA, if the benefits of regional trade liberalization are limited because countries in the region have similar industrial structure, regionalism is not likely to develop into deep integration in the short run. Unlike Northeast Asia, Southeast Asia got a head start in developing regionalism, launching AFTA in January 2002. Nevertheless, Southeast Asia has not shown much interest in extending AFTA to Northeast Asia to form an East Asian FTA. There are several possible explanations for this, and the fact that the industrial structure of Southeast Asian countries is not conducive to economically benefiting from an FTA is one of the reasons. With AFTA, industries in member countries did not stand to gain much from the agreement and thus did not exert pressure to accelerate economic integration.

A considerable part of the manufacturing sector was established through foreign direct investment and major components were brought in from parent companies located overseas. These characteristics made it difficult to satisfy the preferential rules of origin under AFTA. Currently, the volume of intra-regional trade is around 25% of AFTA's total exports, and 60% to 70% of that is composed of transactions between Singapore, Malaysia, and Indonesia. If trans-shipments from Singapore's free port are excluded, the volume of regional trade is only 5%. The only industries that benefited from AFTA were probably the oil and mining sectors. Even in Malaysia, where the volume of regional trade with other ASEAN countries amounts to 20% to 25%, only 3% of the goods exported to ASEAN are subject to AFTA's Common Effective Preferential Tariffs (CEPT). Thus, AFTA has failed to attract the interest and support of the private sector and its expansion to other regions such as Northeast Asia has been limited.

Political factors also negatively affected the development of an East Asian FTA. East Asia has experienced wars and ideological conflicts. With the memory of Japanese occupation still fresh, China, Korea, and several Southeast Asian countries tend to distrust Japan on political issues. *The Economist* (2002) describes Chinese-Japanese relations as "less than cordial," stating that China and Japan mistrust each other.

China experienced ideological conflicts with other East Asian countries because of its socialist system, and Korea, Vietnam and Cambodia were internally divided by ideological differences. ASEAN was created by Southeast Asian countries to confront the fall of Indochina to communism and with the political purpose of strengthening ties and voicing positions. Faced with potential competition over regional leadership in East Asia, neither Japan nor China could initiate regional cooperation through regionalism during the Cold War as any active gesture to establish a trading bloc by either country could provoke the other country. In addition, Japan's history of military aggression makes East Asian regionalism even harder to develop. Eichengreen (2002) says that "Asian governments are suspicious of strong supranational institutions," and "regional integration tends to be organized on the basis of 'soft institutionalism'."

In the case of Europe, economic integration was promoted to dissipate the remaining hostilities of war and as a result, went beyond 'Fortress Europe' to adopt a unified currency and parliament. However, similar developments did not happen in East Asia. Differences between Europe and East Asia arise from the fact that East Asian countries share few economic and political similarities compared to the countries in Europe. East Asia also lacks a leader or leading country to initiate economic integration. In the case of European unification, Jean Monnet and Robert Schuman laid the foundation by insisting that strengthened economic cooperation would help maintain peace.[10] However, such figures have yet to appear in East Asia. In Europe, the main disputing players, Germany and France, took the leading role to influence economic integration and induce the participation of neighboring countries whereas no East Asian country has emerged to play a similar role for East Asian integration. Japan is the most promising country in terms of economic power, but it has not yet taken a leadership role to an extent befitting its stature.

At the same time, Yip (2001) believes that East Asian regionalism has been delayed owing to political factors rather than economic reasons. He points out that many East Asian countries were under a system of regional security established by the U.S., and thus were not able to construct an independent regionalism. After World War II, the U.S., in order to protect its own interests in East Asia, tried to hinder foreign nations from expanding their power and continued to cooperate economically with East Asia while facilitating regional order and security. As a result, the U.S. gained hegemony in East Asia and may react sensitively to East Asia's economic integration efforts that exclude the U.S. in light of the following three concerns: 1) East Asian countries might build up military power through economic growth, and as a result, threaten order and security in the region. 2) Conflicts between East Asia and the West might intensify and East Asia might attain regional leadership through economic integration, 3) The smaller countries of East Asia might unite with a regional power like China and Japan and challenge U.S. hegemony.

On the other hand, there is opposition to economic integration in East Asia within the region. Historically, China has been known to avoid formal economic/political cooperation initiatives that can influence its internal policy decisions. Also there still remains antagonism and competition among East Asian countries stemming from Japan's past imperialism. On the whole, Japan's refusal to make an official apology impedes East Asia's regional integration.

Recently, the politically antagonistic relationships in Northeast Asia seem to

[10] Refer to Fontaine (1992) for the roles of Jean Monnet and Robert Schuman in the early stage of European integration.

have been mitigated to some extent. Munakata (2001a) observed that "trilateral relations among the U.S., Japan and China are improving simultaneously, an unusual situation, since the terrorist attacks," and "Tokyo-Beijing tensions have substantially eased." Munakata (2002) describes this phenomenon by stating, "It is remarkable that the competitive tension among China, Japan and Korea created enhanced momentum for regional cooperation." She also suggests "East Asian leaders should not let this historic opportunity slip away."

4. HOW TO ACHIEVE AN EAST ASIAN FTA

This chapter discussed regionalism within East Asia, which is now in progress, and reasons for its slow development in East Asia. In Chapter *, eight hypothetical FTAs in East Asia were assumed and their economic effects were estimated. The findings show that member countries would benefit from both bilateral FTAs and regional FTAs, like a China-Japan-Korea (CJK) FTA and an East Asian FTA. However, the analysis shows that greater economic benefits would be derived under a regional FTA like a CJK FTA rather than under a bilateral FTA. Although the simulation used in the study estimated that a CJK FTA and East Asian FTA would bring a similar level of economic benefits, the chapter argues that greater benefits would be gained under an East Asian FTA than a CJK FTA. This could be verified with a more sophisticated economic model and analytical method. Here, a question we need to answer is how to achieve the East Asian FTA.

There are several possible ways to promote an East Asian FTA. Under current conditions, it may be difficult to promote an FTA covering the whole East Asian region in the short term, due to various reasons, although it is the most economically desirable approach for the region. Therefore as the second best alternative, an East Asian FTA should be phased in starting with the FTAs currently under discussion. Each country in Northeast Asia may form a bilateral FTA with ASEAN, and gradually develop and expand the bilateral FTAs to an East Asian FTA. A similar scenario is to establish an East Asian FTA based on bilateral FTAs currently under active negotiation. Japan has already concluded an FTA (EPA) with Singapore; Japan and Korea are in the process of reviewing a bilateral FTA; and China and Japan are pursuing bilateral FTAs with ASEAN. Sooner or later, Korea will pursue an ASEAN-Korea FTA. Then, East Asia will observe a web of bilateral FTAs in the region. These FTAs would contribute to regional trade liberalization, and increase the need for an East Asian FTA while fostering a foundation for it.

However, consolidating different FTAs could be tremendously difficult since the different trade regulations under various bilateral FTAs will have to be standardized into one agreement. Young (2002) stated, "It is highly unlikely that an East Asian FTA will evolve by itself as a result of amalgamation of bilateral FTAs." Also, there is a possibility that the competition between China and Japan, countries currently vying for regional leadership, may be intensified through bilateral FTAs with ASEAN, making an East Asian FTA more difficult.

The third option is to have Northeast Asia create a CJK FTA, rather than having multiple bilateral FTAs, and then to move in the direction of consolidating it with

AFTA. Wanandi (2000) supported this approach to the East Asian FTA, asserting that a region-wide FTA can be established in the mid- to long-term through bilateral negotiations and activation of subregionalism in East Asia. He emphasized the AFTA together with the Japan-Korea FTA will play the most important role in forming an East Asian FTA.

Although Japan and Korea are officially discussing a bilateral FTA, it will be difficult for the two countries to ignore China's position, considering the political and economic relations of countries in Northeast Asia. China is negotiating an FTA with ASEAN countries, and having joined the WTO at the end of 2001, it expects to build a stable market economy and be ready to promote FTAs in the near future. China's recent proposal of examining a CJK FTA has complicated the FTA issue in Northeast Asia. Korea supported the Chinese proposal, which was presented at the China-Japan-Korea Summit at Phnom Penh, while Japan proposed that the Japan-Korea FTA currently under discussion be concluded first before pursuing a China-Japan FTA.

As the examination of a CJK FTA starts next year, Japan may wish for an early start on its FTA negotiations with Korea; although it may not be easy for Korea to accept Japan's request. Korea has no assurance of benefiting from an FTA with Japan. Japan absolutely needs an FTA with Korea[11], and although it has a relatively advantageous position in negotiations, it has not been progressive in discussing a balanced agreement that would be acceptable to Korea. Since 1999, Japan has held the position that in an FTA with Korea, agricultural sectors be excluded. Japan has also tried to include the additional FTA plus measures which were included in the Japan-Singapore FTA. Related with this point, it is worth noting Tanaka (2002)'s views on Japan's FTA policy. He criticizes Japan's policy of promoting FTAs with neighboring countries in order to solve its domestic problems; rather, he argues, Japan should reinforce its industrial restructuring and boost domestic demand through economic stimulation prior to promoting an FTA with Korea.

Discussions on a CJK FTA and a Japan-Korea FTA will be carried out simultaneously starting from 2003, but considering the current situation, the Japan-Korea FTA is likely to progress more quickly. This presumption is based on the fact that the two countries have discussed their bilateral FTA since 1999. Furthermore, in addition to discussing their bilateral FTA, Japan and Korea should examine a scheme to invite China to participate in the two countries' FTA. In other words, Japan and Korea should utilize their FTA as a strategic framework for a CJK FTA in the mid term and an East Asian FTA in the long term. Thus when Japan and Korea form an FTA, it should be designed with China in mind as a potential member.

It would be ideal to have China as an initial member, but China is not ready to join. Because of this, China seems to propose a joint study on a CJK FTA. If Japan and Korea complete their FTA, then move to establish another FTA with ASEAN to

[11] Japan wants to conclude an FTA with Korea to escape from the difficulties from its economic recession and industrial structural adjustment, and to cope with China's aggressive FTA policy, etc. Japan's MOFA (2002) indicates that Korea is its most important FTA partner.

gradually initiate an East Asian FTA, China will inevitably feel conflicted about whether to participate in East Asian FTA discussions or to construct its own independent regionalism. From an economic perspective, it is desirable for China to participate in an East Asian FTA. Rather than participating in an FTA of Japan-Korea-AFTA led by Japan, China could cope with a Japan-led East Asian regionalism by concluding an FTA with ASEAN early on and extending it to Korea.

In addition to the technical difficulties involved in consolidating multiple FTAs into a single FTA, the sequencing of FTAs in East Asia can raise other issues such as a hub-and-spoke problem, a struggle over regional leadership, political instability, etc. Also, without a clear understanding of the problems these issues could lead to, it will be difficult to construct a policy direction for East Asian economic cooperation. Countries aspire to become the regional FTA hub country in order to attain the benefits of trade expansion and FDI inflows. For instance, increased competitiveness by importing the most suitable raw materials from multiple spokes customs-free and expanding foreign direct investment inflow are some of the advantages. Also a hub country has many advantages in negotiating new FTAs and is in a better position to persuade its prospective partners to accept the conditions of its existing FTAs or other conditions favorable to itself. In a specific region, a hub country could also display its political and economic leadership. This is one of the reasons that China is promoting an FTA with ASEAN and Japan is promoting bilateral FTAs with Korea and ASEAN.

On the other hand, Wonnacott (1996) theoretically shows that constructing an FTA covering the whole region is more advantageous than a hub-and-spoke system. Investment is made in the most efficient industries only in a hub region, and spill over effects will be limited in the latter approach. In addition, a hub-and-spoke structure is relatively inefficient compared to a regional FTA due to the increase of trade-related costs. Since a hub constructs a complex trade network with multiple spokes, traders' compliance costs increase. Also businesses of the hub will pursue rent-seeking behavior. That is, firms in a hub try to maintain monopolistic positions in the hub-and-spoke structure, hindering a competitor from one spoke from branching out to another spoke. Finally, under a hub-and-spoke system, firms in a hub country are more likely to enforce a managed trade system, resulting in lower gains from specialization and trade. This is because, a spoke may have to accept worse provisions in a one-on-one bilateral negotiation with a hub than it would if it were to join an FTA instead which included that hub. Snape (1996) illustrated that multilateral trade liberalization can be impeded as a hub-and-spoke system develops in a specific region. Since individual spokes have preferential access to a hub, they will resist multilateral tariff reduction for sensitive items. Findlay (2000) concluded that the hub and spoke structure contains many dangers. There are strong incentives for economies to try to become the hub in an attempt to dominate economies in their region, leading to a structure of layers of discrimination and potential conflicts.

If ASEAN concludes bilateral FTAs with each of the Northeast Asian countries, it is possible that AFTA will become the hub and the three countries in Northeast Asia will remain as spokes. Scholars of Southeast Asia, including Chia Siow Yue and Hadi Soesastro hold the position that Southeast Asia can be a hub in an East Asian FTA.[12] According to these scholars, the Southeast Asian region could be a hub through bilateral FTAs with China, Japan and Korea, and the FTA with Australia and New Zealand since Southeast Asia has already launched AFTA and has the longest history of regionalism in East Asia.

However, it is questionable whether concluding multiple bilateral FTAs directly translates into becoming a hub. If the Southeast Asian region concludes bilateral FTAs with Northeast Asian countries, it will formally become a hub region. However, if Japan signs an FTA with ASEAN and further concludes bilateral FTAs with other countries, it is highly possible that Japan will become a de facto hub. A country can be a hub when it is equipped with economic power to lead other regions, advanced trading systems, and possesses political and diplomatic capabilities. Examples from Europe and North America show that either complete economic integration is formed or a country with strong political and diplomatic capabilities or strong economic power becomes a hub.[13] The EU, achieving complete integration, became a hub in FTAs with other regions and the U.S. became a hub in NAFTA due to its economic power and advanced trade system.

In addition to this, the characteristics of the Southeast Asian region can be a problem. Regarding this, Eichengreen (2002), quoting Katsenstein (1996), wrote that the decision-making system of member countries in AFTA interrupts the development of regionalism. "In comparison to Europe, [Southeast] Asian regionalism is not well institutionalized. Operating by consensus in regional organizations, Asian states exercise effective voting powers over collective actions." Not only has the consensus-based decision-making process hindered AFTA from achieving economic cooperation effectively, it will also render AFTA an example of "soft institutionalism" or "weak formal institutions" in the future. Under such circumstances, it is unrealistic for AFTA to lead the East Asian economic integration.

Regarding the hub role of ASEAN, Soesastro (2002) stated that ASEAN needs to decide in the near future whether it will promote an East Asian FTA or bilateral FTAs with China, Japan and Korea. According to Soesastro, bilateral FTAs with individual Northeast Asian countries might be more beneficial for ASEAN; however, in that case, the content of AFTA, which ASEAN countries are forming, must be made more substantial.

Of course, China can be a hub like Japan. China and Japan's competitive pursuit over concluding bilateral FTAs with Southeast Asia, a situation that is happening in Northeast Asia, seems to be in line with their plan to secure a superior position in

[12] Chia Siow Yue strongly advocated the hub role for ASEAN in East Asian regionalism at the Asian Economic Panel Meeting, Keio University, Tokyo Japan, May 14-15, 2002. A similar point is made by Soesastro (2001, pp. 235-236), who states that "ASEAN may become some kind of a hub in East Asia, in which separate relations are developed between ASEAN (AFTA) and each of the three Northeast Asian countries."

[13] For example, although Mexico, a member of NAFTA, has established free trade with 32 countries through 10 FTAs, it is hardly recognized as a hub. In contrast, although the U.S. has for fewer FTAs, it is considered the hub for NAFTA.

East Asia by emerging as a hub in East Asian regionalism. China's conclusion of an FTA with ASEAN will substantially improve its position for regional leadership. However, achieving an East Asian FTA will be even more complicated. A policy proposal made by Japanese Prime Minister Koizumi in Singapore in January 2002 on an East Asian FTA reveals Japan's competition with China over regional leadership.[14] Cao (2002) presented China's position on an FTA with ASEAN. According to him, an ASEAN-China FTA and a Japan-Korea FTA will coexist in East Asia until an East Asian FTA is established through the integration of both FTAs. Yet, he does not hide his opinion that an East Asian FTA would most likely occur with Korea and Japan individually joining the ASEAN-China FTA. Here, we see that China and Japan are competing for the regional leadership through FTAs. If China and Japan are successful at concluding bilateral FTAs with ASEAN, it will be very difficult to build an East Asian FTA by integrating those two bilateral FTAs, because of the leadership struggle between China and Japan.

5. CONCLUSION

With an overview of the progress of worldwide regionalism, this paper discussed regionalism within East Asia, which is in process, and reasons for its slow development in East Asia. In many cases, the negative effects are emphasized more than the positive ones despite the fact that the positive effects exceed the negative ones. Since a social system to make a reasonable decision through a comprehensive evaluation does not always work, an FTA process is inevitably delayed. Winning public support at home is the foremost issue in concluding an FTA smoothly. Governments should endeavor to enhance people's understanding of the economic effects and the strategic importance of FTAs. While minority groups that will suffer from an FTA have voiced their opposition to the agreement, the majority who stand to benefit from it, have been passive in their reaction.

Regardless of how important a China-Japan-South Korea FTA is, in terms of economic gains and strategic goals, such an agreement will not be easy to negotiate because the three countries have very different political, social, and historical perspectives. Unfortunately, mutual distrust among these countries is the greatest impediment to a political decision regarding the FTA. Ohnishi and Yin (2002, 70) pointed out that "building trust among the people of the three countries, rather than presenting the economical calculation of benefits, is the necessary step to realize the Japan-Korea FTA or China-Japan-Korea FTA." Border conflicts, distorted Japanese history textbooks, and the apparent pursuit of regional leadership by China and Japan damage the prospects for mutual trust among the three countries.

The governments must make an effort to resolve such political and social conflicts. It should be recognized, however, that sometimes these conflicts serve to

[14] During a speech entitled "Japan and ASEAN in East Asia-A Sincere and Open Partnership" in Singapore on January 14, 2002, Japanese Prime Minister Koizumi states "our goal should be the creation of a 'community that acts together and advances together.' And we should achieve this through expanding East Asia Cooperation founded upon the Japan-ASEAN relationship."

emphasize the urgent need for concluding an agreement. For instance, one purpose for initiating European economic integration in the 1950s was to strengthen economic cooperation in order to prevent another war between Germany and France.

Since Japan and Korea are in the process of officially reviewing the possibility of an FTA, it is highly possible that the Japan-Korea FTA would be the first FTA in the Northeast Asia region. As previously mentioned, a Japan-Korea FTA is meaningful by itself; however, the two countries should adhere to an open policy to establish a Northeast Asian FTA by allowing China's participation with certain conditions. Improving the relationship between China and Japan could also be a decisive factor in establishing an East Asia FTA. Cheow (2001) asserted, "as long as relations between Asia's two powers (China and Japan) are not clearly ironed out, it is almost impossible to envisage greater and further pan-Asian economic co-operation." However, these political and social conflicts do not always act as obstacles to the development of FTAs. For example, it is well known that the EU was initiated with the purpose of preventing another war between Germany and France by strengthening economic cooperation. Unfortunately, East Asia did not have momentum to convert a hostile relationship into more cooperative one.

REFERENCES

Bergsten, C. F. 2000. "The New Asian Challenge." Institute for International Economics (IIE) *Working Paper* 00-4. Washington D.C.: IIE.
Bustelo, P. 2002. "The Impact of the Financial Crises on East Asian Regionalism." Forthcoming in Liu, Fu-Kuo and Philippe Regnier eds. *Regionalism in East Asia: Paradigm Shifting?* London: Curzon Press.
Cao, S. 2002. "Progress of China-ASEAN FTA and China's Position." Presented at 2002 International Forum on Northeast Asia Trade Policy Cooperation. Nanjing, China.
Cheong, I. 2002. "Korea's FTA Policy: Focusing on Bilateral FTAs with Chile and Japan." Seoul: KIEP.
______. 2003. "Regional Economic Integration in Northeast Asia: Present and Future." Presented at the Fourth Korea-OECD Join Conference on "Korea as a Business Hub of Northeast Asia: Potentials and Policy Recommendations." Held in Seoul, October 14-15.
Cheow, E. 2001. "How to Define a Region of Closer Economic Co-operation in Asia?" Presented at the International Conference on Regional Economic Co-operation in Asia: Challenges for Europe. Organized by the Vienna Institute for International Economic Studies. Vienna. October.
Economist, The. 2002. "A Survey of Japan." April 20th-26th.
Eichengreen, B. 2002. "What to Do with the Chiang Mai Initiative." Presented at the Asian Economic Panel in Tokyo. Organized by KIEP, Center for International Development of Harvard University, and Keio University. May.
Federation of Korean Industries (FKI). 2001. "Korea Industries' Perception of an FTA." Seoul: FKI. (in Korean)
Findley, C. 2000. "Old Issues in New Regionalism." Presented at the 2000 APEC Economic Outlook Symposium. Manila, Philippines. July.
Fontaine, P. 1992. "A New Idea for Europe: The Schuman declaration – 1950-2000." Brussel: European Communities.
Katsenstein, P. J. 1996. "Regionalism in Comparative Perspective." *Cooperation and Conflict* 31: 123-159.
MOFA (Ministry of Foreign Affair, Japan). 1998-2000. *Blue Book on Diplomacy 1998*: Volume 1. Tokyo. December. (in Japanese)
______. 2002. "Japan's FTA Strategy." Tokyo. October. (in Japanese)
Munakata, N. 2001a. "Focus on the Benefits Not Threats of Regional Economic Integration." *PacNet Newsletter*. Jakarta: CSIS. November 16.
______. 2001b. "Evolution of Japan's Policy toward Economic Integration." *CNAPS Working Paper*. The Brookings Institution. December.
______. 2002. "Seize the Moment for East Asian Economic Integration." *PacNet Newsletter*. Jakarta: CSIS. February 1.
Ohnishi, H. and Y. Qing Zhu. 2002. "Effects of the Japan-Korea and Japan-Korea-China FTA Estimated by an Northeast Asian Model." Presented at the Northeast Asian Economics Association Annual Meeting. Seoul: Sejong Center for the Performing Art. February 15.
Snape, R. 1996. "Which Regional Trade Agreement." In Bora, Bijit and Christopher Findley eds. *Regional Integration and the Asia Pacific*. Melbourne: Oxford University Press.
Soesastro, H. 2001. "Towards an East Asian Regional Trading Arrangement." In Tay, Simon S. C., Jesus P. Estanislao, and Hadi Soesastro eds. *Reinvesting ASEAN*. Singapore: ISEAS.
Tanaka, N. 2002. "Choice of Japan in the 21st Century and FTA Issues." The 23rd Symposium on FTA in East Asia. Tokyo. October 7.
UNCTAD. 2002. *World Investment Report*.
Wanandi, J. 2000. "East Asian Institution Building." Remarks made at the 2000 annual meeting of the Trilateral Commission in Tokyo. (www.trilateral.org)
Wonnacott, R. 1996. "Trade and Investment in a Hub-and-Spoke System Versus a Free Trade Area." *World Economy* 19: 237-52.
World Bank. 1993. *The East Asian Miracle – Economic Growth and Public Policy*. London: Oxford University Press.

Yamazawa, K. 2001. "Approaches to Regional Economic Co-operation in Asia and Future Prospects." Presented at Regional Economic Co-operation in Asia: Challenges for Europe. Organized by the Vienna Institute for International Economic Studies. Vienna. October.

Yip, W. 2001. "Prospects for Closer Economic Integration in East Asia." *Stanford Journal of East Asian Affairs*. Vol. 1: 106-111.

Young, S. 2002. "Challenges of Free Trade Agreements in the Asia-Pacific RAegion." Seoul: Korea National Committee for Pacific Economic Cooperation (KOPEC). August. Unpublished Paper.

Part II: Southeast Asian Views on an EAFTA

CHAPTER 4

AN EAST ASIAN FTA: A NEW FRONTIER OF ECONOMIC COOPERATION IN EAST ASIA

TERMSAK CHALERMPALANUPAP

CHAPTER 5

INDONESIA'S FTA POLICY AND ITS PERSPECTIVES ON AN EAST ASIAN FTA

DEDDY SALEH

CHAPTER 6

AN EAST ASIA FTA: A MALAYSIAN PERSPECTIVE

MOHD HAFLAH PIEI

CHAPTER 7

AN EAST ASIAN FTA: A PHILIPPINE PERSPECTIVE

JOHN LAWRENCE AVILA

CHAPTER 4

AN EAST ASIAN FTA: A NEW FRONTIER OF ECONOMIC COOPERATION IN EAST ASIA

TERMSAK CHALERMPALANUPAP

1. EAEG / EAEC REVISIT

In the late 1980s, ASEAN was alarmed by the growing competition from the mushrooming free trade areas (FTA) in the world, including the formation of a single European market, the market integration between the US and Canada and the US and Mexico, which soon led to NAFTA. ASEAN was also dismayed by the slow progress in the Uruguay Round of multilateral trade negotiations. Three significant developments followed that represented ASEAN's response to the adverse situation.

First, ASEAN cooperated with Australia in initiating APEC in 1989. The decision to locate the APEC Secretariat in Singapore in 1993 could be seen as recognition of the active support of ASEAN, and of Singapore in particular, for the APEC process.

Next, came the idea of an ASEAN Free Trade Area first espoused by Prime Minister Anand Panyarachun of Thailand. At the Second ASEAN Summit held in Singapore on 27-28 January 1992, ASEAN Leaders endorsed the idea of an AFTA when they signed the Framework Agreement on Enhancing ASEAN Economic Cooperation. The Framework Agreement spelled out ASEAN Member Countries' commitment to promote cooperation in several areas, most important of which was the cooperation in trade. Also at the Singapore Summit, ASEAN Economic Ministers signed the Common Effective Preferential Tariff (CEPT) Scheme for the ASEAN Free Trade Area (AFTA) to start the realization of AFTA.[1]

[1] In 1992, ASEAN had only six members: Brunei Darussalam (which joined in January 1984 soon after its independence from British rule), and the four founding members namely Indonesia, Malaysia, the Philippines, Singapore and Thailand.
At first, AFTA was to be created in 15 years starting in 1993. Just one year after implementation, the six ASEAN members quickly realized that their original 15-year target was too conservative. The ASEAN Economic Ministers in 1994 agreed to accelerate the realization of AFTA from 15 to 10 years, by 1 January 2003, instead of 2008.
Viet Nam joined ASEAN in July 1995; Laos and Myanmar in July 1997; and Cambodia in April 1999. Each of them was given a 10-year timetable to complete implementing the CEPT Scheme.
At the Sixth ASEAN Summit in Hanoi in December 1998, ASEAN Leaders agreed that the six older

C. Y. Ahn et al (eds.), East Asian Economic Regionalism, 57-74.

Last and of direct interest to this Seminar was the emergence of an idea to establish an East Asia Economic Group (EAEG). Prime Minister Dato Seri Dr. Mahathir Mohamad of Malaysia began to espouse his idea of an East Asia Economic Group (EAEG) in late 1990. His view was that countries in East Asia (Southeast Asia + Northeast Asia) should do more in consultation and cooperation to help lesser-developed economies in the region overcome difficulties, and to help transition economies such as Cambodia, Laos and Vietnam in reform and reconstruction.

Soon after that, the Malaysian Minister of International Trade and Industry visited the other ASEAN countries to explain the EAEG idea. The thinking then was that the EAEG would comprise of six ASEAN members, Japan, Korea, China, Hong Kong, Taiwan and Vietnam. The Group could meet when necessary, either back-to-back with the annual ASEAN Ministerial Meeting and Post Ministerial Conferences (AMM/PMC) of Foreign Ministers, or back-to-back with the annual meeting of ASEAN Economic Ministers (AEM) to discuss issues of common concern to East Asian economies.

ASEAN convened a special Senior Economic Official Meeting (Special SEOM) in Bandung, Indonesia, on 15-16 March 1991 to discuss the EAEG formally for the first time. Subsequently, the EAEG was discussed at the 23rd AEM Meeting in Malaysia in October 1991.

At the opening of the 23rd AEM Meeting, Prime Minister Mahathir stressed the need to work together with the East Asian economies through the formation of the EAEG, because ASEAN members alone were not strong enough to protect trade. He said the EAEG would be GATT-consistent; it would not be a trade bloc because it would stand for free trade, and it would not be detrimental to ASEAN's cohesiveness.

The 23rd AEM agreed to an East Asia Economic Caucus (EAEC), instead of the EAEG, and recommended it for consideration at the Fourth ASEAN Summit in Singapore in January 1992. Some details of the EAEC were described in the Joint Press Statement of the 23rd AEM.

At the Second Summit in Singapore, the EAEC was endorsed by ASEAN Leaders as part of ASEAN's efforts in strengthening and/or establishing cooperation with other countries, regional / multilateral economic organizations, as well as APEC. In the Singapore Declaration, ASEAN Leaders stated, *"With respect to an EAEC, ASEAN recognizes that consultations on issues of common concern among East Asian economies, as and when the need arises, could contribute to expanding cooperation among the region's economies, and the promotion of an open and free global trading system;"*

Subsequently, the Secretary-General of the ASEAN Secretariat,[2] Mr. Rusli Noor

ASEAN members would advance the implementation by one year to complete AFTA in their countries by 1 January 2002.

[2] Until the end of 1992, the head of the ASEAN Secretariat was designated as the Secretary-General of the ASEAN Secretariat. His appointment to a 3-year term was based on alphabetical rotation among the ASEAN members.

Following the major restructuring in 1992, the head of the ASEAN Secretariat was re-designated as the Secretary-General of ASEAN and was accorded the Ministerial status. His selection is based on merit as from Brunei Darussalam, was tasked to study an appropriate modality to realize the EAEC. The study was completed by the new Secretary-General of ASEAN, Dato Ajit Singh from Malaysia, who took over the helm of the restructured ASEAN Secretariat at the beginning of 1993.

ASEAN officials considered the modality of EAEC proposed by the Secretary-General of ASEAN and finally ASEAN Foreign Ministers, at their 26th AMM in Singapore in July 1993, decided that the EAEC would be a "caucus within APEC" and that the AEM would provide support and direction to the EAEC.

The "caucus within APEC" indicated that the EAEC would function independently; it would not be a mechanism of APEC. The Caucus need not discuss only APEC issues; it could determine its own agenda and work program. And the Caucus need not necessarily report to APEC either.

China was interested in joining the EAEC. But China's support would come with a condition that Taiwan and Hong Kong must not be included, even though both along with China had already joined APEC in November 1991. China's preference was to confine the EAEC membership to only sovereign States. Japan and Korea, meanwhile, were reluctant to take a clear stand, especially after the US expressed strong opposition to the EAEC.

The US unfortunately considered the EAEC as both a threat to APEC and to the US presence in the Asia-Pacific region. The US argued that by including some and excluding others in APEC, the EAEC could "weaken APEC or complicate its deliberations." Moreover, said the US in a demarche to the Secretary-General of ASEAN in 1993, "the US would be concerned about anything that raises questions about United States commitment to the region and exclusion from the region."

Nevertheless, ASEAN continued to try to explain the EAEC to win support from especially China, Japan and Korea. The Secretary-General of ASEAN visited these three countries in November 1993 to discuss the EAEC. More importantly, ASEAN Foreign Ministers held a working lunch with Foreign Ministers of Japan, China and Korea in Bangkok on 25 July 1994, on the sidelines of the 27th AMM/PMC.

The Joint Communique of the 27th AMM reported that the Foreign Ministers had a discussion on the EAEC and agreed that the consultations would continue on this informal basis. Incidentally, Dr. Han Sung-joo, the Foreign Minister of Korea at that time, would subsequently play a leading role in advocating East Asia cooperation when he chaired the East Asia Vision Group.

While the ASEAN side learned nothing new from the Foreign Ministers of China, Japan and Korea at the working lunch, one unintended but very significant outcome their informal meeting was the agreement to continue to meet on the same informal basis. This laid the foundation for what would turn out to be the ASEAN+3 process for cooperation in East Asia.

well as nomination from member countries. The Secretary-General is appointed to a 5-year term by the ASEAN Heads of Government/State.
The current Secretary-General of ASEAN, Mr. Rodolfo C. Severino, Jr. from the Philippines will complete his term at the end of 2002. Mr. Ong Keng Yong, press secretary to the Prime Minister of Singapore, has been nominated by ASEAN Foreign Ministers to succeed Mr. Serverino. His appointment is expected at the upcoming Eighth ASEAN Summit in Phnom Penh on 4-5 November 2002.

In 1995-1997, the ASEAN Economic Ministers took the lead in engaging their partners from China, Japan and Korea. In 1996, the AEM reported "increasing receptiveness of the EAEC among the Asia-Pacific countries" and agreed to continue the ASEAN efforts to realize the EAEC. The AEM also agreed to develop programs for development of SMEs and human resources and assigned Malaysia to come up with a paper on this matter. In 1997, again the AEM reiterated the "increasing receptiveness of the EAEC among the Asia-Pacific countries" and took note of the SMEs development program being undertaken.

By 1998, however, the AEM no longer mention the EAEC in the Joint Press Statement. Even when Malaysia hosted the APEC Economic Leaders Meeting in 1998, Prime Minister Mahathir did not pursue the EAEC anymore. Thus the EAEC idea was quietly laid to rest.

2. ASEAN+3 PROCESS

The reason Prime Minister Mahathir need not pursue the EAEC idea anymore was because he succeeded in initiating something even more satisfying and far-reaching. For on 16 December 1997, he played host to the historic inaugural meeting of ASEAN+3 Summit, which was followed by three successive ASEAN+1 Summits with the Chinese President, the Prime Minister of Japan and the Prime Minister of Korea.

Apart from Prime Minister Mahathir, another East Asian Leader who could rightly share the honor of initiating the historic process was Prime Minister Ryutaro Hashimoto of Japan. For in his policy speech in Singapore on 14 January 1997, Prime Minister Hashimoto proposed a "broader and deeper partnership" between ASEAN and Japan. In particular, he proposed, among other things, a "broader and deeper exchanges between Japan and ASEAN at top and all the other levels".[3]

Convening an ASEAN-Japan Summit alone would not be extraordinary. After all, Japan has been one of the most active Dialogue Partners [4] of ASEAN since the early 1970s. And ASEAN Leaders had met two Japanese Prime Ministers in the past: meeting with Prime Minister Takeo Fukuda during the Second ASEAN Summit in Kuala Lumpur in August 1977; at that time, Prime Ministers of Australia and New Zealand also had separate meetings with ASEAN Leaders; and Prime Minister

[3] The other two Japanese proposals in the "Hashimoto Doctrine" called for active cooperation between ASEAN and Japan *"to preserve and restore cultural heritages, and to maintain and development unique cultures"*; and joint initiatives to tackle problems confronting the international community such as *"terrorism, the environment, enhancing health and welfare, food and energy shortages, population growth, AIDS, narcotics, and reinforcing the rule of law"*.

[4] ASEAN's Dialogue Partners are: Australia, Canada, China, the EU, India, Japan, the Korea, New Zealand, Russia, the US, and the UNDP. Pakistan is a Sectoral Dialogue Partner; Papua New Guinea is a Special Observer (with no intention to join ASEAN).

Japan has been an active partner of ASEAN since the early 1970s. Korea was an ASEAN's Sectoral Dialogue Partner in November 1989. The relationship was alleviated to the status of Dialogue Partnership in July 1991. China's first formal contact with ASEAN was in 1991 when the Chinese Foreign Minister met with ASEAN Foreign Ministers on the sidelines of the 24th AMM in Kuala Lumpur. China was accorded Dialogue Partner status in its relationship with ASEAN in July 1996.

Noboru Takeshita in Manila on 15 December 1987 during the Third ASEAN Summit.

The Japanese proposal for "broader and deeper exchanges" "at top and all the other levels" created an opportunity for Malaysia to convince the rest in ASEAN to have an ASEAN-Japan Summit in Kuala Lumpur, back-to-back with the Second Informal Summit.[5] The initiative quickly grew into a more ambitious plan to also invite China and Korea to meet with ASEAN Leaders. The responses from China and Korea were also very positive. Thus the ASEAN+3 process was born.

At first, the emphasis was on strengthening bilateral cooperation between ASEAN-China, ASEAN-Japan and ASEAN-Korea, building on their existing dialogue mechanisms. At the three successive bilateral meetings on 16 December 1997, ASEAN Leaders and their counterparts from China, Japan and Korea issued three Joint Statements on their respective bilateral cooperation towards the 21st century.

In the ASEAN-China Joint Statement, the Leaders affirmed their commitment to *"promote good-neighborly and friendly relations, increase high-level exchanges, strengthen the mechanism of dialogue and cooperation in all areas to enhance understanding and mutual benefit. ..." "China underlined its conviction that the economies of the East Asian region would continue to be one of the fastest growing in the world. ASEAN member States and China agreed on the need to consolidate their close economic relations by promoting trade and investment, facilitating market access, improving the flow of technology and enhancing the flow of and access to trade and investment related information. ..."*

The ASEAN-China Joint Statement also stated the agreement *that "the maintenance of regional peace and stability served the interests of all parties, they undertook to resolve their differences or disputes through peaceful means, without resorting to the threat or use of force. The parties concerned* [6] *agreed to resolve*

[5] After the First Summit in Bali on 23-24 February 1976, ASEAN Leaders met in Kuala Lumpur in the Second Summit in Kuala Lumpur on 4-5 August 1977, which was to coincide with the 10th anniversary of ASEAN (ASEAN was established in Bangkok on 8 August 1967). The Third Summit was held in Manila on 14-15 December 1987 (coinciding with the 20th anniversary of ASEAN). The Fourth Summit was held in Singapore on 27-28 January 1992. In Singapore, ASEAN Leaders agreed to convene a summit every three years. Hence, the Fifth Summit in Bangkok was held in 1995. In Bangkok, ASEAN Leaders further agreed to convene an informal summit in each of the two years in between the two formal summits. The 1st Informal Summit was held in Jakarta on 30 November 1996. The 2nd Informal Summit was held in Kuala Lumpur on 14-16 December 1997. In 1998, the Sixth Summit was in Hanoi on 15-16 December 1998. The 3rd Informal Summit was in Manila on 27-28 November 1999; and the 4th Informal Summit was held in Singapore on 22-25 November 2000.
At the 4th Informal Summit, ASEAN Leaders agreed to meet in an annual summit without the distinction of it being either formal or informal summit. State ceremonies and preparatory meetings would be minimized, while papers and documents reduced to a necessary minimum. The emphasis would be on providing a congenial atmosphere for fruitful discussion of the ASEAN leaders.
The Seventh Summit in Bandar Seri Begawan on 5-6 November 2001 was the first summit held under the new format.
This year the Eighth ASEAN Summit will be held in Phnom Penh on 4-5 November 2002.

[6] The "parties concerned" in the disputes in the South China Sea usually refer to Brunei Darussalam, Malaysia, the Philippines and Viet Nam on the ASEAN side and China. Taiwan has laid claims over many disputed areas in the South China Sea and militarily occupied some disputed islands. But Taiwan has never been involved in the ongoing ASEAN-China process to draw up a code of conduct in the South

their disputes in the South China Sea through friendly consultations and negotiations in accordance with universally recognized international law, including the 1982 UN Convention on the law of the Sea. ..."

In the ASEAN-Japan Joint Statement, Leaders of ASEAN and Japan "*expressed their determination to work together to ensure that future generations would live in peace and stability and that social and economic development would be sustained. With a view to fostering an enhanced partnership, they decided to intensify dialogues and exchanges at all levels.*"

In the ASEAN-Korea Joint Statement, Leaders of ASEAN and Korea "*agreed that the stability and prosperity of Northeast and Southeast Asia were inter-linked and it was essential for both sides to work closely together for the mutual benefit of both regions.*"

2.1. Formation of the East Asia Vision Group

At the second ASEAN+3 Summit in Hanoi on 16 December 1998, it was agreed that Leaders of ASEAN, China, Japan and Korea would meet every year. Another important outcome was a decision to set up an East Asia Vision Group (EAVG).

The EAVG was President Kim Dae Jung's initiative designed to bring together experts from Track-2 to discuss the future of cooperation in East Asia and to submit recommendations to the fifth ASEAN+3 Summit in Brunei Darussalam, scheduled for 5 November 2001. Two representatives from each of the 10 ASEAN Member countries, China, Japan and Korea would form the Vision Group.

Subsequently, former Korea Foreign Minister Dr. Han Sung-joo, now a professor at Korea University, was appointed Chair of the Vision Group. The EAVG Secretariat was run by the Korea Institute for International Economic Policy, whose president, Dr. Lee Kyung-Tae, was also a Korean representative on the Vision Group. The ASEAN Secretariat was invited as an observer to EAVG meetings.[7]

2.2. Joint Statement on East Asia Cooperation (1999)

It was at the third ASEAN+3 Summit in Manila on 28 November 1999 that Leaders of ASEAN countries, China, Japan and Korea began to spell out what they hoped to achieve together in East Asia. In their Joint Statement on East Asia Cooperation, the Leaders said in part that "*They noted the bright prospects for enhanced interaction and closer linkages in East Asia and recognized the fact that this growing interaction has helped increase opportunities for cooperation and collaboration with each other, thereby strengthening the elements essential for the promotion of peace, stability and prosperity in the region.*" "*Mindful of the challenges and opportunities in the new millennium, as well as the growing regional interdependence in the age of globalization and information, they agreed to promote*

China Sea.

[7] Dr. Suthad Setboonsarng, Deputy Secretary-General (Operations) represented ASEAN Secretariat to attend the first two EAVG meetings; the author of this paper attended the last three EAVG meetings.

dialogue and to deepen and consolidate collective efforts with a view to advancing mutual understanding, trust, good neighborliness and friendly relations, peace, stability and prosperity in East Asia and the world."

2.3. Historic Meeting of China, Japan and Korea

Also at the third ASEAN+3 Summit in Manila another historic event took place. Prime Minister Zhu Rongji, Prime Minister Keizo Obuchi, and President Kim Dae Jung had an informal breakfast meeting on 27 November 1999. This was the first meeting among the heads of government of these three countries in modern times. And it was their common desire to work with ASEAN and to develop East Asia cooperation that brought them together.

At the fourth ASEAN+3 Summit in Singapore in November 2000, Leaders of China, Japan and Korea held their second informal breakfast meeting. They agreed to regularize their working breakfast meeting to improve coordination in cooperating with ASEAN under the ASEAN+3 framework. They also established a +3 coordination group to work closely with ASEAN's Working Group on e-ASEAN on ICT cooperation.

2.4. ASEAN+3 Ministerial Meetings

The 1999 Joint Statement on East Asia Cooperation mentioned only the ASEAN+3 Foreign Ministers Meeting as a mechanism to review the progress of the implementation of the Joint Statement. Since then ASEAN+3 ministerial meetings on finance, economic/trade, labor, agriculture and forestry, and tourism have been convened and regularized. ASEAN+3 Ministers of Environment plan to convene their first meeting in November 2002 in Vientiane. ASEAN Ministers on Transnational Crime will convene the first ASEAN+3 on Transnational Crime with China, Japan and Korea in Thailand next October. ASEAN+3 ministerial meetings on science and technology, energy, culture and information are under consideration of relevant senior officials.

At the level of senior officials (SOM), a number of ASEAN+3 bodies have been established to provide support to their respective ministerial meetings. One new addition was the ASEAN+3 Directors-General Meeting, which was formally established in an inaugural meeting in Seoul on 30 August 2002. This newest ASEAN+3 body will have an important role to play in the future direction of East Asia cooperation, including the EAFTA.

2.5. EAVG Meetings

The EAVG met five times: EAVG-I, Seoul, 21-22 October 1999; EAVG-II, Shanghai, 20-21 April 2000; EAVG-III, Tokyo, 2-4 October 2000; EAVG-IV, Bali, 14-16 February 2001 (organized by ASEAN Secretariat); and EAVG-V, Seoul, 27-29 May 2001. In the afternoon of 29 May 2001, the EAVG paid a courtesy call to President Kim Dae Jung. The Korea President emphasized the importance of the task undertaken by the EAVG and his keen interest in awaiting the report and recommendations of the EAVG.

In early October 2001, the EAVG Report was formally submitted to the Leaders of ASEAN countries, China, Japan and Korea. The EAVG Report was formally considered at the fifth ASEAN+3 Summit in Bandar Seri Begawan on 5 November 2001.

2.6. East Asia Study Group

Interestingly, one year before the Vision Group submitted its report, an official group at the SOM level was formed to look into the future of East Asia cooperation as well.

At the fourth ASEAN+3 Summit in Singapore in November 2000, President Kim Dae Jung's proposal to establish an official East Asia Study Group (EASG) was adopted. The Study Group would consist of ASEAN Secretary-General, ASEAN SOM leaders and SOM leaders from China, Japan and Korea. According to its TOR, the Study Group would "explore practical ways and means to deepen and expand the existing cooperation among ASEAN, the People's Republic of China, Japan and the Republic of Korea, and prepare concrete measures and, as necessary, action plans for closer cooperation in various areas". Of special importance is that mandate for the EASG to "assess the recommendations of the EAVG" and "explore the idea and implications of an East Asian Summit". The EASG is tasked to submit its report and recommendations to the sixth ASEAN+3 Summit, to be held in Phnom Penh on 4 November 2002.

The EASG has established a working group, consisting of ASEAN DGs, officials from +3 countries at comparable level and a representative of the ASEAN Secretariat, to assist in its work. The EASG Working Group now also functions as the ASEAN+3 Directors-General Meeting.

3. EAVG REPORT AND RECOMMENDATIONS

3.1. Towards an East Asian Community

The title of the EAVG Report [8] indicated clearly the Vision Group's direction for East Asia cooperation. In its Executive Summary of the Report, the Vision Group explained that in proposing the formation of an East Asian community, *"we seek the following goals:*

- *Preventing conflict and promoting peace among the nations of East Asia;*
- *Achieving closer economic cooperation in such areas as trade, investment, finance and development;*
- *Advancing human security in particular by facilitating regional efforts for environmental protection and good governance;*
- *Bolstering common prosperity by enhancing cooperation in education and*

[8] The EAVG Report is available on the ASEAN Secretariat's web site, at the section about the Seventh ASEAN Informal Summit in Bandar Seri Begawan.

human resources development; and

* *Fostering the identity of an East Asian community."*

The Vision Group put forth altogether 57 recommendations; 22 of them were highlighted in the Executive Summary of the Report, covering the following areas: Economic Cooperation (4 recommendations); Financial Cooperation (3); Political and Security Cooperation (4); Environmental Cooperation (4); Social and Cultural Cooperation (5) and Institutional Cooperation (2).

3.2. EAFTA

In one of the key recommendations under Economic Cooperation, the Vision Group called for an "Establishment of the East Asian Free Trade Area (EAFTA) and liberalization of trade well ahead of the APEC Bogor Goal.[9] "

The Vision Group believed that "In order to facilitate the formation of a region-wide FTA, East Asia needs to consolidate all existing bilateral and sub-regional FTAs within the region."

It then further recommended "the establishment of a ministerial committee to oversee the development of an EAFTA."

It also emphasized that "the regional integration arrangement should be consistent with the World Trade Organization (WTO) agreements so as to reinforce the multilateral trading system."

Finally, the Vision Group called for "the EAFTA to be designed in such a way that will benefit all member economies. We [the Vision Group] also recommend the establishment of GSP status and preferential treatment for the least developed countries in the region."

This was all that the Vision Group proposed about the EAFTA.

3.3. Initial Responses

At the fifth meeting of the ASEAN+3 Summit in Bandar Seri Begawan on 5 November 2001, the Leaders considered the Report of the Vision Group and warmly thanked President Kim Dae Jung for his initiative.

President Kim, who led the discussion on the Report, highlighted three recommendations in it:

* Evolution of the ASEAN+3 Summit to an East Asian Summit, together with institutionalization of the East Asia cooperation process, to create regular channels of communications and cooperation;
* Establishment of an East Asia Forum consisting of government representatives and others from outside the government to serve as an institutional mechanism for social exchanges and regional cooperation in East Asia; and

[9] At the second summit of the APEC Economic Leaders in Bogor, Indonesia, in 1994, the APEC Leaders endorsed the vision of an open trading system in the Asia-Pacific in which the developed member economies would achieve free and open trade and investment by the year 2010 and the developing member economies by the year 2020.

* Establishment of an East Asian Free Trade Area (EAFTA), starting with an interim step of linking existing free trade areas in East Asia together.

The Press Statement issued after the Summit said that the EAVG Report contained key proposals and concrete measures to broaden East Asia cooperation. "Some are bold yet feasible such as establishing an East Asia Free Trade and liberalizing trade well ahead of APEC's goals."

The Press Statement added that the East Asia Study Group (EASG) that the ASEAN+3 Leaders established in 2000 would now assess the EAVG's proposals.

When it was tasked to examine and prioritize the Vision Group's recommendations, the ASEAN Secretariat put the proposal on the EAFTA in the category of "Require Further Studies"[10]. The reason was that ASEAN's priority was, and still is, to concentrate first on accelerating the realization of AFTA and consolidating economic integration among its 10 members and in assisting the four newer ones (Cambodia, Laos, Myanmar and Vietnam) in regional economic integration. In the meantime, ASEAN would continue to strengthen its cooperation with its dialogue partners, particularly China, Japan and Korea, in new and comprehensive economic partnerships. Comprehensive economic linkages between ASEAN and each of the +3 countries in Northeast Asia will constitute important building blocks for economic cooperation in East Asia in the long run. At the same time, the ASEAN Secretariat was of the opinion that China, Japan and Korea must themselves build their economic linkages. So when all parties concerned are ready, then the idea of an EAFTA could be transformed into reality without much pain or difficulty.

The Working Group of the Study Group and subsequently the Study Group itself agreed to the classification of the proposal on the EAFTA as a recommendation requiring further studies. Now in its final report to the ASEAN+3 Summit in Phnom Penh on 4 November 2002, the EASG is expected to propose that the ASEAN+3 Economic Ministers be assigned to conduct a study on the benefits, challenges, and implications of an EAFTA.

This essentially is the state of play of the EAFTA issue in the ASEAN+3 process.

4. SOME PERTINENT ISSUES

4.1. Building Blocks or Stumbling Blocks?

4.1.1. ASEAN and AFTA

When one starts pondering on what the EAFTA should be, one good starting

[10] The three other categories are: Immediate Measures; Medium-Term (2-5 years) and Long-Term (+5 years).
EAVG's recommendations that the ASEAN Secretariat classified as "Require Further Studies" included: the promotion of investment by SMEs and the establishment of an administrative and financial support system; cooperation towards an agreement on the region's peace-keeping objectives; promotion of sub-regional security dialogues; establishment of an East Asian environment cooperative body including a dispute settlement mechanism and an environmental database.

point is to examine what has been achieved on the ground, especially in the ASEAN region in terms of economic regionalism as well as bilateral/external economic cooperation. For the idea of building the EAFTA on the existing building blocks and merging the FTAs may be easy said than done.

Take AFTA for example. ASEAN members have good reasons to be proud of AFTA, especially when compared with the South Asia Association for Regional Cooperation (SAARC) where the idea of a FTA in South Asia remains on the drawing board. However, experts would quickly point out that AFTA is a rather rudimentary FTA, with an emphasis on tariff reduction (down to 0-5%), not tariff elimination. According to the latest statistics, the CEPT tariffs on 96.24% of the Inclusion Lists of the six original signatory countries of the AFTA agreement were reduced within the range of 0-5% on 1 January 2002. About 98% (or 44,162 tariff lines) of all the tariff lines of the six ASEAN members were included in the CEPT Scheme with an average tariff of 2.89% (compared with 12.76% average when they started implementing the CEPT Scheme in 1993).[11]

The AFTA agreement did not include investment, services, dispute settlement, intellectual property rights, government procurement, and competition policy. Investment promotion and protection, services liberalization, dispute settlement, protection of intellectual property rights were already addressed in other ASEAN agreements. It also did not include labor rights. ASEAN has yet to recognize labor rights and illegal migration as regional issues, even though there is a ministerial forum on labor. The receiving countries in ASEAN prefer addressing these issues through national policies and bilateral talks with the sending countries.

For most of the six original signatories of the AFTA agreement, their implementation of the CEPT Scheme has more or less been completed by the beginning of this year. But Vietnam still has until 2006, Laos and Myanmar until 2008 and Cambodia until 2010 to finish their respective implementation. In other words, AFTA will not be completed until 2010.

Meanwhile, negotiations among ASEAN members on services liberalization on all sectors and all modes of supply have made slow progress and produced unsatisfactory results. Now one solution is to pursue the negotiations in specific areas with like-minded member countries. The principle of ASEAN minus X can also be used in service liberalization. In effect this will allow the like-minded countries to liberalize their services faster and exchanging concessions among themselves without having to extend the same concessions to non-participating countries in ASEAN.

Since tourism is one of the key services in most ASEAN members, an ASEAN Tourism Agreement will be signed by Leaders at their Eighth ASEAN Summit in Phnom Penh on 4 November 2002. The new agreement is aimed at facilitating travel into and within the ASEAN region, and enhancing cooperation to improve efficiency and competitiveness of the ASEAN tourism industry.

At this stage, it is reasonable to assume that the EAFTA cannot be more

[11] See the Joint Press Statement of the 16th Meeting of the AFTA Council, held in Bandar Seri Begawan on 11 September 2002.

meaningful than AFTA. The EAVG apparently did not envisage a high level of regionalism for the EAFTA either.

On investment, the Vision Group merely recommended "Expansion of the Framework Agreement on an ASEAN Investment Area to all of East Asia." However, the 1998 Agreement on the ASEAN Investment Area (AIA) has no provision for accession by States outside of ASEAN. In any case, the AIA is not very ambitious. It calls for the immediate opening up of all industries for investment to ASEAN investors as well as granting them national treatment by the year 2010, with some exceptions as specified in the Temporary Exclusion List and the Sensitive List submitted by members, and to all investors by 2020.

Consequently, ASEAN Leaders at their Sixth Summit in Hanoi in 1998 offered new short-term measures to enhance ASEAN investment climate from 1 January 1999 to 31 December 2000. In addition, the AIA Council adopted at their Fifth Meeting in Bandar Seri Begawan on 11 September 2002 a 2-year ASEAN Investment Initiative. And Thailand will host the First ASEAN Trade Fair in Bangkok on 14-20 October 2002 to promote and attract foreign direct investment into the ASEAN region.

4.1.2. ASEAN-China FTA

A big pleasant surprise came from Prime Minister Zhu Rongji of China at the ASEAN-China Summit in Singapore in November 2000. He proposed the setting up of a free trade relationship between ASEAN and China to attract trade and investment and where ASEAN can be a priority for Chinese businesses. He called for the establishment of an Expert Group under the ASEAN-China dialogue relationship to study trade and economic cooperation between ASEAN and China.

The Expert Group's report[12] was considered at the ASEAN-China Summit in Bandar Seri Begawan on 6 November 2001. The Summit endorsed the following proposals of the Expert Group:

* Setting up a framework agreement on economic cooperation (with special emphasis on five priority areas of cooperation: agriculture, ICT, HRD, Mekong River Basin development, and mutual investment)
* Establishment of an ASEAN-China Free Trade Area within 10 years, with special and differential treatment and flexibility to the newer ASEAN members
* Granting "early harvest" for products and services to be determined by mutual consultations.
* Starting the FTA negotiations with a view to concluding the agreement as soon as possible

In addition, China also agreed to grant special preferential tariff treatment for some goods from Cambodia, Laos and Myanmar, which China considered the least

[12] Report of the ASEAN-China Expert Group entitled "Forging Closer ASEAN-China Economic Relations in the 21st Century" is available on the ASEAN Secretariat's web site, at the section on the Seventh ASEAN Summit.

developed members of ASEAN.[13]

ASEAN and China have established the Trade Negotiating Committee (TNC) to iron out details of what has generally billed as the world's largest FTA, for it will cover an estimated combined population of 1.7 billion (1.2 billion on the Chinese side, not including Hong Kong, Macau and Taiwan, and 500 million on the ASEAN side). Within ASEAN, the ASEAN Trade Negotiating Group (ATNG) has also been set up; it is chaired by a deputy permanent secretary of the Ministry of Commerce of Thailand.

The TNC talks tried to tackle significant but muddy issues surrounding the "early harvest," product coverage, modality of the FTA negotiations, and the content of the draft Framework Agreement on ASEAN-China Comprehensive Economic Cooperation. In the direct consultation between ASEAN Economic Ministers and Chinese Minister of Trade and Economic Cooperation, held in Bandar Seri Begawan on 13 September 2002, most of the issues were clarified and resolved.

Their Joint Press Statement reported that the Framework Agreement will contain the following:

* ASEAN-China Free Trade Area (ACFTA), which will cover trade in goods, services and investment and the principles of special and differential treatment and flexibility for the ASEAN member States, especially the new members;
* Specific measures to facilitate trade and investment and enhance economic cooperation;
* An Early Harvest Package, including specific economic cooperation activities which shall be undertaken or implemented on an accelerated basis, and exploring the feasibility of an Early Harvest Program for trade in services;
* Negotiations of specific agreement for the liberalization of trade in goods, services and investment, which will commence in 2003.

On the Early Harvest, the ASEAN and Chinese Ministers also agreed that it would be implemented no later than 1 January 2004 over a period of three years. And a longer timeframe of the Early Harvest would be accorded to Cambodia, Laos, Myanmar and Vietnam.

How ASEAN and China will pursue the negotiations on the FTA and on supplementary agreements on liberalization of investment and trade in services will be very interesting to follow. Most probably, they may have to also adopt the more practical approach of using the ASEAN minus X.[14]

[13] At first China appeared reluctant to grant special preferential tariff treatment to Viet Nam. But in ASEAN, the six older members started extending special preferential tariff treatment on a unilateral non-reciprocal basis to each Cambodia, Laos, Myanmar and Vietnam individually under the ASEAN Integration System of Preferences (AISP). The AISP will extend tariff preferences to nearly US$400 million worth of CLMV's exports a year.

[14] See papers on ASEAN-China economic relations by Ms. Thitapha Wattanapruttipaisan (October 2001, and June 2002) posted on the ASEAN Secretariat's web site, the section of Staff Papers. A paper by Mr. Nguyen M Cuong specifically about the ASEAN-China FTA (August 2002) will be posted on the web site soon.

In view of the emerging and more meaningful ASEAN-China FTA, it is now debatable whether it is sufficient to assume that the EAFTA could not be more comprehensive than AFTA. The ASEAN-China FTA, if indeed it could be realized in the next 10 years, would certainly be the most important foundation on which the EAFTA could build on.

4.1.3. ASEAN-Japan Comprehensive Economic Partnership

One more important building block is the emerging ASEAN-Japan Comprehensive Economic Partnership (CEP). During his official visit to Singapore on 14 January 2002, Prime Minister Junichiro Koizumi of Japan proposed CEP as one of his five initiatives for Japan and ASEAN to "act together, and advance together". Under the CEP initiative, Japan and ASEAN would cooperate in the new Doha round of WTO trade negotiations; strengthen a broad range of economic partnerships on trade and investment to such new areas as science and technology, HRD and tourism.[15]

Mid-level ASEAN and Japanese officials have formed an ASEAN-Japan Closer Economic Partnership (CEP) Expert Group to look into ways and means of enhancing ASEAN-Japan economic relations in trade in goods and services and investment, harmonization and cooperation of systems in facilitating trade and goods, strategies for greater competitiveness, regional mega projects, and "other" cooperation (which could include more sensitive issues – especially to Japan – such as agriculture, forestry, fishery, FTA, food security and rice reserve system, energy security, and the environment).

The EAFTA, undoubtedly, will have to take into serious consideration the issues that Japan considers as sensitive. However, the coverage of the EAFTA will be greatly diminished if trade in agricultural products is to be excluded.

4.1.4. ASEAN-Korea cooperation: CEP or FTA?

Unlike China and Japan, Korea has no direct economic cooperation scheme with ASEAN at the moment. At the ASEAN-Korea Summit in Bandar Seri Begawan last November, ASEAN Leaders and President Kim agreed to explore ways to enhance trade and economic links while encouraging the participation of the private sector in bilateral cooperative efforts, according to the post-summit press statement.

The ASEAN side proposed the establishment of an ASEAN Promotion Center in

[15] The Japanese Prime Minister undertook a swift visit to Bangkok, Kuala Lumpur, Jakarta, Manila and Singapore in January 2002 to put forth his initiatives for Japan-ASEAN cooperation. The effort was widely seen as an urgent Japanese response to the rapidly growing Chinese success in engaging ASEAN, as evident in the ASEAN-China agreement to work toward the FTA.
Another interesting initiative, to which ASEAN has agreed, concerns designating 2003 as the Year of Japan-ASEAN Exchange. The centerpiece of this year long celebration will be an ASEAN-Japan commemorative summit which Japan has proposed for the fourth quarter of 2003.
Yet another initiative of the Japanese Prime Minister involved the convening of a ministerial meeting on the Initiative for Development in East Asia (IDEA), which Japan hosted in Tokyo on 12 August 2002.
For additional details of other regional cooperation schemes involving East Asian countries, see the Table 1 attached.

Seoul to promote tourism, modeled after the highly visible and successful ASEAN Promotion Center in Tokyo, and the establishment of an ASEAN-Korea Business Council.

The ASEAN side also proposed the concept of ASEAN-Korea Closer Economic Partnership (CEP), including the establishment of an FTA, be adopted as the new approach. Korea was of the opinion that a study group could be set up to review the options.

Unfortunately, not much follow-up to the CEP/FTA idea has been undertaken in the ASEAN-Korea dialogue relationship since last November. And here lies a major question: What to do when there are uneven economic linkages among the East Asian countries?

Can the EAFTA take off without closer economic relations between ASEAN and Korea, and, more importantly between China and Korea, China and Japan and Japan and Korea?

4.2. Political Will and Comfort Level

One should bear in mind that the Vision Group's recommendation to establish the EAFTA was part of the Vision Group's overall grand vision of an East Asian community. Thus the Vision Group also recommended the "evolution of the ASEAN+3 Summit into an East Asian Summit" as well as the "institutionalization of regional dialogues" in East Asia. But the Vision Group stopped short of calling for a new regional grouping in East Asia.

However, if one goes through all the major recommendations of the Vision Group, one cannot fail to arrive at the conclusion that the Vision Group was pointing at the need for a new regional organization in East Asia. Take for example the Vision Group's recommendation "to establish and implement effective measures for the prevention and avoidance of conflict, as well as for management of tensions within the region." This would certainly require a strong central authority with broad mandate and immense resources. Even a 35-year-old grouping like ASEAN has no such ambition or capability.

Another recommendation of the Vision Group "calls for a more closely coordinated regional exchange rate mechanism." This will also require a high degree of policy coordination and regular monitoring and adjustment. A highly efficient regional body well staffed with financial experts would be required to undertake such an important task.

Based on ASEAN's experience with AFTA, it is clear that creating the EAFTA would actually require a much stronger regional body to manage the bigger and more complicated process.

Lastly, the Vision Group's recommendation on the evolution of the ASEAN+3 Summit into the East Asia Summit left little doubt in many ASEAN members that the Vision Group – and most probably the Korea -- wanted to replace the ASEAN+3 process with a new regional grouping.

Some ASEAN members are quite concerned that ASEAN as well as individual ASEAN members could be marginalized by a new East Asian grouping. Their preference is to step up efforts in ASEAN integration first. Then go step-by-step in the "evolution" and development of the ASEAN+3 process.

This seminar is most timely as it helps pool information and generates ideas on this very important and exciting issue. All in all, the EAFTA is a new frontier of economic cooperation in East Asia and deserves careful and concerted study.

Table 1. East Asian Nations and Growing Regionalism

Forums	ASEAN 10	ASEAN 7	China	Japan	Korea	DPRK & Mongolia	Hong Kong	Chinese Taipei	Mekong Countries
ASEAN+1	y	n	Y	Y	y				
ASEAN+3	y	n	Y	Y	y				
APEC		y	Y	Y	y		y	y	
ASEM		y	Y	Y	y				
GMS			Y						y[1]
ARF	y	n	Y	Y	y	y			
EALAF	y	n	Y	Y	y				
IDEA	y	n	Y	Y	y				
ACD	y[2]	n	Y	Y	y				
AMBDC	y	n	Y	Invited	Invited				
ACCORD	y	n	Y						
Quadrilateral			Y						y[3]
MRC			Observer						y[4]
Boao Forum for Asia	y	n	Y	Y	y				

Notes: **ASEAN 10** means all the 10 Member Countries of the Association. **ASEAN 7** means the older 7 Member Countries, except Cambodia, Laos and Myanmar. **n** means not applicable.

y[1] The Mekong countries in the ADB-organized Greater Mekong Sub-region (GMS) Economic Cooperation Conference are Cambodia, Laos, Myanmar, Thailand and Vietnam. Cambodia will host the first GMS Summit in Phnom Penh on 3 November 2002 to commemorate the 10th anniversary of the GMS. The President of the ADB and the Chinese Premier has been invited to attend.

EALAF is East Asia-Latin America Forum. ASEAN, China, Japan and the Korea have teamed up to engage 17 countries in Latin America in economic cooperation consultations.

IDEA is Japan's Initiative for Development in East Asia. Japan convened the Ministerial Conference on IDEA in Tokyo on 12 August 2002.

y[2] **ACD** is Thailand's initiative on Asia Cooperation Dialogue. Myanmar did not attend the inaugural meeting in Cha-am, Thailand, last June because of border tensions with Thailand. Thailand will host the second ACD in Chiang Rai next year

ACCORD is ASEAN-China Cooperative Operations in Response to Dangerous Drugs.

AMBDC is ASEAN's initiative on ASEAN-Mekong Basin Development Cooperation. The AMBDC's best known flagship project is the Singapore-Kumning Rail Link (SKRL). Japan and the Korea have been invited to join the AMBDC as its core members; but both of them have declined the invitation, saying that they need more time to study the AMBDC's activities.

y[3] in **Quadrilateral** are Laos, Myanmar, Thailand and China. The Quadrilateral is promoting, among others, river transport on and tourism along the Mekong River.

MRC is the Mekong River Commission based in Phnom Penh. **y** [4] are Cambodia, Laos, Thailand and Vietnam; China and Myanmar are Observers in the MRC. Both China and Myanmar are seriously considering joining the MRC.

The **Boao Forum for Asia** was initiated by China. Though it saw active participation of several government leaders, the BFA is considered as a Track II forum.

CHAPTER 5

INDONESIA'S FTA POLICY AND ITS PERSPECTIVES ON AN EAST ASIAN FTA

DEDDY SALEH

1. INTRODUCTION

The establishment of new regional and cross-regional as well as bilateral preferential trade arrangements involving either Southeast and East Asian or Pacific countries has become new trend since the last few years. The movement to promote free trade agreement (FTAs) in some parts of Southeast and East Asian countries can be considered as a defensive response to other regional and global developments, such as European Union, NAFTA, and AFTA. A lightened burden and stagnancy of the multilateral trading system, such as WTO round could possibly explain the tendency for more countries to propose or join in preferential trade arrangements. Though many of the new regional preferential trade arrangements are located around the two main "hubs" for international trade, like the United States and European Union (EU), now numerous new players are trying to set up preferential trade agreements either bilaterally or regionally. During the last few years, there are a number of preferential trading arrangements being studied or negotiated in Southeast and East Asian countries. One of the greatest regional preferential trading arrangements agreed in principle in 2001 is ASEAN+3 (China, Korea, Japan). Even before that, ASEAN in collaboration with Australia and New Zealand have studied the possibility of setting up ASEAN Free Trade Agreement - Closer Economic Relationship (AFTA-CER). Due to some reasons, however, the proposed FTA could not be implemented yet. Therefore, they are now endeavoring to establish a closer economic partnership (CEP). Further, ASEAN-India is in the process of discussing the terms and conditions of a closer economic relationship, including the possibility of a free trade agreement.

Meanwhile, Singapore, as a member of ASEAN, is pro-active in setting up new free trade agreements with some other countries, such as bilateral or regional FTAs with Japan, New Zealand, Canada, India, Mexico, European Union, USA including Batam and Bintan Island, Australia, and EFTA. Moreover, Thailand has also agreed to establish free trade agreement with Australia as well with Japan. It seems that both Singapore and Thailand are really eager to extend the establishment of

C. Y. Ahn et al (eds.), East Asian Economic Regionalism, 75-94.

preferential trade arrangement with other countries bilaterally or regionally.

In the meantime, several economies in the East Asian region has also proposed and/or negotiated free trade agreements with some countries bilaterally or regionally. Japan has negotiated FTA with Korea, Mexico, Chili, Singapore, and Canada. Meanwhile Korea has also proposed FTA with other countries like Mexico, New Zealand, and Chile, besides Japan and ASEAN.

Those countries that are actively negotiating new FTAs are industrialized or relatively developed economies, such as Japan, Korea, and Singapore, and their approached partners are also advanced industrial countries (Canada, USA, European Union) or relatively advanced developing countries like Chile and Mexico.

Apart from a defensive response, the objectives of regional and cross regional free trade agreements in East Asia are to improve economic integration with Europe and the Western Hemisphere. Now, what are the effects of free trade agreements on countries either member or non-member economies and what is the Indonesian perspective toward on an East Asian FTA? This paper will therefore try to scrutinize and elaborate some merits and demerits of FTA from my personal judgment.

2. THE ROLE OF EAST ASIAN COUNTRIES FOR INDONESIA'S ECONOMY

Korea, China and Japan are the major trading partners for Indonesia not only in terms of export but also in import. Korea and China are the fourth and the fifth largest trading partner for Indonesia respectively, either export or import, while Japan is the first largest trading partner. Furthermore, Japan and Korea are also the main sources of investment for Indonesia for the last three decades. The role of those three countries in Indonesia's economy can be elaborated below.

2.1. Indonesia-China

Indonesia and China are close neighbors with a long history of traditional friendship. Since reopening diplomatic and trade relations between two countries on August 8, 1990, trade relations between the two countries have made big strides.

As illustrated in Figure 1, Indonesian export to China since 1993 has increased drastically by 17.8%, i.e., from $1.25 billion to $3.49 billion in 2001. Notwithstanding, Indonesian export to this country declined 19.22% in 2001 compared with the previous year that reached $4.32 billion. In 2001, Indonesian export to China including Hong Kong was 6.2 % of the total Indonesian export to the world.

The top ten Indonesian exports to this country consist of Lubrications/Fuels/Oils, Wood, Paper & Paper Board, Organic Chemicals, Wood Pulp, Electrical Equipment, Plastics, Fats & Oils, Cotton, and Computer/Machinery. In spite of that, there are ten products that have had high growth during the same period, namely apparel, knitted (173%), pharmaceutical products (153%), optical/medical instruments (152%), book and newspaper (138%), footwear (129%), electrical equipment (128%), coffee, tea, spices (121%), malt & wheat gluten (107%), miscellaneous manufactured articles (104%), and inorganic chemicals (101%).

Figure 1. Indonesia-China Trade Relations

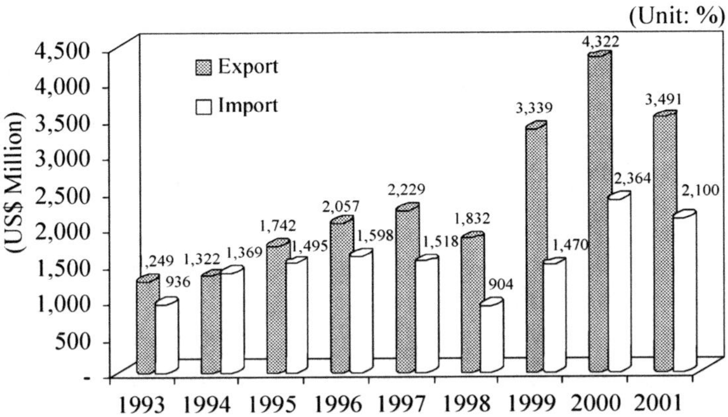

Source: Indonesia Central Bureau of Statistics 2001 (Processed)

On the other hand, Indonesian imports from China also increase drastically, from \$0.94 billion in 1993 to \$2.10 billion in 2001 with the growth of 7.37% annually. Despite that Chinese imports to Indonesia declined 11.18% in 2001 compared with the previous year that reached \$2.36 billion. The main commodities of import from China are lubricants/fuel/oil; computer/machinery; electrical equipment; inorganic chemicals; cotton; organic chemicals; tobacco; cars, truck, autos; edible fruit & nuts; and plastics.

Indonesia and China have huge potential for cooperation particularly in trade and industrial cooperation because of different comparative advantages. Indonesia has an abundance of natural resources such as plywood, cement, rubber, palm oil, fertilizer, rattan, and coffee. Meanwhile, China has a lot of cotton, corns, and technology. The complementary characteristic can support our long-term cooperation mainly to enhance our economic cooperation on the basis of equality and mutual benefit.

Apart from that, China investment in Indonesia has increased steadily since 1997, i.e. from US\$23.5 million in 1997 to US\$156.9 million in 2000. Surprisingly, China tends to be the main player of investment in Indonesia, because China was the first largest investor in Indonesia in 2001 with the total value of investment of US\$6,054.8 million. This figure contributed 40.2% of total foreign investment in Indonesia. It seems that China will become the main player in Indonesia particularly after the establishment of FTA in the near future.

2.2. Indonesia-Japan

Japan is the largest market for Indonesian export, accounting for 23.1% of the Indonesian total export to the world. During the period of 1993 – 2001 Indonesian export to this country, as can be seen in Figure 2, had fluctuated with the trend of 1.27%, i.e., from \$11.17 billion in 1993 to \$13.01 billion in 2001. However, based on non-oil and gas manufactured products, Indonesian export to this country is the second rank after the United States. Of $11.17 billion of Indonesian total export to this country in 2001, $6.70 billion (51.2%) of them were non-oil and gas manufactured products, and the rest of them were oil and gas products.

There are three largest export products to Japan with value of more than one billion dollars, namely lubricants/fuels/oils; wood; and electrical equipment. The other largest export products are fish, ores, computer/machinery, paper & paper board, furniture, aluminum, and plastics.

Even though, Japan is the largest importer for Indonesia, its import to Indonesia for the period of 1993 – 2001 had declined with the growth of minus 8.33%, i.e., from $6.25 billion in 1993 to $4.69 billion in 2001. The highest total import figure of Indonesia from Japan occurred in 1995; a year after Indonesia liberalized its investment, i.e., $9.22 billion.

Figure 2. Indonesia-Japan Trade Relations

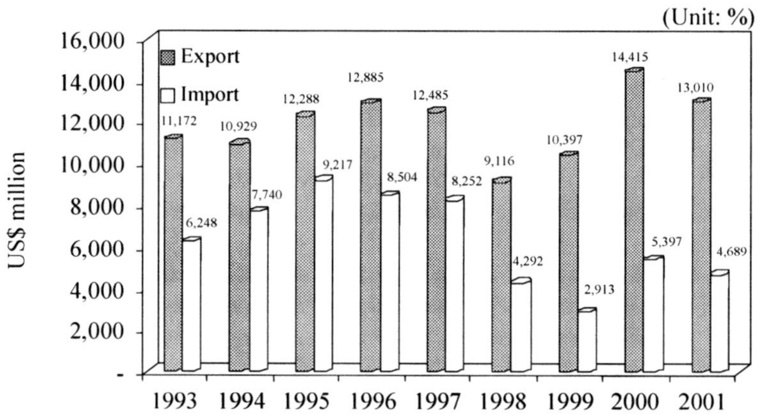

Source: Indonesia Central Bureau of Statistics 2001 (Processed)

The top ten imports of Indonesia from Japan in 2001 consisted of computer/ machinery; cars, trucks, autos; iron and steel; organic chemicals; electrical equipment; articles of iron or steel; plastics; rubber; ships, boats; and man-made staple fibers.

As stated before, Japan is one of the main sources of investment for Indonesia since Indonesia liberalized its investment regulation. In 1997, total Japanese investment in Indonesia recorded US$5,417.8 million, but declined to US$1,330.7 million in 1998 and then dropped to US$639.9 million in 1999. In 2000, however, it increased to US$1,954.8 million and again decreased to US$772.0 million in 2001 or become the fifth largest investor in Indonesia after China, Malaysia, Saudi Arabia, and Singapore.

2.3. Indonesia-Korea

Korea is one of the major trading partners for Indonesia. Korea's role in Indonesian trading is significant as can be proved by export and import performance. Figure 3 shows that for the period of 1993 – 2001, Indonesian export to Korea grew 6.30% per year, i.e., from \$2.22 billion in 1993 to \$3.77 billion. Indonesian export to this country in 2001, however, contracted for 12.63% compared with the previous year (US\$4.32 billion). The most important sector in Indonesian export to Korea are lubricants/fuels/oil; ores; wood; wood pulp; man-made staple fibers; electrical equipment; paper & paper board; organic chemicals; cotton; and rubber.

Figure 3. Indonesia-Korea Trade Relations

(Unit: US$ million)

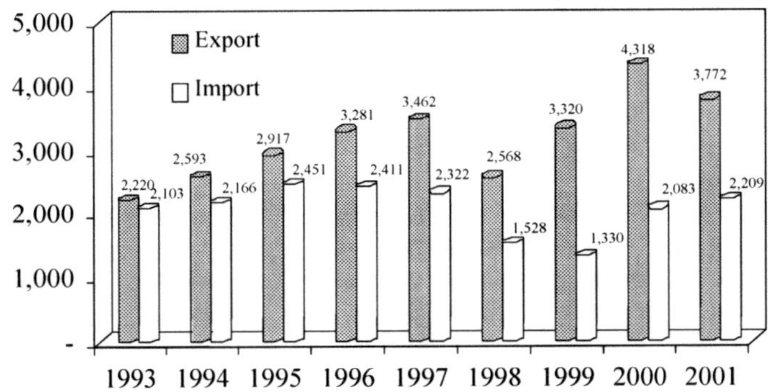

Source: Indonesia Central Bureau of Statistics 2001 (Processed)

In the meantime, the growth of Indonesian import from Korea slightly contracted 2.63% for the period of 1993-2001, i.e., from \$2.10 billion in 1993 to \$2.2 billion. In 2001, however, its import increased 6.09%, from \$2.08 billion in 2000 to \$2.2 billion in 2001. As far as import are concerned, the most important sectors in Indonesian import from Korea are lubricants/fuels/oils; organic chemicals; computer /machinery; plastics; electrical equipment; iron and steel; cars, trucks, autos; man-made filaments, ships, boats; and raw hides & skins.

As mentioned above, Korea is also one of the main sources of investment for Indonesia. Total Korean investment approved by the Investment Coordinating Board of Indonesia in 1997 accounted for US\$1,409.4 million. However, due to the crisis that hit Indonesia since mid-1997, its investment has dropped drastically to US\$202.4 million in 1998 and slightly increased to US\$239.0 million in 1999. In line with the favorable situation either in Indonesia or globally, its investment increased to US\$690.0 million in 2000, but then dropped to US\$369.6 million in 2001. For the period of January -August 2002, total Korean investment in Indonesia was recorded at US\$325.5 million. In 2001, Korea was the eighth foreign investor in Indonesia and contributed 2.5% of total foreign investment.

3. FTA POLICY

Historically, since 1967 ASEAN member countries have initiated economic cooperation in order to increase their economy and to improve their standard of living. The basis for functional cooperation among ASEAN countries was laid down on 8 August 1967 with the signing of the historic Bangkok Declaration. Since then, ASEAN has recorded an impressive record of rapid and sustained economic growth, regional stability and security, as well as close collaboration in scientific, technological and socio-cultural endeavors.

Rapid and sustained economic growth rates during the 1970, the 1980s and the beginning of the 1990s (before the crisis jolted this region in mid-1997) had made ASEAN one of the most economically dynamic regions in the world. ASEAN Leaders made, therefore, the momentous decision to link their economies by establishing the ASEAN Free Trade Area (AFTA) on January 28, 1992. Under a Common Effective Preferential Tariff (CEPT) Scheme, 15 groups of products are scheduled for accelerated tariff reduction from their 1992 level to 0 –5% by the year 2008, as well as to reduce or eliminate non-tariff barriers. It is expected that the CEPT scheme will encourage the spirit of competition and force the business actors to achieve higher efficiency, productivity, as well as to attract more foreign investors to ASEAN countries.

Due to the rapid economic development of ASEAN member countries before the crisis, the so-called "ASEAN Miracle" the ASEAN Leaders accelerated the implementation of AFTA from 2008 to 2003. During the peak of the crisis in ASEAN regions, ASEAN Leaders initiated to anticipate the crisis by accelerating the implementation of AFTA a year in advance (2002)..

Although AFTA is primarily an economic initiative, its implication will spill over into and redefine existing relationship in and outside the economic sector and possibly even outside ASEAN itself. Indonesia, as a member of ASEAN, together with other ASEAN member countries has experienced implementing AFTA through its CEPT Scheme.

To make the Indonesian economy more efficient, in 1994 the Government of Indonesia fully lowered the entry barriers of foreign direct investment. Meanwhile, in 1995, pre-announced tariff cuts to average 5% by the year 2003; the year of AFTA's scheme comes to effect. In short, Indonesia has made significant progress, either in economic growth or social welfare.

Furthermore, Indonesia has so far never proposed any free trade agreement with other countries bilaterally. Nonetheless, Indonesia is now in the process of studying the possibility of free trade agreements with other countries.

3.1. Future Prospects

The prospect of a free trade area among the countries in Southeast and East Asian countries, especially ASEAN+3 in the near future will be greater for this region. ASEAN+3 (Korea, China, and Japan) have some complementary advantages, such as huge potential market, investment source, and technology transfer or capacity building.

Based on some social and economic indicators, the total population of this region is almost 2 billion people covering of 501.54 million in ASEAN region, 45.7 million in Korea, 1,250.7 million in China including Hong Kong, and 126 million in Japan. This huge population means the ASEAN+3 market would have a total GDP of $6,968.0 billion and visible export for $1,271.5 billion and import for $1,115.4 billion per year (in terms of FOB) [1].

Furthermore, the flows of investment, particularly from Japan, Korea, and Singapore to developing economies might possibly increase after taking advantage of liberalization of trade and investment under the framework of free trade agreements. The flows of investment/capital from one country to another heavily depend on each country's attractiveness, business security, business climate, as well as their incentives. The more attractiveness a country the more investment will come. Therefore, a country that offers an attractive and conducive investment climate will be a winner in this region. ASEAN member countries (excluding Singapore) and China will compete with each other to attract more investment to invest in each country. It is believed that the competition to attract foreign direct investment among those countries will be keen.

The movement of people, capital, goods and services intra ASEAN+3 might increase drastically after free trade agreement comes into force, and eventually will increase the regional prosperity.

3.2. *Indonesian Trade Performance in AFTA*

Based on ASEAN experience, the first time CEPT-AFTA was implemented in 1993, the average CEPT tariff of ASEAN-6 (Brunei Darussalam, Indonesia, Malaysia, Philippine, Singapore, and Thailand), was 12.76%, but reduced to 3.21% in 2001, and even in 2003 it will be lowered to 2.37%. The impact of tariff lowering over ASEAN export intra-ASEAN is significant. During the period of 1993 – 2000, the total intra-ASEAN export increased from $43.68 billion (1993) to $90.44 billion (2000) with the growth rate of 7.82% annually. This also gives a positive impact to the Indonesian trade performance as can be seen below.

ASEAN is the most important market for Indonesia because Indonesian export share to this region has increased every year since 1993 up to 1998. In 1993, the share of Indonesian export to ASEAN accounted for 13.57% of its total export to the world and increased to 19.13% in 1998. However, for the period of 1999 – 2000 its export share to this region tended to decline, i.e., 17.01%, 17.52%, and 16.88% respectively.

Since the establishment of AFTA, Indonesian trade structure has improved significantly. Figure 4 shows that for the period of 1993 – 2001, Indonesian export to ASEAN has experienced significant improvement with a growth of 8.79%, i.e., from $4.99 billion in 1993 to $9.51 billion in 2001. Nevertheless, Indonesian export to this region in 2001 contracted 12.6% compared with the previous year that obtained $10.88 billion.

[1] See APEC homepage www.apecsec.org.sg.

The most important sectors of Indonesian export to ASEAN in 1993 were jewelry; lubricant/ fuels/oils; electrical equipment; special woven fabrics; man-made filaments; apparel, not knitted; fish; computer/machinery; rubber; and cars, trucks, and autos. However, in 2001 the structure or the rank of Indonesian export to ASEAN changed significantly to namely electrical equipment; computer/machinery; lubricants/ fuels/oils; paper & paper board; jewelry; organic chemicals; plastics; cars, trucks, autos; articles of iron or steel; and ores.

Figure 4. Indonesia-ASEAN Trade Relations

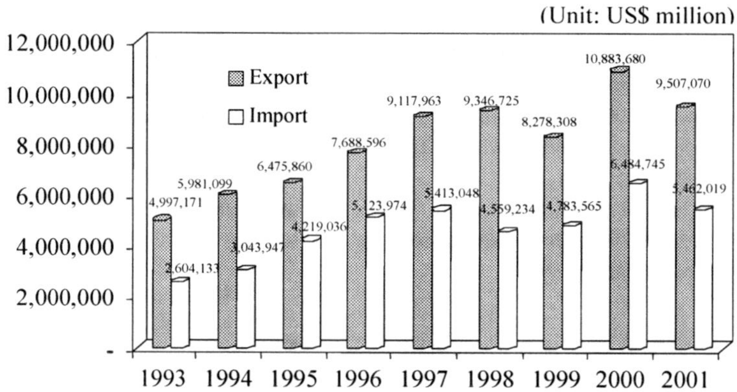

Source: Indonesia Central Bureau of Statistics 2001 (Processed)

On the other hand, Indonesian import from ASEAN had also experienced a positive growth for the period of 1993-2001 with the annual growth of 9.36%. Its import since 1993 up to 1997 increased steadily, i.e., from $2.60 billion in 1993 to $5.41 billion in 1997. In 1998, however, its import dropped $4.56 billion because of the severe impact of economic crisis in Indonesia, but in 1999 it slightly increased to $4.78 billion. The performance of Indonesian import from this region in 2000 increased drastically to $6.78 billion, this was also in line with the increase of Indonesian export to the world as well as ASEAN. Needless to say, its import dropped again in 2001 to $5.46 billion.

As far as import are concerned, the most important sectors for Indonesian import from ASEAN in 1993 were lubricants/fuel/oils; electrical equipment; computer/ machinery; ships, boats; plastics; fats & oils; miscellaneous chemical products; organic chemicals, iron and steel; and articles of iron or steel. However, there was a slight change in the top ten Indonesian import from ASEAN in 2000, with the position of lubricants/fuels/oils; organic chemical; computer/machinery; ships, boats; plastics; electrical equipment; sugar; car, trucks, autos; cereal, and articles of iron or steel.

Despite the competitiveness of Indonesian products in the ASEAN market based on statistical analysis (using the model of Revealed Comparative Advantage, Acceleration Ratio, and Trade Specialization Coefficient) conducted by the Agency for Industry and Trade Research and Development of Ministry of Industry and Trade of the Republic of Indonesia, there are 80 industries (ISIC 5 digits) that are competitive in facing AFTA 2002.Details of Indonesian products competitiveness is as follows:

- Industries under the *maturity stage* consist of 37 industries, covering among others, food industry; textile and textile products; leather goods; footwear; furniture and household equipment; paper, printing and publication; chemical and other chemical goods; plastic goods; laboratory equipment; glass sheets; electronics; jewelry; handicrafts, and other industries.
- Industries under the *growth to maturity stage* consist of 28 industries covering among others, edible oil; beverages; organic chemicals; rubber products; cement; pharmacy; building materials; metal processing machine; office machinery and equipment; camera and optical; musical instruments, and other industries.

  Industries under the *growth stage* consist of 3 industries, covering chocolate powder industry; soap and cleaning preparation; and lifting and hoisting machineries, tractor industry.
- Industries under *import substitution stage* consist of 7 industries, including cosmetic industry; non-ferrous metal rolling; nail, screw and bolts; hinge, and locks; pipe; all kinds of metal containers; metal pipe and pipe fitting; and air conditions, refrigerator and the like industries.
- Industries under *introductory stage* consist of 5 industries, including other plastic products industry; sewing machine; blower, compressor and the like; electric generators, and motor vehicle component and apparatus industries.

In short, the result of the study also suggested that Singapore and Malaysia would benefit the most from the AFTA 2002, then followed by Thailand, Indonesia, Philippines, and Brunei Darussalam.

3.3. Under Progress

ASEAN has extended its economic cooperation with other regional countries (Korea, China and Japan) in order to establish a free trade agreement. Among the three countries of East Asia, ASEAN-China negotiations seem to be more progressive rather than ASEAN-Korea and ASEAN-Japan FTAs. The followings progresses of FTA negotiation between ASEAN with its partners.

❖ *ASEAN-China*

At the ASEAN-China Summit held in Singapore in November 2000, the Leaders of ASEAN and China agreed to look into the implication of China's accession to the WTO. They also agreed to explore measures to further enhance economic cooperation and integration between both sides, including the possibility of establishing a free trade area between ASEAN and China. The decision by the leaders to look into these two issues was a natural response to a number of important global and regional developments during the course of the past decade.[2] At the seventh ASEAN Summit in Brunei Darussalam, leaders from both China and ASEAN member countries agreed to an ASEAN-China FTA.

The establishment of a free trade agreement between ASEAN-China will create an economic growth with 1.7 billion consumers, a regional GDP for approximately $ 2 trillion and total trade estimated at $1.23 trillion. It is believed that the removal of trade barriers between the two sides will reduce costs, increase intra-regional trade and economic efficiency. ASEAN-China FTA will create a sense of community among member countries of ASEAN and China, as well as provide another important mechanism for supporting economic stability in East Asia. The establishment of ASEAN-China will also allow them to have a larger voice in international affairs (WTO) on issues of common interest because both sides are categorized as developing countries.

Based on the ASEAN Trade Negotiation Group (ASEAN-TNG) and ASEAN-China Trade Negotiation Committee meetings held in Bangkok at the end of July and early August 2002, they noted that the ASEAN-China framework is not only a free trade area but ASEAN has to negotiate an early harvest package. In this case China offers an early harvest package of Agricultural Products that only consist of HS Chapter 1 – 8. Meanwhile, ASEAN offers agricultural products + CPO + Rubber + Wood and some manufacturing products.

Furthermore, ASEAN-China agreed to establish a free trade area within 10 years with special and different treatments for new members of ASEAN countries.

- *ASEAN-Japan*

So far, ASEAN-Japan has agreed to set up a Framework for ASEAN-Japan Closer Economic Partnership and Detailed Scope of Study for cooperation, as well as the establishment of ASEAN-Japan Closer Economic Partnership Expert Group.

In terms of Detailed Scope of Study, ASEAN proposed the scope of study covering focus on market access issues, especially on NTMs such as SPS; inclusion of agriculture, fishery and tourism; the time frame to conclude a comprehensive study; emphasis on investment promotion rather than liberalization; concern with the use of the word "harmonization; concern with inclusion of competition policy and government procurements; energy security; transfer of advance/appropriate technology, and dispute settlement mechanism.

- *ASEAN-Korea*

So far, ASEAN-Korea FTA is still extending the basis of cooperation and increasing the awareness of society relationship of Southeast Asia and Korea by improving economic relations and trade through private sectors' participation. It is hoped that through this conference we can get more information about ASEAN-

[2] Executive Summary of Forging Closer ASEAN-China Economic Relations in the 21st Century.

Korea FTA progress directly from the Korean Government experts who were involved in the Conference.

3.4. Future Direction

It seems that ASEAN is eager to establish free trade agreements not only with East Asian countries (Korea, China, and Japan) but also with other countries (like India, Australia, New Zealand). Despite the recent enlargement, ASEAN remains a small player in the international arena. The long-term goal for ASEAN should be to liberalize trade globally without discrimination. To do so, ASEAN remains committed to the concept of "open regionalism", bilateral RTAs between ASEAN and other groupings, like MERCOSUR, SAARC and EU.

4. AN EAST ASIAN FTA

4.1. General Discussion on an East Asian FTA

Even though, the Leaders of ASEAN+3 have committed to establish a free trade area, we should examine the opportunities and challenges that can result from the implementation of an FTA in the near future. Every change has a positive and negative impact. The establishment of a free trade agreement, either bilaterally or regionally, could also bring positive and negative impacts. The followings are merits and demerits of FTAs between ASEAN and East Asian countries, particularly for Indonesia as a member of ASEAN+3 FTA.

4.1.1. Merits of ASEAN+3 FTA

1) As stated above, the establishment of ASEAN+3 FTA will create greater economic growth for the two regions; because each country has some complementary advantages in terms of market, investment source, technology transfer/know how, and so on. With total population for almost 2 billion people and total estimated GDP for $6,968.0 billion and visible export for $1,271.5 billion and import for $1,115.4 billion per year, it can generate prosperity for the region or increase ASEAN welfare.
2) The flows of investment from Japan, Korea, and Singapore to developing economies might possibly increase after taking advantage of liberalization of trade and investment under the framework of free trade agreements. On the other hand, Japan, Korea, Singapore as developed and relatively developed economies can relocate their business activities to economies with cheaper labor costs, such as Indonesia, Vietnam, the Philippines, China, and others regions. ASEAN investment can also be expected to invest there. Relocation of business activity, either industry or trade, is one effective mean for distributing business activities along with respective comparative and competitive advantages.
3) The establishment of a free trade agreement will provide better prospects for

industrial relocation as the final act promises to reduce tariff and non-tariff barrier to international movement of goods and services, including capital goods. Furthermore, it will encourage industrial capital and technology to flow more in line with emerging complementarities and globalization of production to meet the requirement of an increasingly unified international market.

4) Increasing trade and investment will raise productivity through dissemination of technology, and improved productivity will make further progress in capital accumulation.
5) In terms of social aspects, relocation of business activities will constitute significant benefit to the developing countries in terms of gross domestic product growth, employment creation, poverty alleviation, technology transfer, and access to markets and managerial skills.
6) ASEAN-China will have a larger voice in international trade affairs (WTO) on issues of common interest because of the accession of China to WTO.
7) Efficiency and specialization will be promoted with increased efficiency through enhanced competition.
8) Developed countries will provide technical advice and assistance (capacity building) to developing countries, which will create international cooperation .
9) Consumer benefits will increase since people have a wider range of choice in products and services (high quality and lower prices).
10) Regional conflict will diminish and regional security will be enhanced through economic development.
11) The strengthening of economic partnership between developed economies and developing economies will promote Asia as a growth center.

4.1.2. Demerits of ASEAN+3 FTA

1) The preferential reduction of trade barriers would bring with it some loss of tariff revenue.
2) Along with the accelerated flows of positive movements such as, people, capital, goods, and services, there will be negative flows as well, including crime, disease and ecological degradation.
3) Uncompetitive companies will no longer survive.
4) The competition among members will be extremely keen, either in market penetration or attraction of FDI.
5) It is hard for unskilled labor to seek a job.
6) Mainly developing countries will endeavor to create technical barriers in order to protect their domestic industry.
7) There would be no protection for weakness business activities in developing countries.

4.1.3. Major issues related with an East Asian FTA

Some major issues that have been discussed in negotiating free trade agreements, especially between ASEAN-China are as follows:

1) The starting point or commencing date of free trade area has to be agreed. Even though ASEAN-China negotiations have been on-going, a definite time has not been decided except for a 10 year time frame.
2) High sensitive sectors between the two sides need to be discussed. Each country or region has different sensitive sectors, and therefore, they try to protect their public interests.
3) Liberalization of investment,
4) Liberalization of services,
5) The time frame of tariff reduction, and
6) Elimination of non-tariff barriers.

4.2. Economic Factors

Even though ASEAN+3 FTA has not been implemented yet, East Asian countries (Korea, China, and Japan) trade relations with ASEAN have improved significantly. Based on the ASEAN Secretariat data, the total trade (exports and imports) with ASEAN-6 (Brunei Darussalam, Indonesia, Malaysia, the Philippines, Singapore, and Thailand) for the period of 1993 – 2000 had grown 5.6% annually, i.e., from $108.8 billion in 1993 to $200.8 billion in 2000. Thus, those countries are always in surplus with ASEAN for $25.6 billion in 1993 and $1.0 billion in 2000.

Figure 5. ASEAN Foreign Trade Performance with Korea, China, and Japan

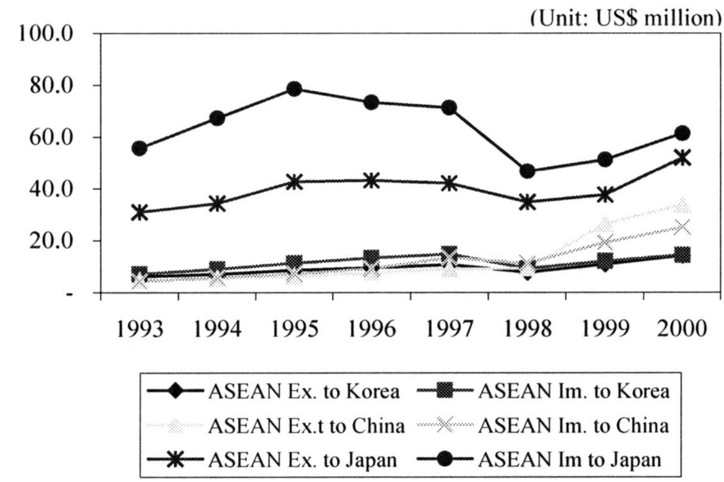

Source: International Trade Center 2002 (Processed)

Even though ASEAN+3 FTA has not been implemented yet, East Asian countries (Korea, China, and Japan) trade relations with ASEAN have improved significantly. Based on the ASEAN Secretariat data, the total trade (exports and imports) with

ASEAN-6 (Brunei Darussalam, Indonesia, Malaysia, the Philippines, Singapore, and Thailand) for the period of 1993 – 2000 had grown 5.6% annually, i.e., from $108.8 billion in 1993 to $200.8 billion in 2000. Thus, those countries are always in surplus with ASEAN for $25.6 billion in 1993 and $1.0 billion in 2000.

Those three countries' exports to ASEAN-6 for the same period had grown for 2.2%, i.e., $67.19 billion in 1993 to $100.86 billion in 2000. Of $67.19 billion, $55.70 billion was from Japan, $7.15 billion from Korea, and $ 4.34 billion from China. Meanwhile, in 2000 their total export increased to $100.86 billion, covering $61.40 billion from Japan, $24.98 billion from China, and $14.47 billion from Korea.

The most important sectors for Korean export to ASEAN consisted of electrical equipment; computer/machinery; lubricants/fuels/oil; organic chemicals; plastics; iron and steel; cars, trucks, autos; ships, boats; articles of iron and steels; and man-made staple fibers. Meanwhile, the top ten Japanese export to ASEAN comprised of electrical equipment; computer/machinery; cars, trucks, autos; iron and steel; plastics; optical/medical instruments; articles of iron or steel; jewelry; and rubber. While the most important sector for Chinese export to ASEAN includes electrical equipment; computer/machinery; lubricants/fuels/oils; cotton; optical/medical instruments; iron and steel; cereals; plastics; inorganic chemicals; and jewelry.

On the other hand, those three countries' imports from ASEAN-6 in for the same period grew 10.3%, i.e., from 41.61 billion in 1993 to $99.91 billion in 2000. Of $41.60 billion in 1993, Japan absorbed $31.0 billion, followed by Korea for $6.1 billion, and China for $4.5 billion. In 2000, however, those countries import from ASEAN increased to $99.9 billion, covering $14.14 billion for Korea, $33.78 for China, and $51.98 billion for Japan.

As far as imports are concerned, the most important sector for Korean imports from ASEAN are lubricants/fuels/oils; electrical equipment; computer/machinery; wood; ores; organic chemicals; miscellaneous chemical products; copper; rubber; and plastics. While the most important sector for Japan's imports from ASEAN are also electrical equipment; lubricants/fuels/oils; computer/machinery; wood; fish; optical/medical instruments; plastics; furniture; ores; and cars, trucks, and autos. Likewise, Chinese imports from ASEAN cover of live animals; meat & edible meat offal; fish; dairy produce; other animal products; live trees; edible vegetables; edible fruits & nuts; coffee, tea, spices; and cereals.

4.3. Sensitive Sectors

Almost every country has sensitive sectors, and that's why each country tries to protect its national interests. If two potential partners are main competitors, the sensitive lists of that country will be longer. On the other hand, if they are highly complementary then the list of sensitive sectors will be limited.

Let's take Indonesia as an example. Based on Indonesia's experienced in AFTA, before the crisis Indonesia had placed many sensitive products in the highly sensitive list such as rice, sugar, soy bean, clove, garlic, and wheat. The reason why many products were included in the highly sensitive list is because Indonesia had many competitors particularly from Thailand and Vietnam. However, since the intervention of IMF during the crisis, nearly all products under the sensitive list were eliminated from the list, except rice, but now Indonesia has included sugar into the highly sensitive list.

I believe there will be many sensitive products requested by countries involved in ASEAN+3 FTA, particularly China and Japan (in terms of agricultural products. Needless to say, China is ASEAN's main competitor, and therefore, it has requested some potential products for ASEAN to be included in sensitive sectors, such as rice, sugar, palm oil, rubber, and plywood.

4.4. Non-Economic Factors

Non-economic factors can also play a significant role in accelerating the implementation of a free trade agreement.

Political Conditions

Generally speaking, the recent political conditions in Southeast Asia and East Asia are quite conducive. ASEAN political conditions are increasingly better compared with the past, though in some parts of ASEAN members countries, like Indonesia and the Philippines, there are still some regional conflicts. Likewise, East Asian countries' political conditions especially in Korea, China, and Japan have been stable.

Thus, the leaders of ASEAN+3 endeavored to establish a free trade agreement in order to increase equal prosperity of the region, particularly in some parts of ASEAN countries. This is good momentum for Southeast and East Asian countries to foster free trade area in this region, and therefore, we should work hand-in-hand to implement what our leaders have agreed.

Social Conditions

Developed, relatively developed countries, and developing countries all have different economic status and thus different social conditions. Developed and/or relative developed countries such as Japan, Korea, and Singapore have a high living standard, and thus, nearly all the population is well educated and healthy. On the other hand, the social conditions of developing countries, particularly new ASEAN member countries such as Myanmar, Laos, and Cambodia are much lower than those of the three countries mentioned above. Most of the population is uneducated, unskilled and unhealthy.

It is expected that an FTA would enhance the social status of developing countries, generate prosperity, and therefore balance out an unbalanced region.

Culture

The cultures of Southeast and East Asian countries are quite different from each other, and ASEAN member countries are heterogeneous in contrast to Korea, China, and particularly Japan This is one of the obstacles for a multinational corporations (MNC) to establish or relocate their business in this region. Most foreign managements are facing with this problem. Thus, they have to learn and understand the social and culture of the country before they establish or relocate a business activity.

4.5. Overall Evaluation

Based on the data and information above, it is believed that the prospect of ASEAN+ 3 FTA in the coming years can generate more activities in the regions not only in the supply side but also in the demand side if they are complementary to each other.

In the supply side, when full implementation of the FTA is commenced, more industries will be established or relocate from developed and/or relative developed countries to developing countries taking advantage of their comparative advantages. The countries with attractive investment climates and good infrastructure will succeed in attracting new direct foreign investment from developed and/or developed countries.

Thus, each developing country will endeavor to generate a favorable investment climate. The investment in both regions will move freely from one country to another and even to the outside of ASEAN+3 taking the benefits of investment privilege existed in both regions. Thus, investment can generate a lot of new jobs and eventually reduce the unemployment rate of the region.

In the case of trade, more products (raw materials, intermediate and finished products) will also move freely from one country to another country. When the FTA is fully implemented, barriers to trade will automatically lessen or disappear. So it is predicted that the exports and imports of both regions will increase progressively.

Yet, will ASEAN+3 succeed? How much progress has been achieved? Are all ASEAN+3 pro-active in negotiations? It seems that among the 3 prospective candidates, only China is pro-active. The ASEAN-China FTA initiative is now a major undertaking, and the Chinese side has largely driven the progress toward its realization.

Moreover, Thailand tends to be more active in encouraging other ASEAN member countries to negotiate with China. Among the ASEAN member countries, it seems to me that Thailand is well prepared compared with other ASEAN member countries like Indonesia. Based on our representative officer's information in Bangkok, Thailand has established many outlets in some parts of China and they are ready to supply their outlets when the ASEAN-China FTA to be implemented.

In this case, Indonesia, as a member of ASEAN, should support the establishment of ASEAN-China, though it is not well prepared yet. Indonesia should show its solidarity with other ASEAN member countries.

Indonesia has a dilemma. Even though Indonesia is not fully prepared, can it support the establishment of an ASEAN-China? If not, Indonesia will be left far behind other member countries. I think Singapore and Thailand are impatient to establish a Free Trade Agreement with Australia and New Zealand, because other ASEAN member countries could not support establishing the AFTA-CER proposed a few years ago.

The success of Singapore and Thailand in establishing a free trade agreement with other countries signals that other ASEAN member countries could not pursue them. Besides that, there is a tendency that other countries try to lessen the ASEAN soundness that has been achieved so far by establishing a free trade agreement with one ASEAN member countries. Furthermore, the recent tendency of more countries to establishing a FTA bilaterally or regionally also indicates the failure of the Seattle Ministerial Meeting to launch a new WTO rounds few years ago.

4.6. Perspectives on an East Asian FTA

The relationship of ASEAN with Japan, Korea, and China for almost two and half decades has contributed significantly Southeast and East regional economy as a peaceful, stable and developed region.

As stated before, Southeast and East Asia countries have different endowment factors and comparative advantages, but they can complement each other. Developed and/or relatively developed countries have huge capital sources including advance technology with well-educated people. While, developing countries, such as Indonesia with their limited of capitals, lack technological mastering and know-how, but have abundant of natural resources and lower cost of labors.

These differences can be used for mutual benefit. Developed and/or relatively developed countries can expand their business activities, either in developing countries and/or in their countries, by exploiting the lower cost of productions and transactions in developing countries. Likewise, developing countries can also utilize the capital and technology from developed and/or relative developed countries.

The demand of goods and services could also progressively increase due to huge number of consumers in both regions. Consumers, either end-users or industries will have many choices at lower prices and best quality. Japan, Korea, China (Hong Kong) can be potential markets for developing countries, due to the fact that their income per capita and consumption are extremely high.

Now what happens if a country has similar comparative advantages or do not complement each other. Let's take ASEAN-China as an example. As already known, China is the major competitor for ASEAN not only between both regions but also globally. Generally, ASEAN and China have similar comparative advantages.

In my point of view, since Indonesia was jolted by the multi-dimensional crisis, Indonesia is not well prepared for entering a free trade area, either in AFTA or ASEAN-China. Nowadays, there are too many Chinese import products in the Indonesian markets legally or illegally with cheaper prices. It is indicated that Chinese products are more competitive than those of Indonesian products. Therefore, I still doubt the success of ASEAN-China FTA, particularly for Indonesia, because they do not complement each other.

What about ASEAN-Korea and ASEAN-Japan? Will those countries succeed in implementing a FTA? Since they are complementary, I think both ASEAN-Korea and ASEAN-Japan FTAs can succeed. Korea and Japan are not the major competitors for ASEAN. Most Japanese and Korean products are high quality and also concentrate on high-class consumers. Meanwhile, ASEAN member countries focus on medium-low consumers.

ASEAN member countries can utilize the comparative advantages of Korea and Japan, namely capital, technology and know-how, as well as their markets. On the other hand, Korea and Japan can also utilize ASEAN member countries' comparative advantage, particularly Indonesia with its abundant of natural resources, low labor costs, and great potential market.

5. CONCLUSION

Economic interdependence is still growing between countries in the region and between regions. It is believed that the establishment of a free trade agreement between Southeast and East Asian regions, particularly ASEAN+3 (China, Korea, Japan) will foster the regional economy with 1.86 billion consumers, a regional GDP of about US$ 6.97 trillion and total trade estimated for US$ 2,39 trillion. Such initiatives will bring greater benefits to its members if it involves a larger grouping, though in practice it will be difficult to achieve because of the very diverse economic interests.

Free trade agreements between ASEAN+3 (China, Korea, Japan), would offer ASEAN member countries some practical trade and investment benefits as well as other strategic benefits. Trade with Japan, Korea and China is very important to ASEAN member countries, especially Indonesia. ASEAN exports to those three countries account for around 26 percent of total ASEAN exports and those three countries are also the source of nearly 31 percent of ASEAN imports.

Taking into account the magnitude of the economic and social problems of the region, it seems that there is no alternative but to strengthen our economic development strategies particularly in trade and investment sectors. As we approach the liberalization of trade and investment through ASEAN+3 FTA, we need to reinforce our deepening economic cooperation.

When ASEAN+3 FTA comes into effect, it can be a modality for both regions to increase regional economic growth and prosperity. The removal of trade barriers between those two regions will, therefore, lower expenses, and increase intra-regional trade as well as economic efficiency. Overall, there are positive economic gains for both regions as a result of establishing a free trade area. Apart from that, an FTA also creates a sense of community among ASEAN member countries and Korea, China, and Japan. It could be used to build a common prosperity of all people of the world, particularly in East and Southeast Asian countries.

Indonesia fully understands that the rapid changes in globalization of the world economy and the scientific and technological progress will generate not only opportunities, but also challenges for Indonesia. Globalization will affect our future, whether we are ready or not, whether we wish it or not, and like it or not. We must prepare well as possible and as soon as possible, if not we will be left far behind. As a result, Indonesia is prepared to face the changing world by anticipating any problem in the future, and actively participating in FTAs regionally or bilaterally.

REFERENCES

Indonesia Investment Coordinating Board. 2002. "Approval Investment Report." December.
Indonesia Central Bureau of Statistics. 2001. Indonesian Foreign Trade Statistics-Exports 1993-2001.
______. 2001. Indonesian Foreign Trade Statistics-Import 1993-2001.
______. 2001. Statistical Year Book of Indonesia. Jakarta.
Indonesian Monetary Economics Statistics. 2002. Indonesian Financial Statistics. December. Jakarta. Bank Indonesia.
Ministry of Industry and Trade of Indonesia. 2002. The Competitiveness of Indonesian Export Product in ASEAN.
Ministry of Foreign Affair of Indonesia. 2002. "The Importance of AFTA and Indonesia's Position." Paper Presented on AFTA Seminar 2002.
Tamboen M.U., Firman. 2001. Preparation of Business Sector Toward Implementation of AFTA 2002. Paper Presented in AFTA Seminar. Jakarta.
Tran, M. D. 2001. CEPT Outreach Programme. National Level Workshop on CEPT Scheme. Jakarta.

CHAPTER 6

AN EAST ASIA FTA: A MALAYSIAN PERSPECTIVE

MOHD HAFLAH PIEI

1. INTRODUCTION

It has been slightly more than a decade since the concept of the East Asia Economic Group (EAEG) was first mentioned by Malaysia's Prime Minister. It was originally conceived of as an informal regional organization to serve as a loose consultative forum where East Asian economies consult each other on issues of common concern as and when the need arises. It was also meant to serve as a defensive strategy to counter the creation of a single Europe and the North America Free Trade Area (NAFTA), as well as to lobby for ASEAN interests in the then ongoing Uruguay Round of the GATT negotiation.

At the time, East Asian economies were growing at a very rapid rate of 8.1 percent per annum on the average (between 1987-91), such that the region had eventually assumed a new role as the regional grouping consisted of some of the most dynamic economies in the world. This growth performance even surpassed those of the developed economies and other parts of the developing world. The NIEs of the East Asian economies had achieved an average annual growth of 8.3 percent , roughly three times the growth rate of the world economy at 2.9 percent while ASEAN's growth rate, excluding the Philippines, was 6.9 percent, more than twice the growth of the world economy. This phenomenal growth performance continued until the Asian economic crisis struck the region in mid-1997.

Rapid growth in the region's economies had been matched and reinforced by their strong trade performance which is characterized by its increasing contribution to world trade, as well as intra-regional trade. Intra-East Asian trade, for example, had grown rapidly from US$196.4 billion in 1987 (a year after the 1985-86 recession) to US$405.4 billion in 1991, thus registering a growth of 106 percent. Meanwhile, exports from the NIEs as a whole grew 73 percent, while their exports to ASEAN countries grew by 125 percent. Total trade between ASEAN and NIEs increased by 156 percent, while Japan's trade with ASEAN increased by 85 percent. Intra-ASEAN trade, in the absence of AFTA which was launched later in 1993, expanded by 114 percent during the same time period. This phenomenal growth, much higher than the world average of 46.9 percent was testimony to the increasing economic linkages between the East Asian economies.

The degree of East Asian economic interdependence was further enhanced by the increasing flow of foreign direct investment (FDI), technology and labor into, and

C. Y. Ahn et al (eds.), East Asian Economic Regionalism, 95-119.

among, countries in the region. All these processes evolved without being based on any co-operation framework of any kind, regional or bilateral, and were completely market driven.

This paper is organized as follows. The next section will highlight some of the major features of the ASEAN economies with special emphasis on its economic relationship with the East Asian countries, China, Japan and Korea. Given the current and potential challenges and circumstances facing the ASEAN member countries, it is argued that it will make good economic sense for ASEAN countries to establish a framework agreement to strengthen its economic co-operation with the three East Asian economies. The next section will discuss the possible architecture of the proposed regional economic co-operation framework which focuses, among others, on the modalities, principles and scope of the proposed initiative. This is to be followed by a discussion on the merits and demerits of the proposed initiatives. The last section will summarize some of the major policy implications of this paper.

2. STRUCTURE OF ASEAN-EAST ASIA TRADE

In the early 1990s, the top five ASEAN exports to East Asian countries were electrical equipment, oil and fuel, computer, machinery, wood, and fish products. Together they formed 75.7 percent, 72.2 percent and 67.7 percent of ASEAN exports to China, Korea and Japan. By 2000, the share of the top five products in the exports of ASEAN had slightly changed where there had been a slight reduction in the share to about 70 percent in the case of China and increased to about 77.9 percent and 71.34 in the case of Korea and Japan respectively. These indicate that ASEAN exports had become more diversified whereas exports to Korea and Japan had become more specialized and concentrated.

Another feature observed in the ASEAN export pattern of the three East Asian economies was that the order of importance of its export items had changed quite distinctively, away from commodities and more towards manufactured products. For instance, in the case of ASEAN exports to China, 'lubricant and fuel', 'wood', as well as 'fats and oils' were the top three exports of ASEAN. Together they contributed 63.3 percent towards ASEAN's exports to China. By 2000, their export shares had sharply contracted to only 17.7 percent. Their positions were taken over by computers/machinery and electrical equipment, which collectively amounted to 48.4 of all ASEAN exports to China.

A similar shift in the pattern of ASEAN exports to Japan and Korea can also be observed, with the exception of 'lubricants, fuel and oil' which still remains at the top of ASEAN exports to Korea, and ASEAN's second most important export item to Japan. This situation will remain for a longer time considering that Japan and Korea are lacking in these natural resources.

With the exception of Japan, ASEAN imports from East Asia can be said to be more diversified than its exports, based on the share of the top 10 or top 5 of ASEAN's import items from the three economies. In 1993, ASEAN's top 5 import items, together, contributed about 36 percent and 55.6 percent toward ASEAN total imports from China and Korea, respectively, compared to 74.3 percent in the case of

Japan. By 2000, ASEAN imports from these countries have become less diversified with the share of the top five import items increasing to 56.8 percent, 70.2 percent and 75.54 percent of ASEAN imports from China, Korea and Japan, respectively.

The above shifting pattern in ASEAN trade relations with the three East Asian economies implies the increasing extent of intra-industry trade with the region and the emergence of a regional production network. This phenomenon is more distinctive in the case of ASEAN's trade with Japan where electrical equipment, computer and machinery together contributed more than 70 percent of ASEAN exports to, and imports from, Japan.

In the case of ASEAN-China and ASEAN-Korea, trade in these products is also high, but they do not reflect a strong regional production network emerging among ASEAN, China and Korea. Most of the machinery and electrical appliances exported by China to ASEAN are those for general or special uses. On the other hand, a substantial part of the machinery and electrical appliances that China imports from ASEAN are electronic components and devices. For example, of the US$2.88 billion worth of machinery and electrical appliances that China imports from Malaysia, more than half of them were kinescope, transistors and integrated circuits, and more than 40 percent were machinery and electrical appliances.

There are several reasons for the rapid growth of ASEAN-East Asia trade during the 1990s, some of which have been discussed earlier. One important factor was the dynamism of the economies in the region as reflected in the rapid growth rate of the real GDP in most regional economies.

Another factor was the falling MFN tariff rates in most economies in the region, particularly in ASEAN and China. At the beginning of 1993, China reduced its tariff on 3,371 import items and abolished import controls on more than 367 commodities. At the 1995 APEC Summit, China's President Jiang Zemin further made a commitment to cut average tariffs to 15 percent by 2000. This new liberalization effort includes substantial tariff cuts on 4,998 tariff lines. China has also eliminated quotas, licensing and import controls on 176 tariff lines, or more than 30 percent of commodities subject to these restrictions. As part of China's commitment for its accession to the WTO, it has agreed to make further cuts in tariffs and NTBs. Table 5 provides data on the weighted average tariff rates for 2001, and the agreed Chinese bound tariff rates reported in the Protocol of Accession to be implemented starting from the date of accession. The decline in China's average tariff rate between the time of its accession and the final year is expected to be from 13.7 percent to 5.7 percent.

Table 1. ASEAN Trade with Japan, China and Korea

(Unit: US$ million)

	1993			1994			1995			1996		
	Expt	Imp	B of Tr	Expt	Imp	B of Tr	Expt	Imp	B of Tr	Expt	Imp	B of Tr
China	4529	4326	193	5304	5759	-455	6201	7130	-922	7474	9218	-1744
Japan	30952	55703	-27751	34300	67302	-33002	42681	78535	-35864	43150	73310	-30160
Korea	6126	7148	-1022	7005	9036	-2031	8574	11346	-2772	9446	13294	-3848
Total	41607	108794	-28580	46609	82097	-35488	57456	97011	-39548	60070	95822	-35752

	1997			1998			1999			2000		
	Expt	Imp	B of Tr	Expt	Imp	B of Tr	Expt	Imp	B of Tr	Expt	Imp	B of Tr
China	9168	13482	-4314	9204	11212	-2008	26407	19184	7223	-33783	24985	8798
Japan	42009	71264	-29263	34717	46693	-11976	37629	51244	-13615	51982	61404	-9422
Korea	10668	14857	-4189	7813	9267	-1454	10878	12110	-1232	14145	14471	-356
Total	61845	99603	-37766	51734	67172	-15438	74914	65338	-7624	99910	100860	-950

Source: ASEAN Secretariat, Jakarta.

Table 2a. Major ASEAN Exports to China

(Unit: %)

HS chapter	Sector	1993	2000
85	Electrical equip.	6.01	31.77
84	Computer/machinery	6.39	16.63
27	Lubricants/fuel/oil	32.30	13.17
38	Misc. chemical products	0.61	5.68
44	Wood	22.64	2.75
29	Organic chemical	1.52	2.10
48	Paper and paper board	0.47	1.86
15	Fats and oils	8.38	1.78
37	Photographic goods	0.01	1.34
	Total	**78.33**	**77.08**

Table 2b. Major ASEAN Imports from China

(Unit: %)

HS chapter	Sector	1993	2000
85	Electrical equip.	11.08	35.96
84	Computer/machinery	9.70	15.69
27	Lubricants/fuel/oil	8.98	4.75
52	Cotton	5.59	2.56
90	Optical/medical instruments	1.03	2.24
88	Iron and steel	2.09	2.13
10	Cereal	3.74	2.08
39	Plastics	0.84	1.84
71	Jewelry	0.12	1.39
28	Inorganic chemicals	2.98	1.39
	Total	**46.15**	**70.03**

Table 3a. Major ASEAN Exports to Japan

(Unit: %)

HS chapter	Sector	1993	2000
85	Electrical equip.	13.06	26.02
27	Lubricants/fuel/oil	28.15	23.08
84	Computer/machinery	7.49	18.8
44	Wood	11.72	3.44
3	Fish	7.29	2.86
89	Ships, boats	0.01	2.08
94	Furniture	2.03	1.68
39	Plastics	0.75	1.86
26	Ores	2.18	1.61
87	Cars, trucks and autos	0.29	1.35
	Total	**72.97**	**82.78**

Table 3b. Major ASEAN Imports from Japan

(Unit: %)

HS chapter	Sector	1993	2000
85	Electrical equip.	30.00	34.57
84	Computer/machinery	23.88	23.39
87	Cars, trucks and autos	11.65	8.61
88	Iron and steel	5.45	5.1
39	Plastics	3.29	3.87
90	Optical/medical instrument	3.68	3.67
73	Articles of iron or steel	3.42	2.12
29	Organic chemical	1.95	1.88
91	Jewelry	0.36	1.45
40	Rubber	0.97	1.03
	Total	**84.65**	**85.69**

Table 4a. Major ASEAN Exports to Korea

(Unit: %)

HS chapter	Sector	1993	2000
27	Lubricants/fuel/oil	36.44	30.86
85	Electrical equip.	9.99	26.15
84	Computer/machinery	7.79	17.16
44	Wood	17.17	2.04
26	Ores	0.89	1.70
29	Organic chemical	1.48	1.54
38	Misc. chemical products	1.70	1.34
39	Plastics	0.53	1.04
40	Rubber	2.61	1.14
74	Copper	1.27	1.23
	Total	**79.87**	**84.20**

Table 4b. Major ASEAN Imports from Korea

(Unit: %)

HS chapter	Sector	1993	2000
85	Electrical equip.	30.39	43.55
84	Computer/machinery	11.96	11.25
27	Lubricants/fuel/oil	4.74	6.20
29	Organic chemical	2.43	4.73
39	Plastics	6.04	4.47
88	Iron and steel	8.70	4.33
87	Cars, trucks and autos	0.98	2.60
89	Ships, boats	0.87	1.91
73	Articles of iron or steel	3.37	1.76
55	Man-made staple filament	5.05	1.32
	Total	**74.53**	**82.12**

Table 5. Post-Accession Reduction in Weighted Tariff Rates for China's Main Imports[a]

Product group	Tariff rate	
	2001	final[b]
Cereal grains	91.1	3.0
Oil seeds	96.9	3.9
Beverages and tobacco products	57.8	10.4
Electronic equipment	10.6	2.3
Vegetable oils and fats	39.3	10.2
Wood products	10.0	3.4
Paper products, publishing	9.3	3.3
Crops	21.7	8.4
Textiles	20.5	8.7
Plant-based fibers	84.3	37.7
Motor vehicles and parts	31.6	14.1
Dairy products	19.0	8.9
Vegetables, fruits, nuts	25.9	12.6
Machinery and equipment	13.4	6.6
Meat products	18.6	9.9
Sugar	77.9	43.8
Processed rice	114.0	65.0
Paddy rice	114.0	65.0
Wheat	114.0	65.0
Ferrous metals	9.1	5.2
Chemical, rubber, plastic products	14.1	8.1
Forestry	2.3	1.3
Food products	16.8	9.8
Fishing	14.2	8.5
Metals	7.0	4.2
Wearing apparel	23.8	14.9
Leather products	11.6	8.0
Meat	14.1	9.9
Transport equipment	5.0	3.6
Metal products	9.7	7.4
Mineral products	14.4	11.4
Petroleum, coal products	8.4	6.7
Manufactures	19.5	15.8
Animal products	9.4	8.0
Product group	Tariff rate	
	2001	final[b]
Average of above	14.6	6.1
All goods	13.7	5.7

Source: UNCTAD, Trade Analysis and Information System (TRAINS) database, based on WTO figures.
a. Weighted by China's imports of relevant items in 2000.
b. At the end of the transition period.

Similar trade liberalizing processes have been taking place in the context of the Uruguay Round commitments, as well as in the AFTA process. Table 6 shows ASEAN post UR-MFN tariff rates. It ranges from as low as 3.12 percent in the case of Brunei to 43.18 percent for Thailand. Tariff rates for Malaysia, Indonesia and Philippines were less than 10 percent, while Singapore is a tariff free city-state.

Table 6. Average MFN Tariffs

Sector	Brunei Darussalam	Indonesia	Malaysia	Myanmar	Philippines	Thailand
Live Animals	0.00	4.74	3.96	8.12	20.00	49.28
Fruits and Vegetable Product	0.00	4.63	2.45	7.50	11.19	48.27
Fats and Oils	0.00	4.86	2.11	2.05	8.45	31.35
Prepared Foodstuffs	0.05	17.57	10.85	13.43	18.76	49.91
Mineral Products	0.00	4.05	2.04	1.42	3.54	18.05
Chemicals	0.64	5.76	1.86	2.34	4.06	32.23
Plastics	2.14	11.14	15.05	2.65	8.43	46.13
Hides and Leather	1.36	6.25	6.91	7.28	8.42	46.67
Wood and Wood Articles	10.44	3.42	1.42	11.21	11.73	36.59
Pulp and Paper	0.00	6.94	9.51	2.78	8.61	32.34
Textiles and Apparel	0.44	13.90	16.70	10.54	18.24	72.07
Footwear	5.33	16.54	19.25	7.41	15.47	79.64
Stone/Cement/Ceramics	0.65	7.26	16.91	3.68	11.01	47.38
Gems	2.41	10.76	2.87	13.65	7.07	33.4
Base Metal and Metal Articles	0.12	9.70	9.36	3.18	8.14	25.37
Machinery and Electrical Appliances	9.22	4.86	8.12	2.77	5.68	36.25
Vehicles	21.24	39.28	52.55	4.68	11.48	47.57
Optical, precision & musical instruments	7.79	7.38	1.82	5.84	4.60	36.75
Arms	0.00	9.29	15.00	9.47	19.00	37.65
Miscellaneous Manufactured articles	2.26	14.70	14.64	7.15	11.23	53.28
Antiques and works of art	0.00	12.86	1.96	4.25	15.00	31.67
Average	**3.12**	**9.34**	**9.42**	**5.55**	**10.08**	**43.18**

A number of the ASEAN countries have also embarked on deregulation and liberalisation measures over the 1990s

- Brunei's applied tariff rates are low, averaging 3.1 percent in 2000, zero for agriculture, and 3.6 percent for non agricultural products.
- Indonesia has undertaken a significant reduction of applied tariff rates, with the lowering of rates going well beyond its WTO commitments. Applied MFN tariffs have been reduced from an unweighted average of about 20 percent in 1994, to 9.5 percent in 1998. Further unilateral tariff cuts are scheduled up to 2003 in accordance with a clearly defined program of tariff reduction. By 2003, the maximum applied tariff for nearly all products will not exceed 10 percent. Already in 1998, tariffs on goods have been reduced to a maximum of 5 percent.
- Malaysia has cut its import tariff by almost one half since 1993, reducing protection for most agricultural and manufactured goods. The average applied tariff rate has declined from 15.2 percent in 1993, to 8.1 percent in 1997. Furthermore, whereas only 13 percent of tariff lines were exempt from import duty in 1995, over half of all lines now bear duty-free applied rates.
- In the Philippines, tariffication and reduction in tariff over the past six years have significantly opened the economy. Applied tariffs were more than halved between 1992 and 1999 from 26 percent to just over 10 percent. The Philippines is in the midst of a tariff rationalization program that will in effect create a uniform tariff structure for manufactured products of no higher than 5 percent.
- For Thailand, applied MFN tariff rates averaged 18 percent in September 1999, compared with 23 percent 1995. Tariff peaks were reduced to 60 percent down from 100 percent in 1995.

3. THE ASEAN FREE TRADE AREA (AFTA)

Arguably, the decision taken during the Fourth ASEAN Summit in 1992 to establish the ASEAN Free Trade Area (AFTA) by year 2008 is the most significant and ambitious step taken by ASEAN so far in terms of regional economic integration. The treaty establishing AFTA was signed in Singapore by the five original founding members, Indonesia, Malaysia, Philippines, Singapore, Thailand, and Brunei. In mid-1995, Vietnam gained admission as the seventh member of ASEAN. Laos and Myanmar followed suit two years later in 1997 with Cambodia joining the bandwagon in 1999.

The main calculus behind the creation of AFTA was the laying of a framework and forum for ASEAN member-states to cooperate with each other whilst moving towards deeper economic integration not only among them but also with the world. AFTA's creation will also help member-economies to lock-on and manage trade reforms more effectively to meet the WTO initiatives collectively. The ASEAN economies that are primarily export-oriented already figure as the central entity in regional trade platforms involving Asia-Pacific economies. Nevertheless, the purpose of AFTA is not simply to promote an increase in intra-regional trade. By increasing and facilitating the free flow of goods within the ASEAN region, the

AFTA is also expected to promote a greater degree of market integration.

The critical tools used to promote trade and liberalization within the region is through the elimination of intra-regional tariffs and the limitation of non-tariff barriers (NTBs). ASEAN's approach to liberalization is one of "open regionalism". This may be characterized as the promotion of regional trade expansion through facilitation and the reduction in the official barriers to regional trade through multilateral reductions in protection. Simply put, it is regionalism with a global orientation (Piei & Abubakar 1998). Apart from promoting and enhancing trade, the AFTA framework also endeavors to promote greater intra-ASEAN investment and foreign direct investment in the region. Simultaneously, AFTA has, since 1995, gone beyond being a traditional Preferential Trading Arrangement and expanded and deepened into other important aspects such as the development and integration in "non-border" areas of co-operation. This is expected to further strengthen the links among ASEAN national markets (Chee 1997). Ultimately, it is also hoped that the region's attractiveness for trade and foreign investment will increase, and thus augment ASEAN's competitive edge as a production base geared for the world market.

The main mechanism for the implementation of AFTA is the Common Effective Preferential Tariff (CEPT). The CEPT is an agreed effective tariff which is preferential to ASEAN member-states, and is to be applied to goods that have been identified for inclusion under the CEPT scheme originating from member-states. To be eligible, several criteria need to be fulfilled, namely;

- The product must already have been included in the 'Inclusion List' of the CEPT scheme of both the exporting and the importing countries. All other categories of products which include those in the 'Temporary Exclusion List' will not be eligible.
- The tariff rate in the exporting country for the same product must be at or less than 20 percent. However, if the tariff in the exporting country is above 20 percent, concessions can only be given when the CEPT of the importing country is also above 20 percent.
- The product in question must be of ASEAN origin and it must have at least 40 percent domestic ASEAN content. This refers to a single country or cumulative ASEAN content.

The original schedule required the CEPT tariffs to be reduced to between 0-5 percent within 15 years, i.e. by 2008, while non-tariff barriers were to be eliminated beginning 1 January 1993. In September 1994, ASEAN agreed to accelerate the establishment of AFTA by reducing the initial time frame from 15 to 10 years. Under the 1994 amended timetable, the full realization of AFTA with tariffs falling between zero and 5 percent was expected by 2003 for the original ASEAN five: Indonesia, Malaysia, Thailand, Singapore and the Philippines as well as Brunei. The deadline for Vietnam was 2006 and for Myanmar and Laos, 2008.

To help ameliorate the effects of the regional crisis and to speed up recovery efforts, ASEAN members announced a further acceleration of the AFTA schedule during the 6th Summit in Hanoi in December 1998. The six original signatories have agreed to advance the implementation by one year from 2003 to 2002. The six also agreed to achieve a minimum of 90 percent of their total tariff lines with tariffs between 0-5 percent by the year 2000. In theory, this would account for 90 percent of total intra-ASEAN trade (ASEAN Secretariat 1999). At the same time, each member-state would individually commit to achieve a minimum of 85 percent of the Inclusion List with tariffs of 0-5 percent by the year 2000. Following this, there is to be an increase to a minimum of 90 percent of the Inclusion List in the 0-5 percent tariff range by 2001. By the year 2002, 100 percent of the items in the Inclusion List would have tariffs of between zero and 5 percent (with some flexibility). It was not until the Singapore meeting in late 1999 that the target of zero tariffs as the ultimate target of AFTA was explicitly endorsed. At this meeting, the Ministers agreed "to eliminate import duties on all products and to target to achieve this objective by 2015 for the six original members and by year 2018 for the new members of ASEAN". Furthermore, as a first step towards this ambitious goal, they agreed that the six original members would eliminate tariffs on 60 percent of their products by the year 2003.

What has been the progress in this direction so far? As of 11 April 2002, the CEPT Scheme had covered 98.09 percent of all tariff lines for the ASEAN-6. Average tariff rates on these products have fallen to 3.89 percent which is well in advance of the agreement that 85 percent of the Inclusion List will have tariff of 0-5 percent. (Table 7 and 8). For the four new members of ASEAN, about half of their total tariff lines (49.94 percent) are in the Inclusion List, 46.88 percent of total tariff lines are in the TEL, 2.18 percent of the total tariff lines an in the GEL, and 1.02 percent of the total tariff lines are in the Sensitive List.

Progress in the level of deeper cooperation notwithstanding, tariff reductions under the CEPT scheme alone may not be sufficient to enhance intra-ASEAN trade if other non-tariff barriers (NTBs) remain in place. This is because the existence of NTBs may limit or perhaps negate the trade liberalizing effect of the CEPT mechanism. To address this issue, the CEPT agreement call on member countries to eliminate quantitative restrictions with respect to products under the CEPT scheme in addition to other non-tariff barriers on a gradual basis within a period of five years.

-*Table 7. CEPT Product List for the Year 2002*

Country	Inclusion List (IL)	Temporary Exception List (TEL)	General Exception List (TEL)	Sensitive List (SL)	Total
Brunei Darussalam	6276	0	202	14	6492
Indonesia	7176	21	68	4	7269
Malaysia	8867	233*	63	73	9236
Philippines	5606	35	16	62	5719
Singapore	5821	0	38	0	5859
Thailand	9104	0	0	7	9111
Total ASEAN-6	**42850**	**289**	**387**	**160**	**43686**
Percentage	98.09	0.66	0.89	0.37	100.00
New Members of ASEAN:					
Cambodia	3115	3523	134	50	6822
Laos	1247	2142	74	88	3551
Myanmar	2387	3017	47	21	5472
Vietnam	3573	1007	196	48	4824
Total	10322	9689	451	207	20669
Percentage	49.94	46.88	2.18	1.00	100.00
Total Asean-10	**53172**	**9978**	**838**	**367**	**64355**
Percentage	82.62	15.50	1.30	0.57	100.00

Source: ASEAN Secretariat

* Covers group of automotive products whose inclusion being deferred to 2005.

Table 8. Average Tariff Rates of Year 1999-2003

Country	Year 1999		Year 2000		Year 2001		Year 2002		Year 2003	
	Tariff Lines	Averag e	Tariff Lines	Average	Tariff Lines	Average	Tariff Lines	Average	Tariff Lines	Average
Brunei Darussalam	6264	1.55	6264	1.26	6264	1.17	6264	0.96	6273	0.96
Indonesia	6931	5.36	7176	4.76	7176	4.36	7176	3.71	7176	2.18
Malaysia	8374	3.22	8417	2.79	8417	2.6	8417	2.43	8417	2.06
Philippines	5431	7.36	5431	5.88	5431	5.24	5431	4.95	5431	3.79
Singapore	5739	0	5772	0	5772	0	5772	0	5772	0
Thailand	9062	9.58	9067	7.29	9067	7.26	9067	5.98	9067	4.63
ASEAN-6	**41801**	**4.8**	**42127**	**3.89**	**42127**	**3.67**	**42127**	**3.18**	**42136**	**2.41**
Cambodia	-	-	3115	10.39	3115	10.39	3115	8.89	3115	7.93
Laos	1247	7.54	1247	7.07	1247	6.58	1247	6.15	1247	5.66
Myanmar	2356	4.45	2356	4.38	2356	3.32	2356	3.31	2356	3.19
Vietnam	3570	7.09	-	-	-	-	-	-	-	-
ASEAN-4	**7173**	**6.3**	**6718**	**7.67**	**6718**	**7.2**	**6718**	**6.42**	**6718**	**5.85**
Total ASEAN-10	**48974**	**5.02**	**48845**	**4.41**	**48845**	**4.16**	**48845**	**3.63**	**48854**	**2.88**

4. ASEAN-EAST ASIA INVESTMENT RELATION

ASEAN had been the top 10 regional FDI destinations in the 1990s, albeit up to the point when the crisis hit the region. The original 5 member countries i.e. Indonesia, Malaysia, Thailand, Singapore, and to a lesser extent the Philippines, had been in the top ten FDI receiving countries during the 1990's. Table 9 shows the net FDI inflow into ASEAN (on a balance of payment basis) between 1995-1999. It is observed that the extra-ASEAN FDI had been more significant than intra-ASEAN investment flows. It can be observed that inflow of total, intra- and extra-ASEAN investment had contracted sharply in 1998 and 1999 (the years immediately after the crisis hit the region). The intra-ASEAN investment share of ASEAN's total investment had contracted from as much as 10.7 percent to 7.2 percent. In 2000, though the regional economies had shown some recovery, and while global FDI flows increased to US$1,270 billion compared with US$1,075 billion in 1999, investment inflows into ASEAN remained on a declining trend at 5.8 percent to US$13.8 billion compared with US$14.7 billion in 1999. In contrast, China and Taiwan recorded an increase in inflows of FDI to US$40.7 billion and US$4.9 billion respectively. FDI into Korea recorded a marginal decline to US$10.2 billion.

Table 9. ASEAN Net FDI on a Balance of Payment Basis

(Unit: US million)

	Intra ASEAN	Total Extra ASEAN FDI	Total ASEAN FDI	Share of Intra-ASEAN FDI in Total FDI
1995	4,653.0	16,668.0	21,321.0	21.8
1996	2,777.7	23,238.4	26,016.0	10.7
1997	5,537.5	22,597.5	28,135.0	19.7
1998	2,019.8	17,575.2	19,595.0	10.3
1999	1,217.5	15,693.5	16,911.0	7.2

Source: ASEAN Secretariat: ASEAN FDI Database

Table 10 shows the stock of FDI in the period 1980-1999. It is observed that the stock of FDI in the region had grown ten-fold from US$24 billion in 1980 to US$249.8 billion in 1999. The bulk of the inflows were absorbed by Singapore, Indonesia, Malaysia and Thailand. Together they accounted for 88 percent of ASEAN FDI, by the end of 1999, ASEAN share of Asian FDI has been showing a sharp decline since the crisis struck to about 29.5 percent in 1999.

Table 11 shows the inflow of FDI into ASEAN by country of origin in the period 1985-1999. The US, Europe and Japan remained the major source of FDI for ASEAN. Together, they contributed more than 60 percent of the total FDI to ASEAN. However, since the crisis, inflows of FDI from Japan had declined sharply from as much as 21.0 percent in 1997 to 5.4 percent in 1999. The share of the three East Asian economies in total ASEAN FDI inflows reduced accordingly to just 9 percent in 1999, from as much as 24.1 percent in 1997.

Table 10. Inward Foreign Direct Investment Stock in ASEAN

(Unit: US$ billion)

	1980	1990	1998	1999
ASEAN	24.0	89.9	232.6	249.8
Brunei	0	0	1.0	1.0
Cambodia	-	0.2	0.7	0.6
Indonesia	10.3	68.8	68.2	65.2
Laos PDR	0	0.14	0.472	0.551
Malaysia	5.2	10.3	45.2	48.77
Myanmar	0	0.1	2.1	2.4
Philippines	1.3	3.3	9.3	11.2
Singapore	6.2	28.6	82.4	79.4
Thailand	1.0	8.2	20.5	26.5
Vietnam	0	294	13.4	15.1
South, East and South East Asia	58.8	181.4	673.9	769.5
Asia	56.7	211.6	741.3	846.7
Developing Countries	131.2	377.4	1,241.0	1,438.5
ASEAN's share of South, East and South East Asia FDI Stock (%)	0.7	9.6	34.5	32.5
ASEAN's share of Asia FDI Stock (%)	42.3	42.5	31.4	29.5
ASEAN's share of Developing Countries FDI Stock (%)	19.7	23.8	18.7	17.4

Source: ASEAN FDI Database

Table 11. Net FDI Inflow to ASEAN by country of origin

(Unit: %)

	1995 (%)	1996	1997	1998	1999	1995 – 1st half of 2000
USA	14.4	15.0	9.3	12.2	15.4	12.9
Europe	23.5	30.0	22.4	23.5	33.2	26.2
Japan	19.5	19.6	21.0	13.2	5.4	15.7
Korea	2.3	2.1	2.9	4.6	2.8	2.8
China	0.6	0.4	0.2	1.5	0.8	0.7
Total (billion US$)	21.3	26.0	28.1	19.6	16.9	112.6

However on a cumulative basis, the share of the three East Asian economies in ASEAN FDI stock between 1995 – the first half of 2002 remains substantial at 19.2 percent, higher than the US at 12.9 percent.

5. THE POTENTIAL EFFECTS OF THE EAFTA

Based on our discussion in the previous section on the economic features of the ASEAN countries and its linkages with the three East Asian economics, it can be concluded that the proposed EAFTA will make both good political and economic sense. The reasons for this are as follows:

5.1. Increased Bargaining Power

The proposed FTA will strengthen the bargaining position of the region, particularly ASEAN, as ASEAN countries would be able to negotiate as a collective, both regionally and multilaterally in areas of common interest. Indeed, the use of regional integration to strengthen the bargaining power of members against a perceived stronger negotiating partner is based on the belief that there is strength in numbers. A prime example is the EEC, whose formation is believed to have been partly motivated by the desire to increase the member countries' bargaining power against the US. Needless to say, one of the prime objectives of the formation of ASEAN, and AFTA, is to enable the consolidation of its regional bargaining position in its dealings with stronger economies and regional grouping. As a group, ASEAN has managed to negotiate better deals from its negotiating counterparts, something which could not have been achieved if individual member countries negotiated individually.

5.2. Signalling the Region's Policy Credibility and Commitment to Reform

The proposed EAFTA will also serve as a signaling device as to the region's policy credibility and commitment to reform. It would send a strong message to other regions, and sub-regions, of each of the EAFTA member country's strong commitment to policy reform including trade liberalization, and thus enhance its position as a credible trade partner. Such a commitment also signals to current and prospective investing firms the advantages of locating their long-term investments in an area committed to open markets and stable macroeconomics.

From the perspective of ASEAN, there is an urgent need to regain, and to enhance foreign investor's confidence in the stability and credibility of policies of member countries in the region. The need is even stronger now than ever before, especially since the advent of the ASEAN economic crisis which had badly damaged the region's economic standings.

5.3. Preparation for Bolder Reforms and Future Challenges

Membership in the proposed EAFTA would prepare prospective member countries in the region to undertake even bolder policy reforms, and confront the challenges of other countries and regional groupings in the future. Country experiences have shown that the first steps toward undertaking policy reforms are often the most difficult, as they are commonly strongly resisted by those with vested interests. The fact that policy reform in the EFTA is circumscribed within a limited number of member-countries would help to overcome the initial difficulties of undertaking the reform. Furthermore, an FTA with China would enable ASEAN member countries to reap an "early harvest" of China's post-accession commitment to liberalize its economy, and this would place ASEAN member countries in a better stead compared to the rest of the world in their economic relationship with China. The fact that the proposed EAFTA would also include two members of the OECD countries, Japan and Korea, will give ASEAN member countries an invaluable experience in their future dealings with the rest of the OECD members. In short, all these will prepare and enhance member countries confidence to embark on bolder policy reforms in response to the onslaught of globalization and liberalization of the world economies.

5.4. Market Enlargement

The proposed EAFTA would lead to an expansion of ASEAN's market size as producers could pool together the markets of the other three East Asia economies. The combined EAFTA market would be about US$6868.1 billion that is about 12 times the current market of ASEAN which stands at about US$570 billion.

A better measure of the market potential of the EAFTA is the size of the "effective demand" that would be created. This can be gleaned from the per capita income levels of the member countries Table 1. It is estimated that China would be the country that would provide most of the additional markets for ASEAN, considering that its population is six times of Indonesia with a per capita income which is 10 percent of Indonesia. Effectively, this means having seven Indonesia's instead of just one in ASEAN/AFTA.

5.5. Trade Creation and Trade Diversion

These are the traditional static effects of a regional economic integration. Trade creation refers to the shift in expenditure or imports of a member country from more expensive domestic sources to a cheaper source within the region. The creation of more trade also refers to the additional and increased variety of exports to other member countries. These exports may be new and non-existent before the integration due to high and restrictive tariffs in the importing member countries. Trade diversion, meanwhile, refers to the shift in imports from a cheaper source outside the region to a more expensive source within the region. Trade creation is welfare enhancing, while trade diversion causes deterioration in the welfare of the importing member countries.

Intuitively, the creation of an EAFTA would be dominantly trade creating as far as ASEAN is concerned. The scope for trade creation is larger than in the case of ASEAN/AFTA, because EAFTA would include lower cost producing countries in a wide range of products, particularly Japan, and to a lesser extent, Korea and China. Conversely, the scope for trade diversion resulting from EAFTA is smaller than in the case of AFTA since the latter would include larger and more developed member countries.

5.6. Efficiency and Enhanced Competitiveness

With the formation of the EAFTA, and with the trade barriers among member countries eliminated, competition among enterprises in member countries would increase, thus promoting specialization, efficiency, productivity and economic welfare. Not only would competition be intensive between and among enterprises of member countries, but strategic alliances between them would also be created in many sectors. The surviving enterprises might become globally competitive too.

5.7. Effects on the Volume and Pattern of Investment

With the removal of barriers to trade, and eventually, of barriers to capital flows within the region, this would result in a more conducive investment climate within the region. There will be more certainty and uniformity in investment policies within the region, besides having an enlarged regional market. All these would be important factors in attracting investors to the region. A more efficient pattern of production would emerge, drawn along the lines of comparative and competitive advantages.

As the EAFTA would comprise of member countries lying across a spectrum of factor endowments and economic development levels, production rationalization would thus take place in consideration of such differences in factor endowment as well as in effective demand across member countries. This could effectively spur growth in agriculture, manufacturing and services. As a result, the proposed EAFTA could have profound implications on investment activity in the region.

6. THE ECONOMIC COST

While the effects of the EAFTA are generally beneficial, it is nevertheless expected to bring with it attendant costs. In particular, the preferential reduction of trade barriers among members of the FTA can bring with it some diversion of trade as explained earlier. From the perspective of ASEAN, the choice is between trade diversion resulting from AFTA only, and trade diversion resulting from ASEAN's integration with Japan, Korea and China in EAFTA. Theoretically, trade diversion resulting from EAFTA should be smaller than those resulting from AFTA. Indeed, the scope for trade diversion is smaller when the following situations occur

- the regional integrated economies are bigger
- the intra-regional trade is higher vis-à-vis its extra regional trade
- the new members of the regional economic integration are more developed
- there is a lower the cost of production in member countries compared with those in non-member countries.

Based on our earlier discussion, EAFTA fulfils all the above criteria. Hence, trade diversion would be small and could be kept to a minimal by taking some pre-emptive measures.

6.1. Decline in Tariff Revenues

The reduction of tariff barriers against member countries following the formation of the EAFTA may lead to some loss in government revenue in some member countries. This will occur as tariff revenues previously collected from import (from non-members) declines as imports are diverted to member receiving preferential treatment at low or zero tariffs.

Within the ASEAN countries, the most affected countries would be the new members, Cambodia, Laos, Myanmar and Vietnam. This is mainly due to their high differential between MFA and CEPT tariff levels. However, this does not constitute real economic losses because it simply amounts to redistribution of welfare to consumers who now may be able to enjoy a lower price for imported goods. Moreover, ASEAN's experience in implementing AFTA has shown that these countries have managed to mitigate these problems by looking for alternative sources of revenue elsewhere in the economy. For example, Cambodia used to receive 56 percent of its total tax revenue from customs duties prior to joining AFTA, two thirds of which were levies on imports from other ASEAN countries. However, membership in ASEAN/AFTA gave the Cambodian government the impetus to introduce a value-added tax in 1999. This has likewise been the experience of other ASEAN countries in the wake of the AFTA implementation. Likewise, the same experience will take place resulting from the formation of EAFTA.

6.2. Adjustment Costs Due to EAFTA

Adjustment costs "encompass a wide variety of potentially disadvantageous short term outcomes that might result from trade liberalization which may include a reduction in employment and output, the loss in industry-specific and firm-specific human capital, and macroeconomic instability resulting from balance of payment difficulties or reduction in government revenue." It must be acknowledged that the formation of EAFTA would result in a dislocation in member economies as proven in the case of AFTA. But these effects would occur as a result of any other policy changes undertaken by an economy such as trade liberalization, and its long-term effect is shown to be relatively small. More advanced member countries may even provide technical assistance and aid to help the affected countries in their effort to readjust to new economic and trade regimes, as was the practice by the more advanced ASEAN countries when implementing the AFTA program. Moreover, the adjustments undertaken by the less-developed member countries would be done more easily and quickly by being members of the EAFTA, compared to them undertaking the reforms individually.

7. THE ARCHITECTURE OF THE EAST ASIA FREE TRADE AREA

In the event that ASEAN and the three East Asia economies, China, Korea and Japan agree to establish a free trade area, there are several modalities to choose from. These include:

- ❑ A region-wide FTA involving all the thirteen countries concerned

- An EAFTA comprising a network of FTAs: ASEAN-China FTA, ASEAN-Japan FTA, ASEAN-Korea FTA, Japan-China FTA, Japan-Korea FTA, and China-Korea FTA
- An EAFTA involving ASEAN and North East Asia FTA similar to the proposed ASEAN/AFTA-CER FTA.

Needless to say, the first modality is the best option as it would involve region-wide economic integration of thirteen separate entities into a single and unified market. The gains from such a comprehensive liberalization, to the region as well as to individual member countries, are expected to be large, while the adjustment process easier, and less costly. Though this choice of regional integration is the most difficult to achieve at the moment, it must be adopted to be the ultimate modality to strive for in the long run.

The second modality is to "weave a web of free trade agreements and areas together across the thirteen economies to finally form a huge East Asia Free Trade Area". Altogether, it would involve six FTAs. To start with, there is already a strong commitment to create an ASEAN-China FTA in 10 years time, and there is good prospect for an ASEAN-Korea FTA to follow soon. The signing of a bilateral free trade agreement (BFTA) between Japan and Singapore may act as catalyst for other ASEAN countries to negotiate an ASEAN-Japan FTA. By doing so, it may neutralize whatever advantages and preferences Singapore may be enjoying in Japan's market, and hence eliminate the bias against them. That will leave another three more FTAs to carve-out among the three East Asian economies. The first one is a Japan-Korea FTA. This initiative which has already been announced is potentially the most influential one of the three possible bilateral FTAs among the East Asian economies. The timing is most opportune given the current improvement in the bilateral relationship between the two economies. There have been suggestions that the Japan-Korea FTA "should logically be extended to include China as well because it otherwise would create serious political tensions". The inclusion of China would effectively rule-out the need to create bilateral FTAs (the China-Japan FTA and China-Korea FTA). Indeed, this would transform the exercise in the direction of a bigger undertaking, that is, the formation of a North East Asian sub-regional arrangement that would eventually be linked to the one already in existence, the ASEAN/AFTA. This represents the third route that may be pursued.

Irrespective of the modality to arrive at the preferred modality, several parameters governing the proposed framework of co-operation need to be clearly spelled-out and adopted. These include, among others, the time frame of implementation, guiding principles, scope and coverage, and special and differential provisions.

7.1. Time Frame

The time frame for implementation will need to consider existing benchmarks. On the one hand, there is the APEC vision to create free trade in the area by 2010 for developed countries and 2020 for developing countries. The proposed EAFTA needs to achieve liberalization of goods earlier than that which has been agreed upon under

APEC, or else this initiative will be made redundant by the latter. This means that the developed countries of EAFTA, Japan, Korea and possibly Singapore, should proceed at a faster pace than APEC i.e. earlier than 2010, while the remaining countries should proceed not later than 2020. For the ASEAN-6, this should not be much a problem because under AFTA they are targeting CEPT zero tariff by 2010. Subject to any new arrangements pertaining to AFTA, the pace of liberalization of EAFTA should not normally go beyond the pace of liberalization to which ASEAN members have already agreed under AFTA i.e. elimination of tariff by 2010 for ASEAN-6 and 2015 for the new members. Consideration is to be given to the CLMV countries which need more time to adjust to the required market-opening policies. Hence, they should be accorded some amount of flexibility and differential deadlines in their liberalization commitments.

7.2. Scope

The EAFTA should be as comprehensive as possible to cover trade in all goods, services, investments, tariff liberalization, non-tariff barriers, technical barriers to trade, and mutual recognition arrangements (MRAs). Other areas could possibly be included as and when the need arises. This is to ensure that the FTA is trade-creating, and hence would lead to efficiency gains for the region as a whole, and to the member countries individually.

In the case of trade in goods, agriculture will be one sector that could pose some problems due to its sensitive nature in almost all economies, except for Singapore. The ASEAN/AFTA approach in phasing in the agricultural products into its CEPT scheme may be used as a model for the three East Asian countries to adopt. Under the AFTA, agricultural raw materials and unprocessed agriculture produce are categorized into two: sensitive and highly sensitive unprocessed agricultural products (UAPs). All sensitive UAPs (altogether 181 tariff lines) would have to be included by 2005, and their tariff rates to be reduced to 0-5 percent by 2010. Meanwhile, the highly sensitive UAPs, which are relatively few in number, need to be phased in by 2005 and their terminal tariff are allowed to be greater than 5 percent by 2010. As for rice, which is considered as highly sensitive in most ASEAN countries, the indicated terminal tariff would be less than 20 percent.

7.3. Tariffs

Subject to the time frame discussed earlier, the overall objective is to achieve free trade in goods by 2010 for the ASEAN 6 and China, Japan and Korea and 2015 for the new members of ASEAN. As a guide, ASEAN could consider extending the AFTA tariff rates to the three East Asian (China, Japan and Korea) countries and the latter would progressively reduce tariffs for ASEAN from the conclusion of negotiation, reaching free trade by 2005. For Japan, and to a lesser extent Korea, the fact that they are developed economies places them in a better position to achieve free trade vis-à-vis ASEAN at an earlier date. For the new members of ASEAN, the rest of the EAFTA would consider to offer them a special preference similar to the

ASEAN Generalized Scheme of Preference for their product to enter the rest of the EAFTA.

7.4. Rules of Origin

To avoid the possibility of trade deflection, FTAs normally adopt rules of origin (ROO) which specify the degree of value added the goods must embody before they can be considered as a regional product which entitles them preferential treatment when traded within the FTA. In the case of AFTA, the ROO is 40 percent domestic and/or regional cumulative content for all goods and for all member countries. It is too simplistic and favors the more developed member countries.

In the case of the EAFTA, ROO of 40 percent is too low, as input from Japan, China and Korea will be considered as local or regional input. A higher percentage of regional content is preferred, and it should be varied by the type of goods traded, and by the country that produced the goods. Sensitive products, where there is greater possibility of trade deflection to occur, are assigned a higher percentage of local/regional content. Similarly, more developed countries like Japan, Korea and Singapore may also be assigned a higher percentage of regional content.

7.5. Non-tariff Barriers

Under the AFTA process, member countries are obliged to eliminate all NTBs, upon enjoyment of the CEPT treatment. Similar rulings need to be instituted in FTAs with the three East Asian countries.

7.6. Technical Assistance

The EAFTA would need provisions on technical assistance particularly from the more developed members. Such technical assistance should cover the following areas:

- technical assistance in the development, strengthening and diversification of the production and export bases of the new member of ASEAN in particular
- assisting of the ASEAN new members in their capacity building
- facilitating the transfer of know-how to the ASEAN countries

It is to be acknowledged that the more developed members of the EAFTA have been the major providers of technical assistance to the less developed member of ASEAN either bilaterally, or through collaboration with ASEAN and other multilateral agencies, particularly in the Greater Mekong Development Projects. With the establishment of the EAFTA, this initiative would be enhanced further in a sustainable manner.

7.7. Trade Facilitation

The EFTA should include trade facilitation activities to enhance the effect of the trade liberalization process. Trade facilitation activities are already underway in

AFTA, as well as in the APEC. What is needed is to ensure that these activities are strengthened so as to bear some tangible benefit in the short term. These activities include harmonization of customs nomenclature and procedures, harmonization of standards, MRAs, and SPS Conference etc.

7.8. Investment

The EAFTA should contain a framework of investment principles and rules which would increase and secure capital flows to and within the region. This aspect has already been taken care of in the case of ASEAN under its Framework Agreement of the ASEAN Investment Areas (AIA, 1988) whereby all barriers to investment in ASEAN are to be removed by 2010. Non-ASEAN investors would enjoy the same privileges by 2020. The ultimate aim is to promote the ASEAN region as a single international destination for investment. To accommodate the non-ASEAN members of EAFTA, the implementation could be accelerated, and in return the latter could consider reciprocal arrangement for the ASEAN investors.

There are other aspects that need to be covered by the proposed EAFTA, but they are beyond the scope of this paper. These include among others such matters concerning the inclusion of the services sectors, intellectual property rights, and e-commerce, etc.

8. CONCLUSION

This paper has highlighted salient features of the economic relationship between ASEAN and the three East Asian economies, China, Korea and Japan for the last decade or so. It has showcased the growing strength of economic interdependencies within, and among, members of the regional economies concerned, and the further scope for greater regional economic integration that exists. All the member economies have benefited from this development, and more gains are expected if regional economic co-operation strategies are to be pursued via the EAFTA proposal.

This paper has also outline the possible modalities of the proposed EAFTA as well as it objectives, principles and coverage and several special provisions that need to be instituted for the efficient implementation of the proposed EFTA.

REFERENCES

ASEAN Secretariat. 2002. "Framework Agreement on Comprehensive Economic Cooperation between the Association of South East Asian Nations and the People's Republic of China." Jakarta.

Harding. H. 1995. "International Order and Organisation in the Asia-Pacific Region." In Robert S.Ross ed. *East Asia in Transition: Towards a New Regional Order*. Singapore: Institute of South East Asian Studies (ISEAS).

Piei, M. H. 1999. "Steps Towards Economic Integration: The ASEAN Free Trade Area." *Panorama*. Manila: Konrad Adenauer Stiftung.

______ & S. Y. Abubakar. 1998. "Promotion of Trade and Investment in ASEAN: Policies and Result." Kuala Lumpur : MIER.

Tay S., J. Estanislao & H. Soesastro eds. 2000. "A New ASEAN in a New Millennium." Jakarta: Centre for Strategic and International Studies.

UNCTAD/UN. 2002. *Trade and Development Report 2002*. New York: United States.

CHAPTER 7

AN EAST ASIAN FTA: A PHILIPPINE PERSPECTIVE

JOHN LAWRENCE AVILA

1. The Evolution of Asian Regionalism

Economic integration in Asia has been, for the most part, market-driven. Trade and investment exchanges contracted mainly by private entities have helped build a web of intra-regional linkages between Asian economies. One major factor was the appreciation of the Japanese yen after the 1985 Plaza Accord that led to the relocation of Japanese manufacturing industries to the rest of Asia. Concern over the rising cost of doing business in Japan and the need to remain competitive forced many local firms to transfer their operations overseas.

The outflow of capital from Japan helped propel the export-driven economies of East Asia, particularly in Singapore, Taiwan, Hong Kong and South Korea – the so-called NIEs – and later in Southeast Asia. The growth of foreign investment, including those made later by South Korea, Taiwan and other progressive Asian economies, contributed to closer and deeper integration of the region. This established horizontal and vertical production linkages and the expansion of business networks, particularly among overseas Chinese. The increasing interdependence of Asia provided a strong impetus for Asian governments to seek closer collaboration.

Governments also played a significant role in this process. Economic reform policies aimed at the opening up the domestic market encouraged the flow of trade and investment in the region. National governments themselves undertook most of these efforts on their own. Unilateral policies directed at liberalization, deregulation and privatization made these countries more fully integrated into the world economy. In particular, the open-door policies of China brought about the increase of foreign investment and trade in the region. Faced with growing competition from China, other countries sought to advance market-opening measures and further regional integration efforts.

At the regional level, the formation of the Association of Southeast Asian Nations (ASEAN) helped bring about economic integration of the region. Early attempts at economic cooperation were largely unsuccessful with political and security concerns dominating the early formative years of the grouping. The 1976 Preferential Trade Arrangement (PTA), which extended margins of preferences to

C. Y. Ahn et al (eds.), East Asian Economic Regionalism, 121-137.

intra-ASEAN merchandise trade, was an early attempt at fostering trade cooperation and liberalization. However, the PTA did not go very far because of the rather selective and flexible approach to tariff reductions by its members.

Concern about growing regionalism elsewhere and declining competitiveness, ASEAN member-countries agreed to establish a free trade area among themselves in 1992. The main mechanism for this would be the Common Effective Preferential Tariff (AFTA-CEPT), which aims to bring tariffs on intra-ASEAN trade to within 0-5 percent. The desire to remain attractive to foreign investment was a major compelling reason for AFTA. ASEAN decided to accelerate the completion of the CEPT by advancing the deadline twice to 2003. ASEAN has likewise moved towards the reduction of non-tariff barriers, liberalization of regional trade in services, and harmonization of measures to facilitate trade and investment.

There was also much discussion about promoting economic cooperation in the region that would be primarily inclusive rather than exclusive. Given that the most important markets for a significant portion of Asia's exports remain outside the region, an arrangement that would include these major trading partners was considered necessary. This concept took formal shape during the low-key inauguration of the Asia-Pacific Economic Cooperation (APEC) association in 1989. APEC is an inclusive organization bringing together all major economies of the Pacific Rim, both developed and developing countries. Open regionalism was to be the key feature of the organization, which is based on "concerted unilateral MFN trade liberalization" favoring an open rather than closed trade bloc.

There remained, however, underlying aspiration for an all-Asian grouping that presumably would advance and promote the economic interests of Asian countries. The chief proponent of this idea was Malaysia who sought to establish an East Asian Economic Group (EAEG) as an exclusive Asians-only association. The Malaysian proposal received lukewarm support from neighboring countries, both from within ASEAN and from Japan. At that time, these countries were rather reluctant to offend excluded trading partners like the United States. In fact, pressure from Washington, DC led to the dilution of the proposal to a looser informal caucus.

In an attempt to bolster APEC as the main regional economic institution, the United States elevated the 1993 Blake Island meeting into a summit of leaders thereby raising its political profile. APEC's ambition peaked at the 1994 Bogor meeting when members agreed to establish a free trade area in the region by 2010 for developed economies and 2020 for developing economies. Subsequently, voluntary individual and collective plans were mapped out to achieve these goals.

Enthusiasm for APEC, however, waned after the failure of the Early Voluntary Sectoral Liberalization (EVSL) scheme that sought to advance the liberalization of fifteen priority sectors. Japan's opposition to the inclusion of fisheries and forest products led to the scuttling of the EVSL. National intransigence led to the collapse of efforts to open up trade ahead of the Bogor schedules. From then on, APEC seems to have lost its momentum as a regional mechanism for trade liberalization.

A similar effort at promoting inter-regional linkages was pursued to boost ties with Europe. In 1992, the Asia-Europe Meeting (ASEM) was inaugurated to promote the facilitation and liberalization of trade and investments between Asia and Europe and fill in the "missing link" in inter-regional relations. With ASEAN, China,

Japan and South Korea as members, ASEM was to be the genesis of increased political and economic dialogue between the Northeast and Southeast Asian regions. The ten Asian members of ASEM had to organize themselves on a regional basis considering the fact that their counterpart was relatively more institutionalized.[1] Prior to each ASEM meeting, a hitherto unknown process of regional cooperation took place among the Asian members to coordinate and come up with joint positions. ASEM helped bring about a grouping similar in composition to the Malaysian EAEC proposal.

The Asian financial crisis hastened this process of intra-Asian dialogue. The crisis somewhat served as a wakeup call to many in Asia that they have to deal with the region's problems on their own without external help. Many realized that in order to avoid future economic crises and reduce their reliance on external support, they should cooperate more closely. ASEAN have had regular series of meetings with their Northeast Asian neighbors through their dialogue mechanism. These have included annual meetings of the ASEAN ministers of foreign affairs, trade and investment, and finance, with counterparts of the three Northeast Asian countries. Since the 1997 crisis, these exchanges have intensified. Annual summitry between the leaders of these countries now takes place alongside periodic meetings of trade, finance and foreign affairs ministers. These encounters have been highly useful and beneficial particularly in building confidence between Southeast and Northeast Asia. These high level exchanges have institutionalized the economic cooperative effort between these countries.

In November 1999, the thirteen countries signed an unprecedented joint declaration pledging to intensify cooperation in economic, political, security, monetary, and financial issues. Among others, ASEAN+3 leaders agreed to enhance monetary and financial cooperation by strengthening policy dialogues, coordination, and collaboration on financial, monetary, and fiscal issues. Members recently concluded bilateral currency swap arrangements to forestall another foreign exchange crisis. They also promised to intensify coordination and cooperation in various international and regional forums such as the WTO, APEC and ASEM as well as in regional and international financial institutions. An East Asian Study Group has since been established to identify long term cooperative goals for the grouping, which included among others a plan to set up an East Asian Free Trade Area (EAFTA).

The proposal to establish an EAFTA is taking place alongside other projects to create preferential trading arrangements in the region (see Table 1). In November 2001, the heads of government of China and ASEAN entered into a new Framework on Economic Cooperation including an agreement to establish a free trade area by 2010. A China-ASEAN FTA will create a 1.7 billon strong market representing about US$ 2 trillion in combined GDP. Bilateral trade has been growing at an average annual rate of 15 percent since 1995 estimated at US$1.2 billion. Working level negotiations are currently taking place including talks on defining an "early harvest" package prior to the full implementation of the arrangement.

[1] See Avila (2001).

Following China's announcement, Japan also advanced its own proposal, referred to as the Initiative for Japan-ASEAN Comprehensive Economic Partnership. The plan included the creation of a free trade accord between Japan and the individual members of ASEAN. Japan's proposal goes beyond the traditional scope of a free trade area and includes cooperation in investment, technology exchange and human resources development. Apparently, Tokyo is concerned about maintaining its economic leadership in the region and is apprehensive of the growing economic power of mainland China.[2]

There has likewise been a dramatic resurgence of bilateral trade initiatives across the region. Nearly every country in Asia is exploring or have entered into bilateral free trade agreements. The foremost advocate of this trade strategy is Singapore, which has recently concluded FTAs with New Zealand, Japan, the European Free Trade Area (EFTA) and Australia. The city-state is also currently negotiating similar arrangements with the US, Canada, South Korea, Chile, and Mexico.[3] Thailand, the Philippines, Malaysia and Brunei are similarly exploring free trade arrangements with several countries. Japan and South Korea are currently engaged in extensive consultations to set up an FTA between their two economies. South Korea has proposed expanding the grouping to include China in a Northeast Asian FTA. Both Japan and Korea are also holding separate talks with a number of potential partners including Mexico, New Zealand and Chile.

[2] ASEAN is likewise negotiating a CEP arrangement with Australia and New Zealand. A possible FTA with the United States, India and South Korea is also under consideration.

[3] Singapore has also been pushing the idea of the Pacific-Five (P-5) FTA Initiative, which includes itself, the US, Australia, New Zealand and Chile.

Table 1. Preferential Trading Arrangements in Asia

Partners	Type of Arrangements	Status	Year
ASEAN	Free Trade Area	Implemented	1993
Singapore-New Zealand	Closer Economic Partnership	Implemented	2001
Singapore-Japan	New Age Economic Partnership	Signed	2002
Singapore-EFTA	Free Trade Area	Signed	2002
Singapore-Australia	Closer Economic Partnership	Signed	2003
South Korea-Chile	Free Trade Area	Signed	2003
ASEAN-China	Free Trade Area	Under negotiation	2001
South Korea-US	Free Trade Area	Under negotiation	2001
Singapore-Mexico	Free Trade Area	Under negotiation	1999
Singapore-Canada	Free Trade Area	Under negotiation	2001
Singapore-US	Free Trade Area	Under negotiation	2000
Singapore-Chile	Free Trade Area	Under negotiation	2000
AFTA-Australia/New Zealand	Closer Economic Partnership	Official discussion/study	1999
ASEAN-Japan	Comprehensive Economic Partnership	Official discussions	2002
ASEAN-South Korea	Free Trade Area	Official discussions	2002
Japan-Chile	Free Trade Area	Official discussions/study	2001
Japan-Malaysia	Free Trade Area	Official discussions/study	2003
Japan-Mexico	Free Trade Area	Official discussions/study	1998
Japan-South Korea	Free Trade Area	Official discussions/study	1998
Japan-South Korea-China	Free Trade Area	Official discussions/study	
South Korea-Mexico	Free Trade Area	Official discussions/study	2000
South Korea-New Zealand	Free Trade Area	Official discussions/study	2000
South Korea-Australia	Free Trade Area	Official discussions	2000
Hong Kong-New Zealand	Closer Economic Partnership	Official discussions	2001
Singapore-India	Closer Economic Partnership	Official discussions	2003
ASEAN-India	Closer Economic Partnership	Proposal/Study	2003
Japan-Canada	Free Trade Area	Proposal/Study	2000
Japan-Thailand	Closer Economic Partnership	Proposal/Study	2002
Japan-Philippines	Closer Economic Partnership	Proposal	2002
Japan-Taiwan	Free Trade Area	Proposal	2002
Japan-Brunei	Free Trade Area	Proposal	2003
Pacific-5	Free Trade Area	Proposal	1998
Singapore-Taiwan	Free Trade Area	Proposal/Study	2002
South Korea-China	Free Trade Area	Proposal/Study	
South Korea-Thailand	Free Trade Area	Proposal/Study	2001
Thailand-United States	Free Trade Area	Proposal	2002
Philippines-United States	Free Trade Area	Proposal	2002
Indonesia-United States	Free Trade Area	Proposal	2002
Singapore-South Korea	Free Trade Area	Proposal	2002

Note: EFTA – Switzerland, Iceland, Liechtenstein, and Norway
Pacific-5 – Singapore, Australia, New Zealand, United States and Chile

The proliferation of FTAs apparently stem from the realization that working exclusively under the auspices of the World Trade Organization do not guarantee trade benefits for the participating countries, particularly developing ones. After the failure to launch a global trade round at the WTO Ministerial conference in Seattle, many governments in Asia now doubt the continued viability of the multilateral system. In fact, there were misgivings among developing countries about the outcome of the last Uruguay trade round. Many feel shortchanged and question the unequal balance of benefits and concessions made after acceding into the wide-ranging treaty. The slow pace of liberalization in the textiles and garments trade and the lack of substantial reduction in agricultural subsidies are some of the problems faced by these countries. Developing Asian countries are also increasingly concerned that proposals to include labor and environmental standards could undermine their competitiveness.

Despite the inauguration of a new round of multilateral trade negotiations in Doha, there is lingering apprehension about the capacity of the world trading system to carry out trade liberalization that is truly beneficial to developing countries. The lack of substantive progress in agricultural trade negotiations and contention over access of cheap medicine reflects the limitations of the multilateral process. The slow pace of multilateral negotiations in the current Doha round is indicative of the inordinate amount of time needed to build consensus among the 144-member trade organization.

The level of expectation has also declined somewhat for ASEAN and APEC as vehicles for regional trade liberalization. Many in the region feel that both institutions have lost their momentum following the fallout of the Asian Financial Crisis. The liberalization process envisioned under the ASEAN Free Trade Area (AFTA) and the drive towards deeper economic integration has slowed down with some countries seeking additional exceptions from their trade commitments. After the failed EVSL scheme, APEC seems to have lost its focus on trade and investment liberalization casting reservations whether the organization can realize the goals set at Bogor.

There is the perception that multilateral and regional trade regimes have had little positive impact on developing countries. Waning confidence in the multilateral trading system and on existing regional arrangements have led many countries to take a more serious look at their respective national positions and consider other policy options to advance their trade interests. The bilateral route is seen as an alternative strategy to the present multilateral and regional trade mechanisms, which are perceived to be too weak and slow in pushing forward the liberalization process. These FTAs are meant to sustain the momentum of promoting freer trade in the face of the ineffectualness of present institutions.

2. WEIGHING THE BENEFITS OF AN EAFTA

The EAFTA proposal is one other alternative to the trade liberalization and economic integration efforts in Asia. This would create a trading consortium with a combined GDP of approximately US$6 trillion. According to 2000 data from the

WTO, an EAFTA would represent around 21.3 percent of global merchandise exports and about one fifth of the world's total imports. An East Asian free trade area would become the world's second largest trading group after the EU. The grouping accounts for nearly half of the world's high-tech exports and two-fifths of the world's exports of textiles and clothing.

Two-way trade between ASEAN and Northeast Asia amounted to over US$200 billion in 2000, up by 28.7 percent from 1996 (see Charts 1 and 2). Trade between the two regions has recovered from the depression caused by the Asian Financial Crisis. ASEAN countries imports more from the region as a whole valued at over US$100 billion in 2000 compared to exports of US$99.9 billion. Much of this trade is with Japan, comprising of more than half of total trade with ASEAN. However, trade between ASEAN and China has been on the up trend. ASEAN exports to China grew more than three fold between 1996 and 2000 while imports almost doubled during the same period.

Figure 1. ASEAN Exports to NE Asia

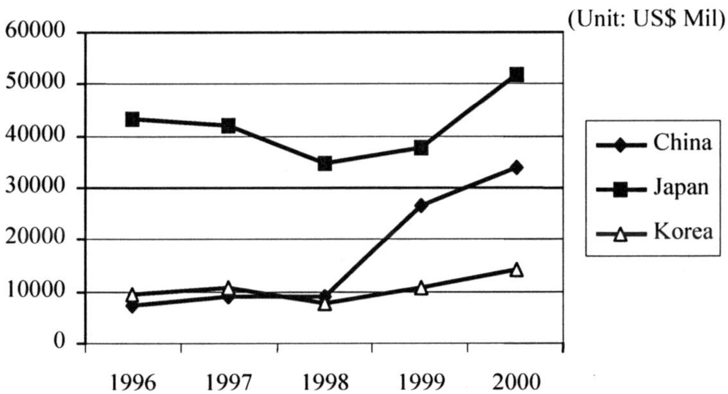

Source: ASEAN Secretariat

Trade flows are likely to increase when the partner's structure of exports is complementary with the structure of exports of the home country. A partner is said to have a complementary (as opposed to competitive) export structure if its comparative advantage reside in sectors in which the other country does not have such an advantage. To get an indication of the complementarities of the export structures of the prospective members of an EAFTA, a comparison of the revealed comparative advantage indices (RCA) can be undertaken. Note that the RCA is just an indicator of the comparative advantage, not the definitive measure[4]. Apart from the conceptual limitations of RCA indices as measures of comparative advantages, it

[4] It is defined as the ratio of a country's share in the world export of a particular good to the share of the country's total exports in world total exports. A value greater than one indicates that the country specializes in the export of that good and has therefore "comparative advantage."

should be noted that the RCA might be sensitive to the level of aggregation of the data.

Figure 2. ASEAN Imports from NE Asia

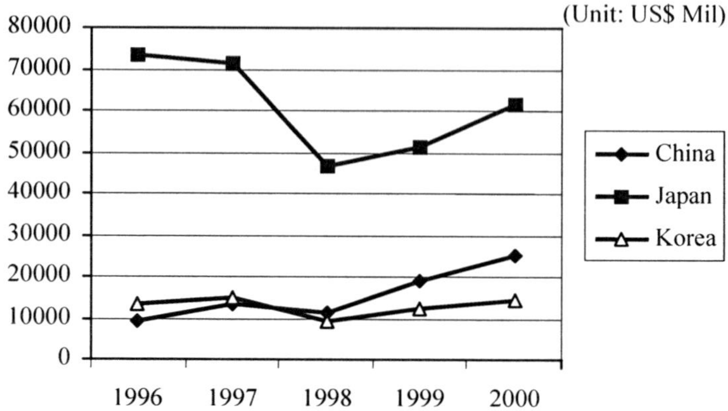

Source: ASEAN Secretariat

Looking at Table 2, we can have some idea of the relative complementarity of the trade between EAFTA members. Japan's comparative advantage lay in non-electric machinery, transport equipment, electronic components, consumer electronics, and miscellaneous manufacturing. China's RCA lay in such products as clothing, leather products, textiles, consumer electronics, basic and miscellaneous manufactures. South Korea's RCA is in textiles, consumer electronics and electronic components. ASEAN countries have different RCAs reflecting different export structures. Malaysia and the Philippines enjoy comparative advantage in consumer electronics and electronic components. Indonesia and Thailand have advantage in leather products. Vietnam's RCA is in fresh food, clothing, minerals and miscellaneous manufacturing.

Conventional economic analysis regarding preferential trade arrangements such as free trade areas highlights the benefits of market opening measures to the domestic and regional economy. An FTA will result in tariff reductions on a faster timeline or to a greater magnitude than in the multilateral level. In principle, the elimination of tariff and quota restrictions among member states lead to improved market access, greater consumption possibilities and realignment of resources towards efficient sectors.[5] A move towards freer trade directly benefits exporters as there will be improved access to existing and new markets. An FTA will also be good for consumers as a greater variety of goods at cheaper prices become more available.

[5] To be consistent with GATT Article 24, two essential conditions must apply: (i) the agreement should substantially cover all trade, and (ii) the agreement should not leave non-members worse off than before. However, there is a difference of opinion on whether free trade areas lead to trade diversion or creation.

The benefits of free trade areas, even in the short-term, go beyond trade. Intra-regional labor mobility, FDI and financial capital flows will directly benefit members. To the extent that harmonization of policies and lower transaction costs between members can help facilitate such movements, an FTA will be desirable. Apart from the trade benefits, FTAs also generally enhance the attractiveness of the area for foreign investments. An FTA will also attract FDI not only from the partner country but also from non-members as well.

Table 2. Specialization Index 2002

	China	Japan	Korea	Indo	Mal	Phil	Sing	Thai	Viet
Fresh food	0.93	-	0.24	1.53	0.39	0.61	0.25	1.85	4.00
Minerals	0.33	-	0.48	2.46	0.84	0.18	0.86	0.42	2.40
Chemicals	0.52	0.86	0.93	0.56	0.41	0.10	0.68	0.71	0.11
Processed food	0.68	-	0.19	1.15	1.22	0.68	0.41	2.52	1.41
Basic manufacturing	1.09	0.88	0.98	0.60	0.40	0.30	0.30	0.67	-
Wood products	0.54	0.17	0.34	3.36	1.38	0.38	0.16	0.76	0.62
Textiles	2.50	0.58	2.85	2.18	0.50	0.30	0.25	1.12	0.81
Non-electric machinery	0.46	1.69	0.59	0.18	0.29	0.14	0.58	0.57	0.15
Misc. manufacturing	1.81	1.29	0.50	0.43	0.57	0.41	0.94	0.84	4.10
Leather products	4.92	-	1.22	2.62	-	0.79	-	2.11	0.15
Transport equipment	0.29	1.77	1.12	0.08	0.07	0.16	0.13	0.32	-
Clothing	4.49	-	0.90	2.37	0.71	2.05	0.41	1.72	3.83
Consumer electronics	1.40	1.29	1.81	0.97	3.14	2.03	2.61	1.74	0.08
Electronic components	0.93	1.73	1.78	0.39	2.36	4.83	3.00	1.53	0.39

Source: ITC (Calculations based on COMTRADE of UNSD)

Certainly, there will be adjustment costs arising from the formation of a free trade area. An FTA would place considerable pressure on import competing industries, which will bear the brunt of the adjustment costs arising from the arrangement potentially leading to factory closures and greater unemployment. These industries will seek to defer or delay this process by seeking additional protection or the provision of so-called safety nets to help mitigate the costs. Thus to the extent that the employment generated from foreign investments can make up for the losses of the import competing industries that fail to compete, joining an FTA can be welfare enhancing. Most analysis concludes that, in the end, the benefits accruing from the FTA will more than make up for the costs.

However, the different levels of development and industrial structures of Asian countries make symmetrical gains almost impossible. Das (2001) observed that larger economies negotiating an FTA enjoy greater bargaining power in the grouping.

In an EAFTA, members like China or Japan can successfully extract concessions of all kinds not just in trade but also in non-trade issues from smaller economies like the Philippines or Thailand. The resulting trade liberalization would be largely confined to concessions given by the smaller partners of the FTA, not by the larger economies. Developed country partners like Japan or Singapore generally have fairly, if not quite, liberalized economies. Consequently, developing country partners like the Philippines can only expect small tariff concessions, because the larger partners of a proposed EAFTA already have low tariffs. Panagariya (1999) also observed that the agenda for deeper integration is likely to be determined by the larger, not by their smaller FTA partners. Hence, smaller economies would have little say over the direction of the FTA.

Consideration of the non-traditional gains associated with the formation of FTAs may be more significant here. Firstly, an EAFTA may help lock in and reinforce domestic economic reform efforts. Trade liberalization fosters competition and creates pressure for market reform throughout the national economy. Entering an FTA will bind governments to their trade commitments and prevent them from giving in to rent-seeking industries opposed to these reforms. Membership in an FTA will prevent succeeding administrations from backtracking on their commitments and succumbing to renewed protectionism for fear of inviting retaliation from the other FTA members. As long as the costs of exiting an FTA outweigh the gains, members will advance reform measures and resist policy reversals

This rationale is significant when the proposed EAFTA includes a number of transitional economies as well as countries still struggling from the aftermath of the Asian Financial Crisis. An EAFTA will help ensure market reform in China, Vietnam and the other former command economies in Asia. It will also guarantee that Japan, South Korea, and other ASEAN governments press ahead with their own reform efforts. An EAFTA would also force ASEAN to move more rapidly in developing its own regional FTA and perhaps advance towards a common market. The potential trade gains arising from an EAFTA should also help these countries offset the cost of adjustment accruing from trade liberalization. An EAFTA will also help 'broadcast' or make known to the international community the region's commitment to the free market and hence stimulate investments.

Secondly, an FTA can also act as insurance against the threat of market closure and trade diversion from other trading blocs. The formation of an EAFTA is viewed by many as a defensive response to the growing regionalism in North America and Europe. The United States is seeking to expand NAFTA to Latin America with the establishment of the Free Trade Area of the Americas (FTAA) by the year 2005. The European Union, already encompassing most of Western Europe, is expanding to Eastern Europe and planning to complete the creation of a Euro-Mediterranean Free Trade Area by 2010. There is growing demand for Asian countries to act together in order to counteract these developments and balance their interests against a more unified EU and a strong NAFTA.

For smaller and developing countries in Asia, the formation of an Asian trade bloc will provide continued access to markets particularly in the more developed and larger economies of the region. Should a global trade war flare up, an EAFTA will have an internal market sufficient to compensate for trade losses from market closure elsewhere. Fearful of being left outside these trade blocs, a small developing member like the Philippines may find assurance by partnering with larger and more developed members like China and Japan in an EAFTA.

This leads us to our third reason. Asian countries can enjoy increased bargaining power vis-à-vis the United States or the European Union if they band together in an EAFTA. Asian countries can leverage their market power and negotiate as a group in the World Trade Organization. An EAFTA will facilitate the coordination of the positions of its members and enable them to achieve greater trade gains in multilateral trade negotiations. Indeed, Asian countries will be able to more effectively resist the trade actions of powerful countries like the US or groupings like the EU compared to acting separately of each other.

3. DIFFERING MOTIVATIONS

Until recently, China, Japan and South Korea were not very much interested in forging preferential free trade deals. Now, these three countries have taken the initiative to establish bilateral accords with other regional states though for different reasons. After its accession into the WTO, China proposed a FTA with ASEAN partly as a diplomatic move to assuage ASEAN countries' fears of an economically dominant China. While attracted by its huge market, there is widespread anxiety about the ability of Southeast Asian firms to compete with low cost manufacturers in the Chinese mainland. Many firms in Southeast Asia are worried that cheap Chinese goods may flood their markets once a free trade agreement is entered into with China. From Table 2 above, we can see that many Asian economies are in direct competition with each other since many of them export the same goods, particularly in textiles and garments, electronic components and consumer electronics, etc. ASEAN governments are also troubled by the fact greater amounts of foreign direct investment are being diverted away from the region and into China. In fact, China already has the lion's share of FDI to developing countries. With a China-ASEAN FTA, ASEAN will have an opportunity to attract some of this FDI and access the Chinese market on preferential terms.

The success of the China-ASEAN FTA depends on an agreement on an early harvest package favorable to ASEAN. China has already agreed to grant preferential tariff goods to less-developed members of ASEAN including Cambodia, Laos and Myanmar. However, concessions will also have to be given to the other members of the Southeast Asian grouping. So far, China has been reluctant to open up services trade and its agricultural sector, particularly rice and palm oil – two critical export commodities of ASEAN.

Emergence of China as a regional competitor is perhaps the primary motivating factor behind Japan's own trade initiatives. Heretofore a staunch multilateralist, Japan has undertaken a major shift in its trade strategy and economic diplomacy.[6] After the announcement of an ASEAN-China FTA, Japan accelerated its own discussions with potential trade partners. It has recently concluded its first FTA with

[6] See Munakata (2001) for an explanation of Japan's shift to preferential trade.

Singapore and is currently negotiating with other ASEAN countries. However, Prime Minister Koizumi made it clear that a Japan-ASEAN FTA should be linked to East Asian cooperation as a whole and would be open to the inclusion of other regional partners.

Greater access to the Japanese market, which is five times in income terms as large as China's, is more attractive to many in Southeast Asia. Many ASEAN economies enjoy complementarity with Japan thus increasing the potential for trade gains. However, it is difficult for Japan to advance on any kind of free trade area without basic resolution of its underlying structural problems. The Japanese government has been unable to undertake fundamental reform necessary to bolster its deflationary economy. Moreover, the strength of Japan's farm lobby prevents the inclusion of agricultural products in any FTA. Japan only managed to conclude its first FTA with Singapore because agricultural trade between the two countries is insignificant. Government protection of Japan's inefficient textile and food processing industries through its system of restrictive non-tariff barriers are also potential obstacles. Japan is also reluctant to open up its services sector, particularly in the movement of natural persons.

Fear of being left out from the trend towards growing regionalism prompted South Korea to consider a shift in its trade strategy.[7] By entering into its own FTA, Korea is seeking to avoid the negative effects of exclusion and possible trade diversion. Concern about guarantees on trade access and lowering barriers to Korean exports is primarily motivating Seoul's FTA policy. With its so-called "open trading country" strategy, Seoul is seeking to enter into strategic alliances with neighboring countries to ensure the country's competitiveness and attraction to foreign investment. The government expresses a wish to establish an FTA with Japan, which is to be the nucleus of a larger Northeast Asian economic trade bloc including China and, consequently, an expanded East Asian economic grouping. Like Japan, however, continued protection of Korea's agricultural sector would be an obstacle in any FTA project.

ASEAN member-countries also have different motivations and feelings about free trade areas. Trade-dependent Singapore is aggressively seeking bilateral trade ties with a range of nations in Asia, Europe and the Americas to ensure its economic survival.[8] Seeking to capitalize on its first-mover advantage, Singapore is erecting a network of free trade deals to ensure that it remains a trade hub in Asia. Such deals are also meant to keep Singapore attractive to foreign investment, particularly in high-technology and service-based industries.

Other ASEAN countries are less sanguine about all these developments. Critics of Singapore's bilateral strategy argue that such moves could provide a backdoor entry for non-members into the AFTA market. Non-ASEAN products could derive the commercial benefits of AFTA by entering into duty-free Singapore. There is also concern that these bilateral and regional projects would distract ASEAN from advancing on its own program for creating a free trade area. The ASEAN Free Trade

[7] See Cheong (2002) for a study of South Korea's FTA policy.
[8] See Rajan and Sen (2002) for a discussion of Singapore's bilateral strategy.

Area still faces many problems in implementing the CEPT scheme. The temporary exclusion of Malaysian cars, and Philippine sugar and petrochemicals from the scheme threatens to weaken AFTA and delay regional integration. Moreover, ASEAN talks aimed at freeing up services trade are currently going nowhere. The 1997 Asian financial crisis has dampened somewhat ASEAN's drive towards liberalization and the trend towards bilateralism could distract them further.

Proposing an EAFTA might lead to diversion of scarce political capital. There is danger that the domestic constituencies in ASEAN are already experiencing liberalization fatigue, particularly with the persistence of economic difficulties. A proposal to free up the domestic market under yet another free trade agreement might test the tolerance of the public for further trade liberalization. Domestic industries in ASEAN already opposed to the AFTA-CEPT will be less inclined to accept another liberalizing scheme.

Furthermore, negotiating one or several FTAs strain the capacity of ASEAN governments. Trade policymakers who are negotiating and operating multilateral and regional agreements will have less time and fewer resources available for bilateral negotiations. Many ASEAN governments are faced with the basic problem of a shortage of negotiating capacity. Many governments simply lack trained or skilled personnel, particularly trade lawyers and negotiators. Resources and personnel are already spread too thinly to cover the various trade forums. Moreover, the capacity for analysis and research on trade matters is very limited making trade officials hesitant and reactive in dealing with new issues.

With a new WTO trade round, members will be preoccupied with the work program in Geneva. Moreover, much remains to be accomplished in AFTA particularly in non-tariff barriers and trade in services to keep trade official busy. Though not in the form of formal binding negotiations, the official meetings of APEC make demands on the capacity of ASEAN countries. The problem is more severe in the less developed countries of Southeast Asia, like Laos, Cambodia and Myanmar. Following the "scarce-negotiator-resources" argument, time spent on an FTA presumably leaves less time or capital to spend on other initiatives. EAFTA, though desirable, will likely be a lesser priority and more of a long-term goal for ASEAN.

In general, ASEAN plays an important role in Asian regionalism. Andrew Elek (1994) noted that ASEAN has been at the core of the process of economic cooperation and regime formation, particularly in APEC and ASEM. Regionalism in Asia has come to adopt the so-called "ASEAN way", which emphasizes consensus decision-making, non-intervention in each other's domestic affairs, conflict avoidance rather than conflict resolution, and informal incrementalism. The emphasis here is on the process rather than the creation of formal institutions. This method observes the formal equality of its members given the disparities in economic development, size, and political systems. These principles and norms also form the basis of economic integration and institution-building in Asia.

ASEAN governments are generally uneasy about efforts to strengthen regional institutions formally for fear that a wider organization might dilute ASEAN's position. This reluctance also stems from concerns about large power domination. ASEAN fears being overwhelmed by either China or Japan once it enters into free trade agreement with these two countries. Consequently, ASEAN will seek to preserve its position in regional forums. In APEC, for instance, ASEAN resisted formal and contractual arrangements preferring instead to move ahead through consensus and on a voluntary basis. Under the 1990 Kuching consensus, ASEAN stated its identity and cohesion should not be eroded and all its cooperative efforts should be preserved. ASEAN officials demanded that the grouping should be limited to consultations and constructive discussions on economic issues and that it "should proceed gradually and pragmatically as regards its eventual institutional structure". How ASEAN will participate in the process of establishing the EAFTA will have a direct impact on its outcome. As long as ASEAN does not move forward in its own integration efforts, an EAFTA proposal is not likely to advance.

4. REALIZING EAFTA

The mushrooming of bilateral preferential arrangements complicates the formation of an EAFTA. The competing forces of trade bilateralism may or may not serve as building blocs for an East Asian economic grouping. These various initiatives may result in what some have called "competitive regionalization" or the formation of competing blocs that may ultimately lead to the rise of protectionism. Anne Krueger (1997) highlighted the problems inherent in overlapping free trade areas, arguing that differing rules of origin increases the scope for protection and weakens the process of further liberalization. Others see the proliferation of preferential arrangements as a process of "competitive liberalization". Richard Baldwin (1995) sees that bloc formation as naturally expansive as he argues a "domino" effect, will lead more and more non-members to become insiders and for FTAs to join up with others. The bilateral arrangements between the Asian countries could complement the formation of an EAFTA as long as they remain open to the admission of other regional countries.

The question of overlapping FTAs could serve to undermine the multilateral trading order under the World Trade Organization (WTO). Opposing blocs of EU, NAFTA and an EAFTA could in the end raise barriers and undermine global free trade. On the other hand, the formation of a three-bloc world has been viewed by some as likely to complement rather than undermine the multilateral trading system. It would be easier and more efficient to organize WTO negotiations and move the world toward free trade faster. Negotiations between three main blocs would make the exchange of concessions easier to achieve and will help persuade reluctant members to support further trade opening measures. Reciprocal trade concessions and gains will most likely be more evenly distributed in a three-bloc trading system. Thus, an EAFTA can serve as a positive force in advancing global free trade.

More significantly, trade initiatives in Asia go beyond the WTO agenda thereby providing the basis for deeper integration of the region. The so-called "New Age" free trade agreements include the liberalization of services trade, investment protection and adoption of competition policy framework, harmonization and mutual recognition of standards and certification, protection of intellectual property rights, opening of government procurement markets, streamlining and harmonization of customs procedures and the development of dispute settlement procedures. Some contain provisions on bilateral cooperation on a wide range of "new" issues in electronic commerce, science and technology, environment, and trade and investment promotion. In this regard, cooperation in EAFTA can help move the WTO negotiations forward and even go beyond the existing agenda.

Such initiatives could likewise negatively impact on other regional arrangements such as APEC and AFTA. As mentioned above, work devoted to the formation of an EAFTA could shift scarce resources and attention away from present endeavors. However, such as a scheme can also hasten the process of liberalization and integration in APEC and AFTA by acting as a positive pressure on its members. An EAFTA will help developing Asian countries in APEC advance their compliance with the goals defined in Bogor and force ASEAN countries to move forward towards fuller and deeper integration.

Yamazawa (2002) argued that EAFTA would have to follow the APEC principle of open regionalism. He advocated that the EAFTA should remain open and supportive of an open world trading system and should be APEC and WTO consistent. Trading patterns in Asia, he points out, make it unlikely that a closed economic bloc would be preferred. The United States and Europe remain the main end-markets for most of Asia's exports as well as major sources of investment. Heavy reliance on external markets, capital and technology make an exclusive closed bloc impractical. To the extent that an EAFTA initiative may be perceived as a discriminatory bloc, it may invite retaliation from the rest of the world particularly from major trading partners like the US. The possibility of inter-bloc trade warfare will have severe repercussions on the economic welfare of the region.

In this regard, the development of bilateral FTAs will help ensure that EAFTA does not develop into an inward-looking discriminatory bloc. Proposals to set up free trade areas between Singapore and the US, Singapore and Canada, Japan and Chile, Japan and Mexico, South Korea and Mexico among others can serve to bridge separate continents and support the multilateral trading system. Yamazawa termed this as "open regional cooperation" when bridging effects of bilateral FTA ensure that regional preferential trading blocs like EAFTA remain consistent with the goal of global free trade.

Domestic support for an FTA will be present if the gains outweigh the losses. Given that fewer members are involved, it should be easier to gain political backing for EAFTA compared to multilateral trade arrangements. The benefits of a plurilateral FTA will be more apparent and quicker to achieve. In the process of instituting a free trade area, however, there are abundant opportunities for trade-sensitive industries to manipulate the process, particularly those sectors that might be adversely affected. Also individual industries in an FTA negotiation will seek to exploit rules of origin to enhance extent of protection.[9]

An EAFTA will have to overcome resistance from domestic constituencies and lessen protection of uncompetitive industries. This is especially relevant in the case of Japan and South Korea, whose trade policy is vulnerable to powerful domestic

[9] Frankel and Wei (1998)

lobbies particularly in the agricultural sector. Excluding agriculture from the scope of the EAFTA will weaken it. There is also concern about Japan's commitment to trade openness given its domestic economic problems. Its inability to address its macroeconomic and financial troubles limits Japan from playing a leadership role in this matter.

The wide divergence among Asian countries in terms of standards of living and political persuasions may also make regional economic integration difficult to achieve. Developing countries in Asia will particularly encounter problems in carrying out adjustment measures and liberalization policies. Sovereign issues will also make negotiations complex. Issues such as capital controls, cross-border labor movement and protection of the agricultural sector are just some of the problems that could bog down negotiations to establish an EAFTA. An EAFTA will have to exempt the less-developed countries of Southeast Asia and provide them with differential treatment. This could lead to a two-tiered EAFTA with less-developed Asian economies largely left out of the benefits of the liberalizing effects of the free trade area. In this regard, significant technical assistance and support program must form part of any EAFTA to enable developing members to participate more fully in the project.

More important, lingering animosities between Asian states threaten regional peace and can become major obstacles to greater regional cooperation. The major powers in Asia have been political rivals and an atmosphere of distrust and enmity still exists between them. An EAFTA can help reduce political tensions and promote harmony between Asian countries but it will require enormous political will to push integration ahead.

Yamazawa (2002) and Panagariya (1998) are equally pessimistic about the short-term future of the proposal. Munakata (2002) contended that such a scheme will take some time. What is more likely in his view is that competitive bilateral or smaller plurilateral arrangements will develop in parallel with each other. He referred to this as the multilayered regional framework. In this sense, existing preferential trading arrangements in Asia such as ASEAN or the many bilateral FTAs will expand and deepen and hopefully link up into a larger regional FTA. Progress on ASEAN's FTA and the proposal to set up a Northeast Asian FTA will be crucial in the realization of an EAFTA. On the other hand, a hub-and-spoke arrangement could lead to the eventual establishment of an EAFTA with ASEAN acting as the core having separate FTAs with China, Japan and South Korea.

An East Asian free trade area will be an ambitious undertaking. An EAFTA would have to hurdle many of these problems. Support for the initiative will only be forthcoming if these concerns are sufficiently addressed. A considerable degree of convergence of policy and economic structure should take place first before negotiations on a free trade proposal can begin. Given the discussion above, most Asian governments would prefer a gradual and managed process that takes into consideration their domestic needs. Moreover, continued reliance of external markets will mean that any trade liberalization scheme must be pursued in a non-discriminatory manner consistent with the principles laid down by the WTO.

REFERENCES

Asian Development Bank. 2003. *Asian Development Outlook 2002.* Manila : ADB.

Avila, J. L. 2001. "APEC and ASEM: Reconciling Two Regional Agendas." In W. Villacorta ed. *Coalition-Building and APEC.* Makati City: Philippine Institute for Development Studies.

Baldwin, R. E. 1995. "A Domino Theory of Regionalism." In Baldwin, Richard, Haaparnata, P. and Kiander, J. eds. *Expanding Membership of the European Union.* Cambridge, U.K.: Cambridge University Press.

Cheong, I. 2002. "Korea's FTA Policy: Focusing on Bilateral FTAs with Chile and Japan." Discussion Paper 02-02. Seoul : Korea Institute for International Economic Policy.

Das, D. 2001. "Regionalism in a Globalizing World: An Asia-Pacific Perspective." CSGR Working Paper No. 80/01.

Elek, A. 1995. "APEC Beyond Bogor: An Open Economic Association in the Asia Pacific Region." *Asian Pacific Economic Literature,* Vol. 9 No. 1.

Frankel, J. and S. Wei. 1998. "Regionalization of World Trade and Currencies: Economics and Politics." In J. Frankel ed. *The Regionalization of the World Economy.* Chicago: University of Chicago Press.

Munakata, N. 2002. "Seize the Moment for East Asian Economic Integration." *The Center for Strategic and International Studies PacNet Newsletter.* (February)

________. 2001. *Evolution of Japan's Policy toward Economic Integration.* Center for Northeast Asian Policy Studies. Washington, D.C.: The Brookings Institution.

Panagariya, A. 1998. "Should East Asia go Regional?" In H. Lee and D. Roland-Host eds. *Economic Development and Cooperation in the Pacific Basin: Trade, Investment and Environmental Issues.* MA: Cambridge University Press.

________. 1999. "The Regional Debate: An Overview." *The World Economy,* Vol. 22. No. 4.

Rajan, R. and R. Sen. 2002. *Singapore's New Commercial Trade Strategy: the Pros and Cons of Bilateralism.* Discussion Paper No. 0202. Centre for International Economic Studies. Australia: delaide University.

Ravenhill, J. 1998. "The Growth of Intergovernmental Collaboration in the Asia Pacific Region." In A. Mcgrew and C. Brook eds. *Asia Pacific in the New World.* London: Routledge.

Yamazawa, I. 2002. "A Case for East Asian Regionalism." Paper presented during the International Conference on East Asian Cooperation: Progress and Future Agenda, 22-23 August. Beijing, China.

Part III: Assessment of East Asian Regionalism

CHAPTER 8

ESTIMATION OF ECONOMIC EFFECTS OF FTAS IN EAST ASIA – CGE APPROACH

INKYO CHEONG

CHAPTER 9

ASIAN REGIONALISM: PROMISES AND PITFALLS

RICHARD E. BALDWIN

CHAPTER 10

EU'S STRATEGY TOWARDS EAST ASIAN INTEGRATION AND REGIONALISM

SUNG-HOON PARK

CHAPTER 8

ESTIMATION OF ECONOMIC EFFECTS OF FTAS IN EAST ASIA – CGE APPROACH

INKYO CHEONG

1. INTRODUCTION

Despite political and social barriers, there is much to be gained from an East Asian FTA. Factors such as geographic proximity, complementary endowments of production factors, and growing economic ties after the crisis will help in making this goal come true. East Asia accounts for one-third of the world's population and one-fifth of the world's GDP and trade volume. In terms of population and GDP, excluding the inflow of the FDI, East Asia is evaluated to have a similar economic potential as the EU and NAFTA. What benefits could an East Asian FTA offer member economies? As East Asia becomes a free market with the elimination of tariffs and non-tariff barriers, businesses will be able to expand exports and enjoy economies of scale. Moreover, the creation of a huge free market will bring dynamic benefits since the region will attract more foreign direct investment, which will subsequently create more jobs and facilitate the transfer of advanced technology.

Other forms of dynamic benefits also exist. First of all, common standards for production technology, product regulations, distribution, and after-sales service can be expanded across countries in the region. Even if these standards are in conflict with the standards of North America or the EU, the Asian countries can gain leverage during international standardizing negotiations by presenting a unified front, as suggested in Igawa and Kim (2001).

The rapid emergence of China in discussions on Northeast Asian or East Asian economic cooperation is also a matter for consideration as East Asian countries need to strengthen cooperation with China. With China's admission into the WTO and its hosting of the Olympics in 2008, its economic and political position will improve. An East Asian FTA offers a way to effectively access the Chinese market and at the same time strengthen economic cooperation with China.

Some have proposed the restructuring of East Asia's development model after the financial crisis.[1] So far, East Asian countries have achieved economic growth through increased exports to the U.S. market. However, since the U.S. demand for

[1] Refer to Ahn (2001) for discussions on new East Asian development models following the financial crisis.

C. Y. Ahn et al (eds.), *East Asian Economic Regionalism*, 139-155.

imports may wane with the fierce competition in its markets and the expansion of its trade deficit, it is time for East Asia to create its own demand; establishing an East Asian FTA seems to be the best way to go about it.

An East Asian FTA will improve the economic and social stability of East Asia and contribute to strengthening the region's presence in the international community. An East Asian FTA can weaken the conflicting positions of China and Japan for regional leadership through the conclusion of bilateral FTAs, and in the long term, secure stability in East Asia, if North Korea joins in the future.

This chapter will estimate the economic effects of various forms of East Asian regionalism using a computational general equilibrium (CGE) model. After reviewing existing studies on an East Asian FTA, this chapter will briefly describe the basic information of the simulation, such as the database, parameters, and the simulation model used. Finally, the chapter will discuss the results of the simulation.

2. Existing Studies on an East Asian FTA

East Asian economic integration has been a topic of study since the mid-1990s. The World Bank (1994) emphasizes the necessity of East Asian economic integration, observing that despite the worldwide economic downturn of the early 1990s, East Asia achieved rapid growth due to the high growth of trade and investment within the region. It specifies that it is the markets within the region that have played a crucial role in the economic growth of East Asian countries. However, noting that the growth of trade within the region will be limited; it is necessary to expand trade with areas outside the region or to design measures to boost trade within the region. That is, mechanisms that facilitate economic integration through trade and investment liberalization such as FTAs should be promoted.

Young (1993) pointed to the high non-tariff barriers in East Asia, asserting the need to develop trade liberalization measures within the region. Moreover, arguing that the establishment of an economic cooperative bloc will facilitate economic growth, Young (1993) recommended that East Asian countries reverse their protective positions. On the other hand, Panagariya (1994) discussed the possibility of the East Asia Economic Group (EAEG) proposed by Malaysia's Prime Minister Mahathir, expressing skepticism about the feasibility of such types of economic integration in the region. Panagariya argued that such integration would be difficult to realize due to the complexity of the non-tariff barriers of East Asian countries. However, there have been drastic changes and developments in East Asia since the study was published, which have increased the viability of economic integration in the region.

In the late 1990s, there were numerous studies on East Asian trade liberalization and trade relations using analytic models. Researchers focused on analyzing trade relations between East Asian countries using the gravity model, or on estimating the impact of trade liberalization using the computational general equilibrium (CGE) model to make policy recommendations. Kreinin and Plummer (1994), Choi (1996), Thorpe and Zhang (2000), Dutta (2002), Lee and Park (2002), and Kim (2002) discussed competitive relations, intra-industry trade, and desirable directions for economic integration by analyzing the East Asian trade structure. Martin, Petri and Yanagishima (1994), Oh and Cheong (1997), Brown, Deardorff and Stern (2001), and Park (2001) are some studies that used the CGE model.

Table 1. Existing Studies on East Asian Economic Integration

Authors	Methodology	Major Findings
Kreinin and Plummer (1994)	Concept of "natural trading bloc"	East Asian economic integration is likely to be realized.
Panagariya (1994)	Descriptive Analysis	Because of high NTBs, East Asian economic integration will not be feasible.
Lee and Park (2002)	Gravity model	An East Asian FTA is more feasible than a China-Japan-Korea FTA.
Martin, Petri and Yanagishima (1994)	Global CGE model	China and ASEAN will be the biggest winners under an East Asian FTA.
Oh and Cheong (1997)	Global CGE model	Japan and Korea can collect the highest gains from an East Asian FTA.
Brown, Deardorff and Stern (2001)	Global CGE model	An East Asian FTA may have disruptive effects on sectoral employment in some regions.
Park (2001)	Global CGE model	North-South FTAs are more economically desirable than South-South or North-North FTAs in East Asia.

Source: Cheong (2002)

Kreinin and Plummer (1994) studied the possibility of economic integration in East Asia using the concept of a "natural trading bloc" to conclude that an East Asian economic integration encompassing ASEAN, other developing East Asian countries, and Japan was highly likely to take place. Kreinin and Plummer (2000) analyzed the effects of NAFTA and the expansion of the European Community (EC-1992) on ASEAN and Korea. According to their findings, NAFTA would create trade diversion effects on the trade of ASEAN and Korea amounting to 4% and 5% of North America's total exports respectively, with the expansion of the EC bringing even greater disadvantages than the effects of NAFTA. Such expansion and deepening of regionalism in North America and Europe will result in a decrease of FDI in East Asia and instead increase FDI in North America and Europe.

Choi (1996) empirically tested the increase in East Asia's trade share of the world economy, examining the possibility of a free trade area including ASEAN, Japan, Korea, and other developing countries using the gravity model. He concluded that the formation of a regional trade bloc in the region would have positive effects, such as increasing the region's global trade share and strengthening the region's bargaining power against other blocs.

Using the gravity model, Lee and Park (2002) also examined the feasibility of trade blocs in East Asia to reach a conclusion similar to Choi (1996). According to their analysis, an East Asian FTA is more economically feasible than a

(China-Japan-Korea) CJK FTA. On the other hand, Kim (2002) examined the growing trade intensity among the ASEAN+3 countries using a standard gravity approach. The author shows that there is no proper evidence that trade relations have intensified over time beyond the gravity factors, observing the change of patterns in the gravity residuals. Based on his findings, he negatively evaluated the feasibility of economic integration in East Asia.

Most studies that use CGE models present a positive assessment of FTAs in East Asia. Martin, Petri and Yanagishima (1994) examined the economic feasibility of a free trade agreement in East Asia, defining the East Asian FTA as encompassing ASEAN, China, Japan, Korea, Hong Kong, and Taiwan. They predicted that China and ASEAN countries would gain the most benefits from an East Asian FTA.

Brown, Deardorff and Stern (2001) estimated the economic impact of an East Asian FTA, and find that the FTA will produce positive gains with disruptive effects on sectoral employment in some regions. They also suggested that some countries may suffer from the FTA, depending on its contents. Park (2001) emphasized the importance of the grouping of FTA partners. That is, an FTA between developed countries in the region (i.e., Japan and Korea) or between developing countries in the region (i.e., China and ASEAN) is not desirable. Instead, he asserted that Japan and Korea should promote FTAs with China, while ASEAN should promote an FTA with Japan rather than Korea.

Prior studies discussed various issues and supported their positions with empirical tests. The gravity model and CGE model are adequate tools for analyzing the economic feasibility of a regional trade agreement. In this study, eight FTA scenarios will be proposed and the economic impact of each scenario will be systematically evaluated using a CGE model. This study will then analyze the economic losses of countries that will not participate in the formation of FTAs in East Asia, and hint that a subregional FTA in East Asia may also set off a domino effect of regionalism. This situation may lead to multiple bilateral FTAs, which might eventually turn into barriers to regional trade. In order to avoid such a situation, the author emphasizes the importance of promoting an East Asian FTA that covers the entire region.

3. DATABASE, PARAMETERS, AND THE ECONOMIC MODEL

Many difficulties accompany the building of a CGE model. Constructing a database necessary for the model's simulation, takes much time and effort. A database construction for a multi-country CGE model requires I-O tables of the relevant regions, along with statistics on production, consumption, trade of each industry and country, etc. In order to save on time and resources, researchers can use products developed by academic institutions like the Global Trade Analysis Project (GTAP), which construct databases for CGE models and then sell them commercially. This study used the GTAP database, version 5, documented by Dimaranan and McDougall (2002).

In this paper, the world economy is categorized into the five regions of China,

Japan, Korea, Southeast Asia[2] and the Rest of World (ROW), and each economy is aggregated into 15 sectors. The 15 production sectors and main parameters used in the simulation are shown in Table 2. Parameters are related to the behavior of economic agents, and since estimating parameters also requires much effort, GTAP parameters are used.

The advantage of the CGE model is that it can systemically estimate the effects of policy changes on economic variables. Trade liberalization in an FTA will have systematic effects on the economy in general, and the CGE model can analyze changes in macro variables such as GDP, welfare level, prices of goods, as well as the interaction between economic agents like producers, consumers, and government. In contrast, the partial equilibrium approach has limitations in estimating the trade liberalization effects of an FTA.

Table 2. Classification of Production Sectors and Major Parameters

	Armington	Elasticity	Elasticity among
Agriculture	2.31	4.5	0.33
Forestry	2.8	5.6	0.2
Fisheries	2.8	5.6	0.2
Energy	2.8	5.6	0.2
Food	2.44	4.78	1.12
Textiles	2.2	4.4	1.26
Clothing	4.4	8.8	1.26
Chemistry	1.9	3.8	1.26
Metals	2.8	5.6	1.26
Auto, Parts	5.2	10	1.26
Otrn (other transportation equipment)	5.2	10.4	1.26
Electr (electric/electrical products)	2.8	5.6	1.26
Mach (machinery)	2.8	5.6	1.26
Omanf (other manufacturing)	2.42	5.06	1.26
Services	1.94	3.85	1.38

Source: GTAP Database (version 5)

The basic structure of a model, encompassing production, consumption, and market clearing conditions is discussed in Cheong (2001). The CGE model used for this research is constructed with the following assumptions. First, the model is based on an assumption of full employment and constant return to scale of all industrial sectors in each region. Second, it is assumed that each economy maintains the initial state of equilibrium. Accordingly, there is no excess profit in any kind of economic activity (production, imports and exports, etc.). Third, production factors can move freely between

[2] Because of the availability of data, Southeast Asia covers only the countries of Indonesia, Malaysia, Philippines, Singapore, Thailand, and Vietnam.

production sectors in a country; however, transfers between countries are not possible except for capital. Fourth, consumers maximize utility while producers maximize profit.

Since the original model is perfectly static, it may be unable to capture the dynamic effects of an FTA, consequently underestimating the economic effects.[3] Besides trade liberalization, an FTA will lead to the improvement of trade rules inducing the inflow of capital from both within and outside the region. That is, as trade, investment and economic growth have interactive and dynamic synergy effects, the effects of concluding an FTA could be amplified. Literature on this aspect includes studies by Levin and Renelt (1992), Grossman and Helpman (1995), and Baldwin and Venables (1995). Among these, Levine and Renelt (1992) asserted that there is a positive relation between economic growth and investment ratio to GDP, and also that the investment ratio to GDP is positively related to the trade ratio to GDP. Baldwin and Venables (1995) asserted that trade liberalization will bring investment incentives besides the static effects, and the accumulation of such investment will provide motives for new economic growth. They dubbed this phenomenon the "capital accumulation effects." Such investment effects could be an important factor in estimating the economic effects of an FTA.

Recently, some CGE researchers have endeavored to reflect the relations of an FTA and capital accumulation in the model. The most representative literature in the field is by Francois, McDonald and Nordstrom (1997). When estimating the effects of an FTA, they tried to model the positive aspects of an FTA by taking into account its capital accumulation effects. A traditional, multi-country CGE model sets the saving ratio as exogenous, and as a result, consumers decide the consumption level for each item based on their income level after savings. However, if the capital accumulation effects are introduced into the model, a consumer will consider his/her savings based on the expected rate of return, resulting from regional differences of capital flow, when he/she decides on the current consumption.

This paper estimated the economic effects of an FTA conclusion under two scenarios: 1) the case where only the effects of trade liberalization are considered (capital accumulation (CA) is not allowed), 2) the case where CA is activated (analyze both effects of trade liberalization and capital accumulation). There are more economic effects when capital accumulation is allowed. Whether capital accumulation is considered or not is controlled with a choice of closures of the model used in this study. When the savings variable is set as exogenous, capital accumulation is not considered; however, by making the savings variable endogenous, capital accumulation is activated in the model. The impact of capital accumulation under the formation of FTAs has not been analyzed in existing studies. However, this report will deal with the importance of investment or capital accumulation in the discussion of simulation results.

4. ECONOMIC EFFECTS OF EAST ASIAN REGIONALISM

This report will assume eight hypothetical FTAs in East Asia and estimate their

[3] On the other hand, the CGE model used for this report does not consider the economic and political costs of structural adjustments. These costs will reduce the net benefits of an FTA.

economic effects. First, the economic effects of the three bilateral FTAs in Northeast Asia (China-Japan FTA, China-Korea FTA, Japan-Korea FTA) and a CJK FTA in Northeast Asia are estimated. Subsequently, the three cases of bilateral FTAs between Southeast Asia's AFTA and Northeast Asian countries (e.g., ASEAN-China FTA) and the case in which East Asia establishes one FTA are examined. For each supposed FTA, the effects of trade liberalization ("TL") and effects of capital accumulation ("CA") in addition to the effects of TL are estimated ("TL&CA"). Trade liberalization refers to tariff elimination among member countries in the GTAP database, published in 2002, which was used to estimate the effective tariff rates of East Asian countries. For a more accurate estimation of economic effects, analyzing the effects of tariff elimination and improvement of non-tariff barriers is also desirable. However, since finding reliable data on non-tariff barriers is difficult, the effects of easing non-tariff barriers are not analyzed.

Recent FTAs are comprehensive, including services, investment, and even trade rules on intellectual property rights, dispute settlement mechanisms and exclusion of anti-dumping rules, etc. But it is not easy to estimate the full economic effects of an FTA. However, it is also very difficult to quantify the degree of improvement in trade rules for the simulation. Because tariff elimination is the most important factor in an FTA, this report will analyze the effects of tariff elimination only.

4.1. Impact on Regional GDP

Table 3 presents the effects of eight assumed FTAs on each regional GDP. According to the findings, while the eight FTAs will bring economic benefits to all member countries, non-members will suffer a loss. For example, if Japan and Korea conclude an FTA, the GDP of the two countries would increase while that of non-member countries, like ASEAN or Rest of World (ROW) could decrease.

As previously discussed, while the economic effects of TL alone are moderate, introducing capital accumulation (CA) effects expands the economic benefits. If the economic effects are estimated under the scenario of a China-Korea FTA, the GDP of China and Korea would increase by 0.12% and 0.76% respectively, considering the effects of TL only. When the effects of both TL and CA are considered, the GDP of China and Korea would increase by 0.45% and 1.76% respectively. In this case, capital accumulation is achieved through increased savings and active investments in the homeland as well as the inflow of FDI from other countries.[4] Such estimation is also clearly shown in bilateral FTAs like the China-Japan FTA and ASEAN-China FTA. For example, when ASEAN and China conclude an FTA, trade liberalization will increase ASEAN's GDP by 0.23%, while the combined effects of trade liberalization and capital accumulation will increase the GDP by 2.08%, approximately five times the effects of TL alone. This is along the same lines as the suggestion made by Chinese Premier Zhu Rongji during the ASEAN-China summit in Singapore in November 2000. Premier Zhu suggested that China's investment in the ASEAN

[4] Since the model used in this research can not identify the source of FDI, there are limitations to analyzing the specific composition of capital accumulation.

region would increase once an ASEAN-China FTA was concluded.

Under Northeast Asian FTAs, Korea is expected to gain relatively more economic benefits compared to China or Japan. Korea is forecasted to gain relatively more benefits from a CJK FTA than from a bilateral FTA with China or Japan. Like other FTAs, it is estimated that greater benefits would be generated by capital accumulation effects rather than trade liberalization effects under an FTA with Japan. This could be because Japanese capital would be invested in Korea, increasing Korea's growth potential.

Table 3. The Impact of FTAs in East Asia on Regional GDP

(Unit: %)

FTAs in Northeast Asia								
	China-Japan FTA		China-Korea FTA		Japan-Korea FTA		CJK FTA	
	TL	TL&CA	TL	TL&CA	TL	TL&CA	TL	TL&CA
China	0.27	1.11	0.12	0.45	-0.01	-0.03	0.34	1.29
Japan	0.05	0.12	-0.00	-0.04	0.01	0.04	0.06	0.13
Korea	-0.05	-0.26	0.76	1.76	0.22	0.92	0.94	2.45
ASEAN	-0.03	-0.36	-0.02	-0.19	-0.01	-0.08	-0.06	-0.59
ROW	-0.00	-0.06	-0.00	-0.06	-0.00	-0.02	-0.01	-0.12
FTAs in East Asia								
	ASEAN- China FTA		ASEAN-Japan FTA		ASEAN-Korea FTA		East Asian FTA	
	TL	TL&CA	TL	TL&CA	TL	TL&CA	TL	TL&CA
China	0.076	0.441	-0.02	-0.12	-0.01	-0.07	0.36	1.39
Japan	-0.007	-0.076	0.04	0.09	-0.01	-0.05	0.10	0.17
Korea	-0.025	-0.177	-0.04	-0.20	0.13	0.65	1.01	2.84
ASEAN	0.229	2.077	0.43	3.19	0.41	2.17	0.73	4.00
ROW	-0.004	-0.075	-0.01	-0.05	-0.00	-0.04	-0.02	-0.22

Source: Author's simulation

According to the estimation, China is found to be a more suitable FTA partner to both Japan and Korea. In other words, both Japan and Korea will gain more benefits by forming an FTA with China rather than concluding a bilateral FTA with each other. This seems to be consistent with the fact that Korean businesses prefer China after the U.S. as an FTA partner.[5] The findings in the report are quite similar to those of Park (2001).

The economic effects grow as regions subject to an FTA expand. Bhagawati and Panagariya (1996) and Schiff (1996) asserted that generally, the economic impact of an FTA increases, as the region it encompasses becomes larger. In order to maximize economic benefits, existing FTA members seek to induce the participation of non-members and link with other FTAs. However, a large FTA entails problems of high industrial restructuring and negotiating costs. Due to these shortcomings, countries initially promote smaller FTAs, and increase the number of member

[5] Refer to FKI (2001) for Korean businesses' preference for FTA partners.

countries gradually.[6]

Although it was estimated that the economic effects would expand as the area covered by an FTA was enlarged as theory suggests, differences would not be great in the case of a CJK FTA or an East Asian FTA. As Table 3 shows, an East Asian FTA will bring more economic benefits to all member countries compared to a CJK FTA, but the difference would not be great. Especially, China can expect a GDP increase of 0.34%-1.29% under a CJK FTA compared to an increase of 0.36%-1.39% under an East Asian FTA, resulting in the small difference of 0.02%-0.10%. This is attributed to the fact that economic and trade scales of Southeast Asia are relatively small. The economic scale of ASEAN is only about one-tenth of the scale of Northeast Asia. For the same reason, Northeast Asian countries can expect smaller benefits under a bilateral FTA with ASEAN than under bilateral FTAs within Northeast Asia.

Some may propose the promotion of a CJK FTA involving only three countries rather than an East Asian FTA involving 13 member countries, since the economic effects of the two agreements are similar. However, promoting an East Asian FTA is appropriate for the following reasons. First, there is a problem with the economic model. The model used in the study attempts to estimate the dynamic effects of an FTA, introducing the effects of capital accumulation. However, since the model is based on the assumptions of perfect competition and static structures, only partial dynamic effects are analyzed with the model. Thus, the model does not properly estimate the dynamic and expanded effects of large-scale FTAs like an East Asian FTA. As a result, the economic effects of an East Asian FTA, as shown in Table 3, may be underestimated.

Second, in this study, only the effects of tariff elimination are considered, which is a part of a comprehensive FTA. Although tariff elimination is important, FTA synergy effects from the elimination of non-tariff barriers, liberalization of services and investment, and the improvement of trade rules will be greater if the FTA covers a greater area. Third, we can consider problems that might arise from bilateral FTAs with ASEAN, which are in progress now. In the case of the development of an ASEAN-China FTA or an ASEAN-Japan FTA, Korea would also consider establishing an FTA with ASEAN, due to concerns about possible damages from exclusion. That is, a domino effect can be realized. When this happens, even though a CJK FTA is established, trade-related costs would increase since the rules of origin differ under each bilateral FTA.[7] In order to reduce such trade costs and maximize the synergy effects of economic integration, an East Asian FTA is necessary.

[6] McMillan (1993) shows that [the Kemp and Wan (1976) theorem can be applied to the point that] "it is always possible to add a country to an existing integration agreement in such way as to improve the welfare of the members of the expanded integration agreement." Although the authors intend to say that FTAs can contribute to multilateral trade liberalization, the theorem can be applied to explain the expansion of existing FTAs.

[7] Protective effects caused by FTA members' preferential rules of origin are called 'spaghetti bowl' effects. Bhagwati (1995) compared these negative effects of regional trading blocs on a multilateral trading system to a spaghetti bowl effect, and this concept could be also used in a regional dimension, like East Asia.

4.2. Impact on Regional Capital Accumulation

The CGE model used in this study is designed to analyze how economic policy changes affect capital accumulation. Recent FTAs include measures on investment such as investment liberalization and other improvements in the investment environment, and thus, investment is now considered a crucial element of an FTA. Because the CGE model is a static model, it cannot directly show investors' decision-making methods. However, it can indirectly estimate the impact of an FTA on regional capital accumulation, through the method in Francois, McDonald, and Nordstorm (1997).

Table 4 illustrates how FTAs affect the regional capital stock. As mentioned in the discussion on the impact on regional GDP, the capital stock of FTA member countries is expected to increase while non-member countries' capital stock will decrease. Also, the activation of capital accumulation is estimated to greatly boost the growth rate of capital stock. Moreover, the impact is expected to be greater in a CJK or East Asian FTA than bilateral FTAs.

Table 4. The Impact of FTAs in East Asia on Regional Capital Stock

(Unit: %)

FTAs in Northeast Asia								
	China-Japan FTA		China-Korea FTA		Japan-Korea FTA		CJK FTA	
	TL	TL&CA	TL	TL&CA	TL	TL&CA	TL	TL&CA
China	0.02	0.21	0.01	0.08	0.00	-0.01	0.02	0.24
Japan	0.00	0.02	0.00	-0.01	0.00	0.01	0.00	0.02
Korea	0.00	-0.05	0.02	0.23	0.01	0.16	0.03	0.36
ASEAN	0.00	-0.06	0.00	-0.03	0.00	-0.01	-0.01	-0.10
ROW	0.00	-0.01	0.00	-0.01	0.00	0.00	0.00	-0.03
FTAs in East Asia								
	ASEAN-China FTA		ASEAN-Japan FTA		ASEAN-Korea FTA		East Asian FTA	
	TL	TL&CA	TL	TL&CA	TL	TL&CA	TL	TL&CA
China	0.01	0.09	0.00	-0.02	0.00	-0.01	0.02	0.26
Japan	0.00	-0.02	0.00	0.01	0.00	-0.01	0.00	0.02
Korea	0.00	-0.04	0.00	-0.04	0.01	0.12	0.03	0.43
ASEAN	0.02	0.33	0.03	0.49	0.02	0.31	0.03	0.58
ROW	0.00	-0.02	0.00	-0.01	0.00	-0.01	0.00	-0.05

Source: Author's simulation

With regard to bilateral FTAs in Northeast Asia, from China's point of view, an FTA with Japan is preferable to an FTA with Korea in terms of capital accumulation. Meanwhile, for Korea, an FTA with China is considered more desirable than an FTA with Japan. This result is the same as the results on the impact of FTAs on regional GDP. On the other hand, for China, Korea is more desirable than ASEAN in terms of regional GDP, and ASEAN is preferable to Korea in terms of capital accumulation. Because FTAs have conflicting impact on different regions, a region-wide FTA such as an East Asian FTA would be preferable to a series of bilateral or subregional

FTAs. It is estimated that Japan will not be affected greatly by any form of FTA, but it may face deterioration in capital accumulation if excluded from FTAs.

4.3. Impact on Regional Welfare Level

In the CGE model, each region's representative agent acts to maximize his/her welfare level. When a policy is changed, the agent will calculate a change in his/her income level, which affects the scale of savings and the consumption scale of each item so that the marginal utility of consumption is identical across goods. Here, price variables are used in the decision-making process for clearing markets. The impact of East Asian regionalism on the welfare level seems to be similar to the impact on GDP. While the welfare level of representative agents in FTA member countries would improve, the welfare level of agents in non-member countries would decline. Since each region's welfare function is different, the impact of East Asian regionalism on regional welfare level is not the same as the impact on regional GDP.

Table 5. The Impact of FTAs in East Asia on Regional Welfare

(Unit: %, mil. $)

FTAs in Northeast Asia								
	China-Japan FTA		China-Korea FTA		Japan-Korea FTA		CJK FTA	
	TL	TL&CA	TL	TL&CA	TL	TL&CA	TL	TL&CA
China	0.50 (4,491)	1.02 (9,111)	0.31 (2,763)	0.52 (4,643)	-0.06 (-498)	-0.07 (-581)	0.55 (4,886)	1.15 (10,251)
Japan	0.25 (9,019)	0.28 (10,067)	-0.03 (-1,247)	-0.06 (-2,230)	0.08 (3,065)	0.10 (3,517)	0.31 (11,301)	0.33 (12,114)
Korea	-0.31 (-1,228)	-0.44 (-1,733)	1.79 (7,025)	2.42 (9,497)	0.29 (1,129)	0.73 (2,874)	1.80 (7,085)	2.77 (10,873)
ASEAN	-0.24 (-1,400)	-0.46 (-2,694)	-0.11 (-639)	-0.23 (-1,316)	-0.06 (-359)	-0.10 (-591)	-0.40 (-2,289)	-0.74 (-4,317)
ROW	-0.04 (-7,472)	-0.08 -(15,919)	-0.02 (-4,097)	-0.06 (-12,511)	-0.01 (-2,199)	-0.02 (-4,166)	-0.06 (-12,736)	-0.15 (-29,223)
FTAs in East Asia								
	ASEAN- China FTA		ASEAN-Japan FTA		ASEAN-Korea FTA		East Asian FTA	
	TL	TL&CA	TL	TL&CA	TL	TL&CA	TL	TL&CA
China	0.37 (3,274)	0.59 (5,271)	-0.15 (-1,288)	-0.19 (-1,720)	-0.06 (-555)	-0.09 (-837)	0.54 (4,814)	1.21 (10,766)
Japan	-0.07 (-2,544)	-0.10 (-3,758)	0.21 (7,623)	0.25 (8,931)	-0.07 (-2,434)	-0.08 (-3,043)	0.45 (16,560)	0.49 (17,870)
Korea	-0.18 (-716)	-0.27 (-1,074)	-0.25 (-1,000)	-0.34 (-1,341)	0.69 (2,716)	1.03 (4,057)	2.16 (8,486)	3.34 (13,146)
ASEAN	0.96 (5,540)	2.25 (13,044)	0.83 (4,819)	2.78 (16,110)	0.94 (5,442)	2.17 (12,614)	1.16 (6,726)	3.48 (20,201)
ROW	-0.02 (-4,533)	-0.07 (-14,426)	-0.04 (-7,223)	-0.06 (-12,559)	-0.01 (-2,808)	-0.04 (-7,008)	-0.11 (-23,009)	-0.25 (-50,495)

Source: Author's simulation
Note: Numbers in the parentheses represent equivalent variations in million dollars.

For example, under a China-Japan FTA, China's GDP would increase by 0.27% if trade liberalization is considered only; meanwhile, it is estimated that the welfare level will increase more extensively by 0.5%.

However, if capital accumulation effects are considered, increases in the rates of welfare levels of FTA members are expected to be smaller than the growth rates of the GDP. Under a Japan-Korea FTA, Korea's GDP is forecasted to increase by 0.92% while the welfare level is estimated to increase by 0.73% if the effects of capital accumulation are considered. Under a model considering the effects of capital accumulation, expected returns of capital are increased with the conclusion of an FTA, and the productivity of capital intensive industries improves as more capital is accumulated. The expectation for higher returns on capital leads economic agents to save, rather than to immediately spend a large portion of their increased incomes, unlike the case in which only the effects of trade liberalization are considered. When the effects of capital accumulation are not considered, a certain proportion of increased income is automatically allocated to increased consumption. In contrast, under a capital accumulation model, the size of savings is first decided according to the expected rate of return on capital, and then the rest of the increased income is consumed. Equivalence variations, changes in welfare level calculated in US dollars, are presented in the parentheses. Under a CJK FTA, Japan is expected to benefit the most (US$12.1 billion per year) followed by Korea (US$10.9 billion per year), and China (US$10.3 billion per year). That is, although Japan's expected growth rate of welfare level is relatively less than that of Korea or China, by participating in a CJK FTA, it is estimated that Japan will gain the most benefits according to the value of equivalence variations. Under an East Asian FTA, ASEAN and Japan are expected to benefit the most.

4.4. Impact on Regional Trade

The impact of East Asian regionalism on regional exports and imports is reported in Table 6 and Table 7. The estimated value is each region's total exports to the world.

In general, the exports of FTA member countries will increase, while non-members' exports will decrease. Non-members will be at a disadvantage as a result of the trade diversion. In the case of a China-Japan FTA, while the exports of China and Japan are estimated to increase by 4.64% and 1.64% respectively, Korea's exports are estimated to decrease by 0.17%. Meanwhile, non-member countries' exports may increase in certain cases, unlike the GDP and welfare levels. For example, when the three Northeast Asian countries conclude a trilateral FTA, the exports of ROW, will improve a little (0.03%) in case of trade liberalization, while it will not happen under an East Asian FTA. Also Japan's exports may increase with a China-Korea FTA and an ASEAN-Korea FTA. The phenomenon of Japan's increasing exports under Korea's FTA with other regions could be explained by Korea's high dependency on Japan for machinery and intermediate inputs.

Under a CJK FTA, Korea will record the highest growth rate in GDP and welfare levels, while China's exports will increase the most. Meanwhile, the export performances of non-members like ASEAN and ROW are anticipated to decline. Under an East Asian FTA, China is forecasted to record the highest growth rate of exports, which are expected to increase by 8.79%. Following China,

Table 6. The Impact of FTAs in East Asia on Regional Exports

(Unit: %)

	FTAs in Northeast Asia							
	China-Japan FTA		China-Korea FTA		Japan-Korea FTA		CJK FTA	
	TL	TL&CA	TL	TL&CA	TL	TL&CA	TL	TL&CA
China	4.64	5.82	2.74	3.26	-0.06	-0.09	6.11	7.51
Japan	1.64	2.03	0.03	-0.03	0.38	0.52	2.03	2.53
Korea	-0.17	-0.41	0.69	2.06	2.07	3.01	2.60	4.69
ASEAN	-0.14	-0.54	-0.03	-0.23	-0.03	-0.13	-0.19	-0.83
ROW	0.01	-0.10	0.02	-0.06	0.01	-0.03	0.03	-0.17
	FTAs in East Asia							
	ASEAN- China FTA		ASEAN-Japan FTA		ASEAN-Korea FTA		East Asian FTA	
	TL	TL&CA	TL	TL&CA	TL	TL&CA	TL	TL&CA
China	2.45	3.04	-0.15	-0.24	-0.09	-0.13	7.17	8.79
Japan	0.04	-0.05	1.01	1.39	0.01	-0.07	3.03	3.82
Korea	-0.09	-0.21	-0.15	-0.31	0.91	1.66	3.32	5.93
ASEAN	1.99	4.28	2.98	6.36	1.72	3.87	3.87	7.88
ROW	-0.01	-0.10	-0.02	-0.11	-0.02	-0.06	-0.00	-0.34

Source: Author's simulation

Table 7. The Impact of FTAs in East Asia on Regional Imports

(Unit: %)

	FTAs in Northeast Asia							
	China-Japan FTA		China-Korea FTA		Japan-Korea FTA		CJK FTA	
	TL	TL&CA	TL	TL&CA	TL	TL&CA	TL	TL&CA
China	5.79	6.25	3.34	3.54	-0.15	-0.15	7.27	7.84
Japan	3.28	3.20	-0.19	-0.19	0.92	0.89	4.08	3.98
Korea	-0.66	-0.78	3.01	3.63	2.77	3.21	5.18	6.13
ASEAN	-0.42	-0.71	-0.15	-0.31	-0.10	-0.16	-0.63	-1.09
ROW	-0.14	-0.18	-0.07	-0.11	-0.04	-0.05	-0.23	-0.30
	FTAs in East Asia							
	ASEAN- China FTA		ASEAN-Japan FTA		ASEAN-Korea FTA		East Asian FTA	
	TL	TL&CA	TL	TL&CA	TL	TL&CA	TL	TL&CA
China	3.40	3.61	-0.44	-0.45	-0.26	-0.26	8.47	9.15
Japan	-0.50	-0.40	2.23	2.32	-0.46	-0.35	5.85	5.90
Korea	-0.42	-0.48	-0.58	-0.61	2.18	2.55	6.63	7.87
ASEAN	3.31	4.89	4.22	6.61	2.72	4.23	5.24	8.06
ROW	-0.13	-0.16	-0.18	-0.16	-0.09	-0.09	-0.49	-0.56

Source: Author's simulation

ASEAN is estimated to increase its exports by 7.88%.

As trade barriers are eliminated and income levels increase, the imports of FTA member countries will grow. Contrary to the case of exports, while FTA member countries' imports increase, non-member countries' imports will decrease unanimously, because of the reduction in income.

As evident in Table 6 and Table 7, the growth rate of East Asia's global exports will only be moderately impacted by East Asian regionalism. However, the impact of East Asian regionalism on intra-regional trade could be a lot greater. It may be useful to examine the growth rates of exports between members under eight different FTAs. As an example, the impact of an East Asian FTA on East Asian trade is presented in Table 8. The table shows that the establishment of an East Asian FTA will deeply impact the intra-regional trade in East Asia.[8]

[8] Although not reported in this paper, the impact of a CJK FTA on China, Japan and Korea is analyzed to be similar to the results presented in Table 8.

Table 8. The Impact of an East Asian FTA on East Asian Intra-Regional Trade

(Unit: %, mil. $)

Exporter	China			Japan			Korea			ASEAN		
Importer	Japan	Korea	ASEAN	China	Korea	ASEAN	China	Japan	ASEAN	China	Japan	ASEAN
Agriculture	134.48	284.37	67.51	35.03	86.39	89.28	37.46	159.73	69.01	51.05	148.27	126.25
	(2,199)	(1,991)	(664)	(35)	(27)	(36)	(22)	(539)	(18)	(574)	(1,578)	(139)
Forestry	7.69	12.01	28.50	42.02	9.48	27.23	17.61	15.26	-3.11	10.15	-5.15	4.74
	(5)	(1)	(1)	(2)	(0)	(1)	(1)	(0)	(0)	(21)	(-23)	(3)
Fisheries	8.13	54.32	40.66	71.70	58.29	48.19	69.72	9.10	-4.00	-3.62	-2.66	79.06
	(30)	(24)	(6)	(18)	(14)	(4)	(5)	(28)	(-1)	(-7)	(-6)	(5)
Energy	-7.25	18.23	15.36	12.60	12.51	10.63	9.09	-6.19	6.42	-4.34	-7.07	10.11
	(-137)	(174)	(50)	(2)	(3)	(4)	(1)	(-2)	(0)	(-48)	(-479)	(260)
Food	105.74	121.24	59.26	32.95	130.74	79.17	93.79	132.27	110.04	84.41	113.56	62.02
	(2,419)	(586)	(545)	(244)	(251)	(300)	(200)	(1,308)	(138)	(1,502)	(4,261)	(382)
Textiles	25.17	37.85	40.46	68.97	29.79	34.05	58.97	20.61	49.43	33.07	16.44	34.12
	(1,052)	(530)	(732)	(2,351)	(162)	(345)	(2,794)	(156)	(743)	(442)	(163)	(90)
Clothing	60.89	52.22	84.62	143.53	41.33	87.78	74.45	58.89	37.84	38.23	67.16	61.38
	(5,813)	(530)	(831)	(831)	(36)	(69)	(879)	(506)	(180)	(81)	(1,060)	(78)
Chemicals	10.60	25.89	29.81	27.92	23.34	20.77	25.29	9.19	21.88	21.54	7.43	18.28
	(223)	(189)	(603)	(1,727)	(961)	(1,379)	(1,525)	(244)	(541)	(1,316)	(236)	(226)
Metals	6.69	22.93	14.94	33.57	28.04	24.62	14.45	7.72	19.20	13.81	8.02	16.53
	(137)	(397)	(304)	(1,900)	(927)	(1,804)	(513)	(177)	(511)	(146)	(125)	(86)
Auto, Part	8.66	78.73	-46.26	124.78	64.77	91.78	154.00	-12.08	343.99	6.14	44.33	117.54
	(12)	(162)	(-46)	(4,097)	(403)	(6,219)	(210)	(-14)	(2,081)	(8)	(100)	(21)
Otrns[1)]	1.57	58.16	25.81	74.87	21.37	65.92	43.94	-12.69	26.45	92.00	10.14	48.53
	(5)	(26)	(115)	(460)	(23)	(1,423)	(62)	(-4)	(134)	(117)	(9)	(7)
Electr[1)]	7.87	34.57	20.11	28.97	21.26	4.06	19.69	-0.42	5.83	7.18	6.70	33.18
	(403)	(348)	(894)	(3,763)	(1,119)	(834)	(833)	(-14)	(410)	(637)	(858)	(948)
Mach[1)]	5.43	34.22	23.14	36.09	27.54	12.30	37.31	-4.63	16.34	13.67	7.94	36.23
	(306)	(275)	(735)	(5,905)	(2,886)	(2,809)	(871)	(-76)	(401)	(514)	(319)	(216)
Omanf[1)]	8.70	27.54	37.47	34.94	26.04	24.89	38.68	-1.18	39.81	31.26	19.37	28.14
	(407)	(213)	(598)	(998)	(379)	(662)	(595)	(-9)	(206)	(780)	(1,049)	(312)

Source: Author's simulation

Note: 1) Otrn - Other Transportation, Electr – Electrical Products and Electronics, Mach – Machinery, Omanf – Other Manufacturing

2) Numbers in parentheses are the values of export growth in million dollars.

REFERENCES

Ahn, C. Y. 2001. "A Search of Robust East Asian Development Models after the Financial Crisis: Mutual Learning from East Asian Experiences." *Journal of Asian Economics* 12: 419-443.

Baldwin, R. E. and A. J. Venables. 1995. "Regional economic integration." In Grossman, Gene M. and Kenneth S. Rogoff eds. *Handbook of International Economics*. Amsterdam: North-Holland/Elsevier.

Bhagwati, J. 1995. "US Trade Policy: The Infatuation with Free Trade Areas." In Bhagwati, Jagdish and Anne O. Krueger eds. *The Dangerous Drift to Preferential Trade Agreements*. Washington D. C.: American Enterprise Institute Press.

_________ and A. Panagariya. 1996. "Preferential Trading Areas and Multilateralism: Strangers, Friends or Foes." In Bhagwati, Jagdish and Arvind Panagariya eds. *The Economics of Preferential Trade Agreements*. Washington D.C.: American Enterprise Institute Press.

Brown, D. K., A. V. Deardorff, and R. M. Stern. 2001. "CGE Modeling and Analysis of Multilateral and Regional Negotiating Options." In Stern, Robert M. ed. *Issues and Options for US-Japan Trade Policies*. Ann Arbor: University of Michigan Press.

Cheong, I. ed. 1999. *A New Strategy for Northeast Asian Economic Cooperation: Regional Economic Cooperation for Trade Issues*. Korea Institute for International Economic Policy (KIEP) Research Paper 99-02. Seoul: KIEP. (in Korean)

_________. 2001. *The Economic Effects of a Korea-Japan FTA and Policy Implications*. KIEP Research Paper 01-04. Seoul: KIEP. (in Korean)

_________. 2002. *East Asian Economic Integration: Recent Development of FTAs and Policy Implications*. Seoul: KIEP.

Choi, Ch. 1996. "Review of East Asian Economic Blocs." *Economic Analysis*, Vol. 2(3). Seoul: Bank of Korea.

Dimaranan, B. V. and R. A. McDougall. 2002. *Global Trade, Assistance, and Production: The GTAP 5 Data Base*. Center for Global Trade Analysis. Purdue University.

Dutta, M. 2002. "Asian Economic Community: Intra-Community Macro-and-Micro Economic Parameters." Presented at the annual meetings of American Economic Association in Atlanta, GA. January 6.

Federation of Korean Industries (FKI). 2001. "Korea Industries' Perception of an FTA." Seoul: FKI.

Francois, Joseph F., Bradley McDonald, and Hakan Nordstrom. 1997. "Capital Accumulation in Applied Trade Models." In Francois, Joseph F. and Kenneth A. Reinert eds. *Applied Methods for Trade Policy Analysis - A Handbook*. London: Cambridge University Press.

Grossman, G. M. and E. Helpman. 1995. "Technology and Trade." Centre for Economic Policy Research Discussion Paper No. 1134.

Igawa, K. and B. Kim. 2001. "A Note on Possibilities about Japan-Korea Free Trade Area: A Theoretical and Strategic Approach." Kobe, Japan: Kobe University. *Unpublished Manuscript*.

Kemp, M. C. and H. Y. Wan. 1976. "An Elementary Proposition Concerning the Formation of Customs Unions." *Journal of International Economics* 6: 95-97.

Kim, H. 2002. "Has Trade Intensity in ASEAN+3 Really Increased? - Evidence from a Gravity Analysis." KIEP Working Paper 02-12. Seoul: KIEP.

Kreinin, M. E. and M. G. Plummer. 1994. "'Natural' Economic Blocs: An Alternative Formulation." *The International Trade Journal*. Vol. 8 no. 2. pp. 193-205.

________. 2000. "Effects of Economic Integration in Industrial Countries on ASEAN and the Asian NIEs." In Kreinin, M. and M. G. Plummer eds. *Economic Integration and Asia*. Cheltenham, UK: Edward Elgar.

Lee, C. and S. Park. 2002. "Formation of Regional Trading Blocs in East Asia and the Roles of Japan and the U.S." KIEP Working Paper 02-13. Seoul: KIEP.

Levine, R. and D. Renelt. 1992. "A sensitivity analysis of cross-country growth regressions." *The American Economic Review*. Vol. 82(4). 942-963.

Martin, W. P., A. Petri, and K. Yanagishima. 1994. "Charting the Pacific: an Empirical Assessment of Integration Initiatives." *The International Trade Journal*. Vol. 4 no. 4. pp. 447-482.

McMillan, J. 1993. "Does Regional Integration Foster Open Trade?" In Anderson, Kym and Richard Blackhurst eds. *Regional Integration and the Global Trading System*. London: Harvestor Wheatsheaf.

Oh, W. T. and I. Cheong. 1997. "Evaluation of Economic Effects of a Free Trade Area in the East Asia." *Kukje Kyungje Yongu*. Vol. 3(3): 65-90. (in Korean)

Panagariya, A. 1994. "East Asia and the New Regionalism in World Trade." *World Economy*, Vol. 17.

Thorpe, M. and Z. Zhang. 2000. "An Assessment of East Asia's Intra-industry Trade and Adjustment." Presented at the 7th Convention of the East Asian Economic Association. Singapore. November 17-18.

Young, S. 1993. "Globalism and Regionalism: Complements or Competitors?" In Bergsten, C. Fred and Mark Noland eds. *Pacific Dynamism and the International Economic System*. Washington D.C.: IIE.

CHAPTER 9

ASIAN REGIONALISM: PROMISES AND PITFALLS

RICHARD E. BALDWIN

1. INTRODUCTION

In this paper, I wish to provide an outsider's perspective on Asian regionalism. My basic point is that I believe that regionalism has not really started in East Asia, but it may, provided at least one major free trade agreement (FTA) gets signed with Japan – a Korea-Japan being perhaps the most likely at the moment.

There is a danger that this bilateralism might not take an optimal form. I make two suggestions on how some of the negative aspects of bilateralism might be mitigated. I close by arguing that Asian regionalism is likely to be good for trade and good for the world trading system. I believe that trade liberalisation begets trade liberalisation. The important thing is to get the liberalisation ball rolling and here FTAs can help.

2. ASIAN REGIONALISM: TALK VS ACTION

Until quite recently, East Asia was one of the few regions in the world where regional trade agreements were rare. This is changing rapidly. The ASEAN FTA, AFTA, the Japan-Singapore accord and recent initiatives between China and ASEAN are just some of the highlights. Yet despite all the headlines, trade patterns within East Asia have not yet been substantially altered by preferential agreements.

Table 1, for instance, shows that intra ASEAN trade actually fell between 1995 and 2000. Trade throughout the region has been depressed, as the rest of column shows, but the drop in intra-ASEAN trade is not notably less than the drop in ASEAN's imports from other regions. For example ASEAN exports to Japan fell by no more than intra-ASEAN trade despite the absence of any ASEAN-Japan preferential liberalization.

How is it possible that AFTA is proceeding but not really affecting trade patterns? A conclusive answer would require a very detailed examination of bilateral trade flows, but at a broad level, two factors seem responsible. The first concerns the level of intra-ASEAN trade. Leaving aside the highly unusual cases of Singapore's trade (dominated by entrepôt shipments) and Brunei's trade (dominated by oil), ASEAN really does not yet trade very much with each other. The second concerns

C. Y. Ahn et al (eds.), East Asian Economic Regionalism, 157-174.

the nature of the preferential liberalization. AFTA was announced to the WTO under the so-called enabling clause, which would have more accurately been called the disabling clause since it suspends most of the WTO disciplines. As a consequence, ASEAN member countries are not required to obey the standard Article 24 dictates that tariffs should go to zero on substantially all trade within a reasonable period of time. Each AFTA chooses its own preferential tariff on every product line. This matters in two ways. First, since ASEAN does not really trade much, it is possible for a good deal of liberalization to occur without it affecting intra-ASEAN trade. Indeed, standard political economy logic would suggest that the items that are liberalized preferentially are items in which there is little trade (this allows the government to announce a liberalization without facing the anger of import competing firms). Second, the same sort of logic suggests that the size of preferential tariff cuts is smallest on products where much trade could arise.

Table 1. Intra-ASEAN Trade Growth in context, 1995 to 2000

From \ to	ASEAN	Korea + China + HK	Japan	US
ASEAN	-22%	-3%	-23%	14%
Korea + China + HK	-17%	-8%	-13%	75%
Japan	-107%	-67%	0%	-43%
ANZ	-10%	-2%	-11%	3%
US	-28%	-37%	-55%	0%

Source: TRAINS database, UNCTAD

In short, East Asian regionalism has not really started yet. The world is filled with hundreds of preferential trade agreements but only a handful has actually liberalizes enough trade to make a difference. Presidents and Prime Ministers throughout the developing world find the thought of preferential trade among fellow developing nations to be politically attractive. However, once the proclamations are signed, day-to-day special interest politics prevents effective liberalization. And since Article 24 mandates do not apply, there is really no cause for complaints.

I do think, however, that East Asian regionalism could get started rather soon.

3. DOMINO THEORY: ASIAN VERSION

I would like to start with a prediction. If Korea and Japan do manage to conclude a free trade agreement, it seems likely that many more real and effective FTAs in Asia will follow. There are two good reasons for believing this, one historical and one logical.

3.1. The Historical Case

Let me begin with historical analogies. During the wave of regionalism that occurred since the early 1980s, a pattern has emerged. I call this the domino effect since it notes how falling trade barriers in one set of countries tends to trigger a fall in the trade barriers of other countries.

3.1.1. Domino effect: The Americas

One domino effect began in the Western Hemisphere when the US and Mexico announced their intentions of forming a free trade area in 1990. Their motives were mainly geopolitical (the desire to foster stability in Mexico by boosting growth and by locking in pro-market reforms) and philosophical (the Bush and Salinas administrations were both pro-free traders). The entire Mexican economy is smaller than that of the Los Angeles basin, while European, and Japanese markets account for more than half the world's economic activity. It thus seems highly unlikely that the US views this politically exacting, yet commercially unimportant, initiative as substituting in anyway for global trade liberalization.

Announcement of the US-Mexico Free Trade Agreement (FTA) destroyed the political economy status quo in the Americas, thereby touching off a domino effect. Other North, Central and South American nations, which are heavily dependent on the US market, faced what appeared to be a fait accompli. Mexico-based producers would gain preferential access to the US market. This could be expected to harm the profits and market shares of firms based in third countries. Moreover, the preferential access to the US could be expected to divert foreign investment to Mexico at the expense of third countries. Canada, which depends very heavily on the US market, decided that it had to be at the negotiating table and the North American Free Trade Agreement was born. This choice was made despite continuing domestic opposition to its first regional liberalization – the US-Canada FTA. Other countries in the Hemisphere, such as Chile, Brazil, Argentina, Uruguay and Paraguay, formally or informally approached the US to begin bilateral FTA talks. Moreover, interest in President Bush's Enterprise for the Americas Initiative boomed in 1991 with 26 countries signing so-called Framework Agreements (these require the countries to make unilateral concessions on trade and investment to the US in exchange for the promise of closer US relations leading eventually to an FTA).

The same sort of dynamic can be used to explain the emergence and enlargement of the Mercosur. As Brazil and Argentina started to liberalize bilaterally, other nations in the region – Paraguay, Chile, Bolivia, for example – asked to join the club. And as the club grew in size, it became even more important to join.

3.1.2. Domino effect: Europe

In Europe, the political leaders of the EC-12 (as it was known at the time) decided in 1985 to create a Single Market as a means of renewing their drive towards monetary and political unity in Europe. Again, the primary motives were geopolitical and philosophical, rather than commercial. Regardless of its raison d'etre, the EC 1992 project posed a threat to non-EC exporters who depended heavily on the EC market. In particular cheaper and easier intra-EC trade was expected to reduce the relative competitiveness of non-EC firms, thereby harming their sales and profits. Non-EC exporters throughout the region recognized the threat and called for their governments to counter their losses. Moreover, since non-EC firms could be expected to react by shifting manufacturing to the EC, many non-EC industrial labor unions echoed the call for action. The EFTA governments' original solution, the European Economic Area arrangement, was quickly eclipsed by a drive for full membership. In 1989 and 1991 respectively, Austria and Sweden decided to join. And now the domino effect began to operate.

The pending EC enlargement made the potential loss of competitiveness even more threatening. That is, the members of the European Free Trade Association (EFTA) – who were heavily dependent on the EC-12 market – individually faced the prospect of losing out in the EC-12 markets and in the markets of those EFTAs acceding to the EC. This enlargement effect was especially important for Finland and Norway due to their heavy dependence on the Swedish market. Since the combined EC and EFTA markets on average account for three-quarters of EFTA exports, the pressure on the holdouts mounted. Finland, Norway and Switzerland requested EC membership in 1992. (The Icelandic government, which is giving much thought to joining, has so far been deterred by the EC's common fishery policy.) Note that accession would force all these countries to liberalize radically their agriculture and services markets as well as adopting a zero-for-zero reduction of remaining EC-EFTA trade barriers. The domino effect caused by the Single Market Program continues. Turkey, Cyprus, some Magreb countries and virtually all of the Central and East European countries have expressed interest in joining.

3.1.3. The Asian analogy

The major difference in Asia is that until very recently, the big market in the region – Japan – avoided all preferential arrangements. This meant that there was never any initial spark to set off the regionalism wildfire in Asia. This, of course, has now changed. It seems perfectly natural to assume that the spreading regionalism that took hold in Europe, North America and South America would also catch on in Asia.

Let me turn now to a logical argument supporting my assertion that regionalism will spread rapidly in Asia if Korea and Japan sign an FTA.

3.2. The Political Economy Logic of Spreading Regionalism

The logic is based on what I call the 'domino theory of regionalism'. I developed this theory about 10 years ago to account for spreading regionalism in Europe (Baldwin 1993), and I have applied it to the North American case (Baldwin 1997). The application to Asia is somewhat different, so I shall here modify the underlying logic – the political economy implications of trade diversion – to fit the circumstances in Asia.

We start with a puzzle. Let us suppose that the level of a nation's import protection is determined by the balancing of pro-trade and anti-trade forces within each nation. The resulting protection is the level that the government finds optimal, after balancing all the demands it faces. If this is true, and I think it is, then trade liberalization is a bit of a puzzle. Why should a government find it politically optimal to remove barriers that previously it found optimal to maintain? The point of asking this question is to stress the necessity of focusing on what has *changed* in the political arena. The domino theory is just one way of explaining how the signing of one FTA can change the arrangement of political forces in *other* nations.

A shock to a bilateral trade relationship – the Korea-Japan FTA in this case – can trigger requests for further FTAs from countries whose governments were previously happy without FTAs. The basic logic is simple. The stance of a country's government concerning an FTA is the result of a political equilibrium that balances anti-FTA and pro-FTA forces. (Typically the pro-FTA group is made up of exporters who would like better market access; the anti-FTA group is made up of import competing firms and workers employed by them.) Since closer integration between Korea and Japan is detrimental to the profits of firms based in other nations – this being due mainly to the preferences that the FTA grants Korean firms in the Japanese market – the FTA signing stimulates exporters in *other* Asian nations to engage in greater pro-FTA political activity. Now if one of the other nations' governments was previously close to indifferent, politically speaking, to signing an FTA with Japan then the extra political activity of their exporters may tilt the balance, leading the country to sign an FTA. This can be thought of as one domino knocking down the next one (think of the first FTA signing as someone pushing over the first domino, and the second FTA as the second domino falling).

To be a bit more explicit, if Korea signs an FTA with Japan, then other Asian nations are also likely to want an FTA with Japan. After all, the Korea-Japan FTA gives Korean firms an advantage in the big Japanese market and this, quite directly, puts non-Korean firms at a disadvantage in the Japanese market. The only way to counter this new disadvantage is to push for an FTA with Japan.

The story does not stop here, however.

After the second FTA is signed, firms based in two Asian nations have preferential access to Japan. And this, in turn, puts firms based in non-FTA nations at *an even greater* disadvantage than when faced with only the Korea-Japan FTA, since a wider range of their competitors enjoys preferential access. As a result, non-FTA firms will have to cut their prices and accept smaller shares of the Japanese market as a result of the second FTA. In the political sphere this new disadvantage will result in greater political pressure – pressure on their own governments to negotiate an FTA with Japan – from the exporters who have lost. If the government of a third nation was previously close to indifferent to signing, this extra pressure may tilt the balance in favour of an FTA. A third FTA gets signed with Japan. And the cycle repeats.

The basic idea is that costs of *not* having an FTA with Japan rise as more of your competitors have them. Thus the political pressure that non-FTA governments face from their exporter is likely to rise as more and more FTAs are signed. This process only stops if everyone who really depends upon the Japanese market is in, or if the non-FTA governments have very strong non-economic reasons for staying away from FTAs.

Notice that this Asian-dominos story is much closer to the North American story that it is to the European story since neither the Americas nor Asia has an institution like the European Union. Preferential trade agreements in America are bilateral – even NAFTA is just a collection of 3 bilateral FTAs (US-Canada, US-Mexico and Mexico-Canada). As a consequence, the automatic market-size effect does not kick in the North American case. Nor will it in the Asian case – at least if things evolve as I think they will, namely in a hub-and-spoke manner.

4. POSSIBLE TRIGGERS

Above I suggested that a Japan-Korea FTA would be a likely trigger. In this section, I consider the logic of what constitutes a trigger and compare the Japan-Korea trigger with others.

4.1. Some Important Facts

The chain reaction that knocks down a row of dominos can be easily triggers. However, the initial push must be large enough. When it comes to the domino theory of regionalism, size depends upon market size and various nations' dependence of other markets. The first order of business is thus to review the facts on market sizes in East Asia.

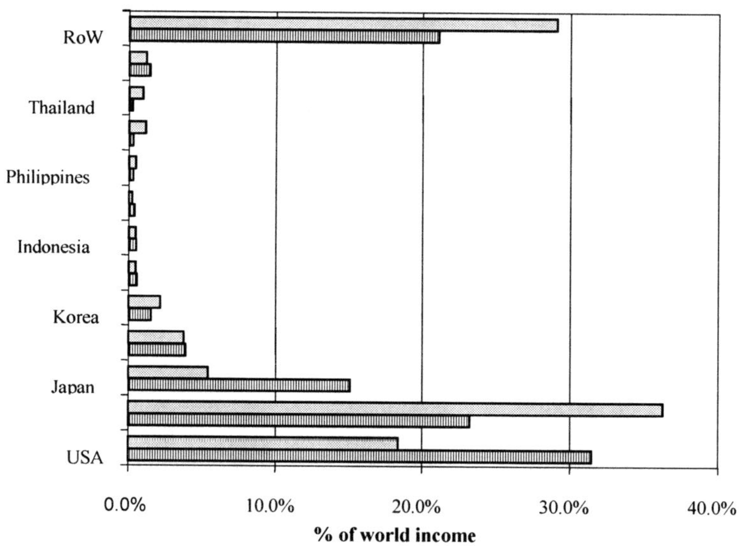

Notes: Real GDP is measured in 2000 USD, not adjusted for domestic price levels.
Source: GDP = World Bank World Development Indicators, adjusted to 2000 base and estimated values developed by the Economic Research Service, Imports from International Trade Statistics, WTO 2002.

Figure 1. Size of Markets

The world of trade politics is dominated by market size because exporters want their governments to get them good access to big markets. One simple measure of potential market size is income. As we can see from the Figure1, the ASEANs have very small markets. Even taken together, their income is about the same size as Korea's income. By comparison, Japan's income is almost 9 times bigger, and China's is more than twice. The figure also shows a more direct of what might be called market access power, namely each nation's total imports as a share of world imports. Here we see that the Asians tend to have a large share of imports than they do of income (with the notable exception of Japan). However, even by this measure Asian markets – apart from Japan, China and Korea – are tiny by world standards.

4.1.1. Mercantilist matrices

The heart of the domino-theory logic is a sort of political economy jealousy. If a nation's exporters are harmed by an FTA involving one of its important trade partners, they tend to react by pushing their government to join the FTA. The next order of business is therefore to establish which markets that various East Asia nations care about.

Bilateral trade flows depend upon much more than raw market size. Distance, in particular, has an enormous role in determining a nation's 'natural' trade pattern, i.e. the pattern that would emerge without manmade trade barriers. The role of distance can be quite clearly seen in the direction of trade matrix shown graphically in Figure2.

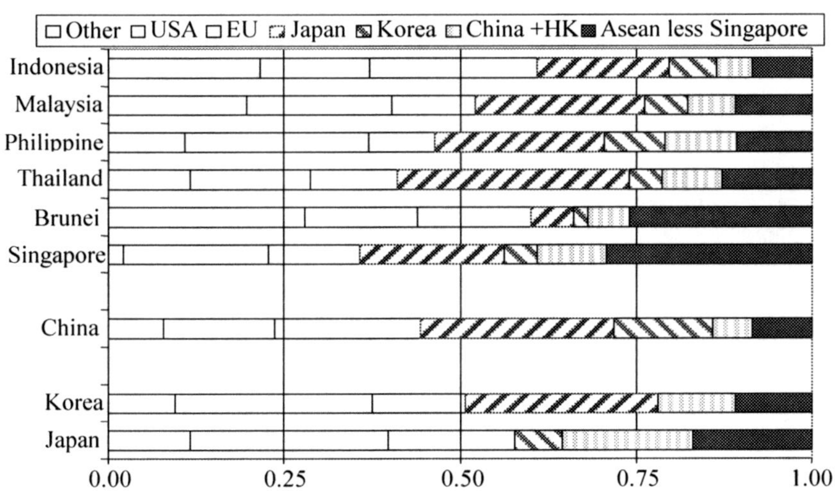

Figure 2. Direction of Exports

The importance of the "trigger logic" lies in the fact that FTAs among many of the listed nations just would not affect enough trade to make a difference to exporters. The first point to note is the low level of dependency of ASEANs on intra-ASEAN trade. Except for Singapore and Brunei – whose trade is quite particular (Singapore being an entrepôt centre and Brunei an oil exporter) – the ASEANs send over 80% of the exports to non-ASEAN nations. The situation is quite different, if one takes the ASEAN+3 grouping as a single export market. Most of the ASEANs send between 40% and 50% of the exports to these markets. The dominance of Japan in the ASEAN+3 market is also plain.

There are many other interesting aspects to be found in this diagram. First, consider the impact of a China+HK FTA with ASEAN (excluding Singapore since its imports will remain duty free to all in any case). Again ignoring Singapore and Brunei, none of the ASEAN countries depends excessively on this grouping. Consequently, any such initiative is likely to be implemented in a lackluster fashion and thus is likely to have little effect on trade patterns. Taking 25% as an arbitrary limit, we see that only Japan cares much about this grouping. Combining this with the fact that a China+HK+ASEAN FTA is unlikely to lead to very marked discrimination, I concluded that such a grouping is unlikely to trigger a domino effect in East Asia.

A more precise way of quantifying such reasoning is to calculate what I call "exclusion indices."

4.2. Exclusion Indices

Exclusion, or the threat of exclusion, is the key to the logic driving the domino effect. This directs us to investigate how much various nations would care about being excluded from various trade blocs. The answers are shown in Table 2. Specifically, for the country listed in each row, the figures show the percentage of that nation's exports that go to the markets indicated in the columns.

4.2.1. AFTA cannot be the trigger

The tables make is clear that the ASEAN free trade area by itself is not likely to trigger a domino effect, even if it is fully implemented. As inspection of the first column of Table 2 reveals, none of the Asian nations listed are heavily dependent on the ASEAN market (we exclude Singapore import data given its small economic size and role as a transhipment centre). As before, Brunei and Singapore are exceptions, but it is important to note that from the perspective of the domino-theory logic these relatively high dependency ratios are not important. Singapore has long applied a policy of unilateral free trade, so its attitude towards regional trade blocs cannot matter (it does not contribute to the discriminatory effects of a trade bloc when it joins since it has no barriers on third parties).Brunei's trade, which is dominated by oil, is not typically highly susceptible to preferential liberalisation initiatives. The key point here is that AFTA by itself is not a big "threat" to exporters based in other nations.

Table 2. Exclusion Indices for Various Trade Blocs, Focus on ASEAN

	ASEAN ex. Singapore	China + ASEAN ex. Singapore	Korea + ASEAN ex. Singapore	Japan + ASEAN ex. Singapore	China + Japan + Korea + ASEAN ex. Singapore
Indonesia	9%	14%	15%	27%	39%
Malaysia	11%	18%	17%	35%	48%
Philippines	11%	21%	19%	35%	54%
Thailand	13%	21%	18%	46%	59%
Singapore	29%	39%	34%	50%	64%
Brunei	26%	32%	28%	32%	40%
China	9%	14%	23%	36%	56%
Japan	17%	36%	24%	17%	42%
Korea	11%	22%	11%	38%	49%

Source: TRAINS database, exports in 2000.

Table 3. Exclusion Indices for Various Trade Blocs, Focus on Japan, Korea and China

	Korea +China FTA	Japan-Korea FTA	China + Japan FTA	China + Japan + Korea FTA	China + Japan + Korea + ASEAN ex. Singapore
Indonesia	12%	26%	24%	31%	39%
Malaysia	13%	30%	31%	37%	48%
Philippines	19%	33%	34%	43%	54%
Thailand	13%	38%	41%	46%	59%
Singapore	15%	25%	30%	35%	64%
Brunei	8%	8%	12%	14%	40%
China	20%	41%	33%	47%	56%
Japan	25%	7%	19%	25%	42%
Korea	11%	27%	38%	38%	49%

As far as the ASEAN is concerned, the result is little changed by adding either Korea or China to AFTA. In both cases, the dependence of the big ASEAN (Indonesia, Malaysia, Philippines and Thailand) ranges from 10% to 20%. For Japan, the exclusion index is 36% and this suggests that Japanese exporters would indeed care about such an FTA if it actually did lead to substantial trade diversion. I note, however, that the sort of goods that Japan exports to these markets are probably not very good substitutes for goods produced in China and AFTA, or at least not yet. The importance of this remark is that even a well-implemented China-AFTA FTA would have limited impact on Japanese exports to the region since the goods that would be preferentially liberalized are not highly competitive with Japanese exports.

4.2.2. *A single "Northeast" FTA could be a trigger*

The picture is quite different when considering any bilateral agreement between Japan and either of the other Big-3 (Japan, China and Korea). Take, for example, a Korea-Japan FTA. As the second column in shows, such an arrangement would threaten to harm exporters based in China and the all of ASEAN with a loss of competitiveness (via trade diversion) in the Korean and Japanese markets. Particularly important is the fact that China sells about 40% of its exports to those two markets, so exclusion, or the threat of exclusion, would generate a great deal of political pressure within China for joining. Of course, if China joined, thus forming a Northeast Asia FTA, the gravitational force would be greatly amplified. Column 4 depicts the consequences. A preferential arrangement among the Northeast-3, would threaten exports between 35% and 45% of the big ASEANs' exports. To avoid this, exporters based in these nations would push their governments to join.

A Japan-China deal is also likely to trigger a domino effect. The combined markets of Japan and China account for almost 40% of Korea's exports, so any loss of competitiveness in these markets would yield substantial domestic pressure on the Korean government to redress the discrimination by negotiating membership in the arrangement. Again, the result would be a Northeast-3 trade bloc, which would, as before, generate irresistible forces for inclusion.

The remaining combination, a Korea-China trade deal, might not lead to a Northeast-3. As column 1 shows, the big ASEAN are not very dependent on the joint Korea-China market.

4.2.3. *Caveats*

It is worth pointing out that there is a big difference between signing an FTA and implementing it. As Section 2 argued, free trade arrangements between developing nations rarelyend up freeing trade. If tr ade is not actually liberalized, then such arrangements will not generate a gravitational pull on third nations. Here is seems worth pointing out that the ongoing China-ASEAN liberalization appears incapable of triggering a domino effect given the slow and piecewise nature of the promised liberalisation.

5. PROMISE AND PITFALLS

I turn next to considering the implications of East Asian regionalism should it really get started.

5.1. *Pro Multilateral Regionalism*

Is Asian regionalism good for Asia and the rest of the world?

I would argue that FTAs in Asian are likely to act as a powerful pro-liberalization force. Not only will they directly lower trade barriers, but they will also change the array of political forces within Asian nations in a way that will facilitate multilateral liberalization. To explain this, allow me a slight deviation.

A few years ago, the World Bank held a conference on regionalism. The most memorable moment was an exchange between Larry Summers – who was head of the World Bank research division at the time – and Nobel-to-be Jagdish Bhagwati. Larry Summers embraced regionalism: "I like all the 'isms', multilateralism, regionalism and unilateralism." Jagdish Bhagwati stood up and railed against regionalism, claiming it to be an important threat to the world trading system (please refer to his book with Anne Krueger, *The Dangerous Drift to Preferential Trade Agreement*).

I tend to side with Summers. To illustrate my approach, consider what I have dubbed as the 'juggernaut theory of trade liberalization' (Baldwin 1994, Baldwin and Baldwin 1996), taking the example of how WTO rounds started a liberalization-dynamic in industrialized nations. Announcement of a reciprocal trade talk, like the Doha Round, multiples the ranks of pro-trade forces by making exporters - normally indifferent to domestic protection - opponents of domestic import barriers. The reason is simply that the principle of reciprocity requires them to fight protection at home, if they are to win better market access abroad. The same goes on in other nations, so the resulting political equilibrium involves liberalized domestic and foreign markets. While the liberalizations are phased in, export interests get stronger as they expand output and employment. Import-competitors get weaker as they scale back or shutdown. A few years down the road, another WTO Round is launched and the cycle is repeated. This time with lower initial import barriers and relatively stronger pro-trade forces.

Now let us apply the juggernaut logic to Asian regionalism. An FTA that is effectively implemented produces some trade liberalization and this tends to expand the ranks and prosperity of exporters while thinning and weakening the ranks of import competing firms. What this means is that after an FTA, the nation's political line-up should be less opposed to any type of further liberalization – including multilateral liberalization – than it was before the FTA.

Seen from this perspective, FTAs that involve Japan may be an excellent way of promoting liberalization in developing nations. The point is that most Asian nations, but not Japan, were exempted from the WTO-GATT-Round-dynamo that has been operating for 50 years (due to 'special and differential' treatment, developing-country exporters were not required to face-down protectionists in their own countries as a condition for winning expanded market access overseas). It is hardly surprising that WTO-GATT Rounds had such little impact on Asian import barriers. This is where North-South FTAs come in.

If these FTAs require all members to bring their tariffs to zero on substantially all trade, then all nations will, indirectly, face world prices. Since Japanese industrial tariffs are negligible (except in a few small sectors), Japan's FTA partners would indirectly face world prices, even though they maintain barriers against other exporters. Inefficient, anti-liberalization industries in the FTA nations are thus likely to shrink. By direct (market access) or indirect (general equilibrium) means, such FTAs will also boost the sales and power of southern export interests. All this should make Asian nations less resistant to further liberalization in multilateral talks.

6. POSSIBLE PITFALLS

Watching against creating new anti-trade constituencies

At first glance, this seems to support Larry Summers' argument that all the trade liberalization 'laterals' (uni-, bi-, pluri- and multi-) are good. This is largely true, however there are exceptions. For example, the EU's Common Agriculture Policy (which arose from Europe's regional liberalization of the food trade) created a powerful anti-liberalization force. A similar story has occurred in Latin American in the car industry. Regionalism has created a trans-national lobby against liberalization of the car sector.

Broad coverage is good, consistent coverage bad

One way to avoid such problems is to include all or most industrial sectors in the FTA. Moreover, if sectors are excluded then it is better to have them excluded on a nation-by-nation basis, rather than consistently (e.g. excluding cars from all Asian FTAs would be foster a pan-Asian lobby against any multilateral liberalization of auto trade).

Beware of Hub-and-Spoke Bilateralism

As a general operating principle, more trade liberalization is better than less. Asians and the rest of the world should welcome Asian regionalism, if the alternative is the status quo. Here, however, I would like to point out that the particular form of preferential liberalization that is likely to emerge from the domino-logic has some drawbacks when compared to other forms.

I shall begin by explaining why I believe that a 'hub-and-spoke' arrangement is the most likely outcome in Asia. (A 'hub' is the center of a bicycle wheel and 'spokes' are the wires attaching the tire to the hub).

Doing so, however, requires a bit of background. From a political perspective, exports are good and imports are bad. A more subtle expression of this idea is the trade is good because trade creates jobs. No matter how it is expressed, this idea is nonsense from the medium- or long-run economic perspective. Be that as it may, the important fact is that this mistaken reasoning points governments in the right direction. It leads them to conduct trade negotiations based on an exchange of market access. Specifically, since exports are good and imports bad, if country A wants better access to country's B's markets, then country A is expected to 'pay' for this market access by opening its own market to B's exports.

Usually, the market opening that result from this mistaken reasoning is good for all nations involved. A drawback of this mechanism, however, is that may create a sort of law of the jungle. That is, with market access as the currency of exchange, big countries are rich and small countries are poor. The rules of the GATT correct this imbalance with the principle of Most Favoured Nations (MFN) treatment. However when it comes to negotiating regional trade arrangements, MFN does not apply, so the law of the jungle may prevail.

Political economy forces created by an application of this law of the jungle support hub-and-spoke bilateralism. Let me illustrate with an example of European regionalism in the 1990s. Take a country like the Czech Republic. On the pro-liberalization side, Czech exporters had a large interest in the EU market, but only a minor interest in the market of, say, Estonia. On the anti-liberalization side, Czech import-competing industries dislike imports whether they come from the EU, Estonia or elsewhere. Now consider what the line-up of political forces looked like inside the Czech Republic in the early 1990s. Czech exporters are willing to fight quite hard for market opening with the big EU market. They are willing to fight much less hard for market opening with Estonia. In other words, there are strong political forces backing market opening with the "hub" but very little support for market opening with other "spokes." Since Czech protectionists simply want to reduce import competition from any source, the protectionists are likely to win when it comes to blocking spoke-spoke liberalization, though they lose when it comes to hub-spoke liberalization.

What all this goes to say is that if Asian regionalism gets rolling, it is likely that a string of FTAs will be signed between Japan and other Asian nations. In other words, it would result in a 'hub-and-spoke' trade arrangement with Japan as the hub and the other partners as the spokes. The point being that many Asian nations rely fairly heavily on the Japanese market, but other trade flows in Asia are more modest. Note that this sort of arrangement is fairly common in the world – there is one around the European Union and one around the US, but such arrangements tend to marginalize the spoke economies. Let me explain.

Marginalizing Effects of Hub-and-Spoke Bilateralism

The marginalizing tendencies of hub-and-spoke FTAs can be illustrated with a numerical example. Figure 3 shows a hypothetical example, which intentionally puts to the side several important issues. Imagine there are three locations being considered as the site for a new manufacturing facility, Japan and two other Asian sites, one in Korea and one in Malaysia. For simplicity, assume the division of sales among markets is fixed irrespective of costs, with 75% sold in Japan and 12.5% sold in Korea and Malaysia. (This simplification lets us divorce cost considerations from demand considerations.) Imagine the unit production costs would be 10 if the plant is located in Japan, 8 if the plant is located in Korea or Malaysia and 15 if three separate plants are built. Economies of scale explain the high cost of separating production; wages explain why the Japanese location means higher production costs.

To start that analysis, suppose initially there are no FTAs, and unit trade costs amount to 6 for all three trade flows (i.e. it costs 6 to ship a unit between any two nations). Internal trade costs are assumed to be zero. The simplified problem facing the potential manufacturer is to choose the location with the lowest costs. Without FTAs, the cost minimizing location for the plant is Japan. The average cost in Korea or Malaysia is 13.25 -- 8 for production plus an average trade cost of (3/4)*6 plus (1/8)*0 plus (1/8)*6. This surpasses the costs of producing in Japan (this equals

11.5) since the high unit production cost in Japan is more than offset by the better market access (i.e. lower average trade cost).

Envision the impact of hub-and-spoke bilateralism on this outcome. Presume Japan-Korea and Japan-Malaysia FTAs take effect cutting the unit cost for bilateral trade to 3. Korea-Malaysia trade costs remain at 6. Arithmetic shows that the average unit cost of locating the plant in the Japan is still lower (10.75) than locating in Korea or Malaysia (11). Although the FTAs lower trade costs bilaterally, trade costs within Japan is lower yet, so there is still some market size effect favoring the Japanese location. In short, location in the hub, Japan in this case, confers preferential access to *all three* markets, not just two.

The morale of this simple arithmetic example is that a hub-and-spoke system of trade arrangement tends to favor location of industrial firms in the hub.

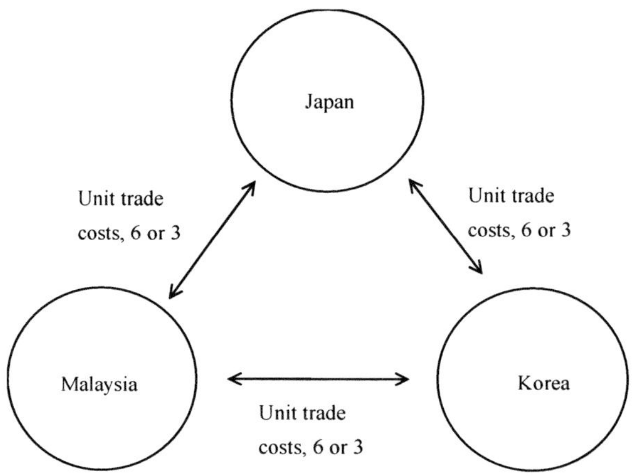

Figure 3. Hub-and-spoke bilateralism: a numerical example

Lastly, consider the impact of turning the hub-and-spoke FTAs into a free trade zone by implementation of a Korea-Malaysia FTA. Here we see that the total unit costs of locating in Korea or Malaysia are now lower (10.625) than locating in Japan (10.75). Although location in the EU implies zero trade costs for 75% of the manufacturer's sales, the lower East European production cost finally become the dominant issue.

Of course, this simple illustration is not general, and we do not mean to say the filling in the gaps between "spokes" will lead to a tidal wave of foreign investment into Korea and Malaysia. Nevertheless, the basic message is clear. Hub-and-spoke FTAs tend to marginalize the "spoke" economies, since factories in the "spokes" have artificially lower market access than factories in the hub. Consequently, hub and spoke FTAs render an artificial deterrent to investment in the outer economies. Filling in the gaps with spoke-spoke FTAs removes this policy-induced investment deterrent.

Another way of saying this is that signing bilateral trade deals with the hub, without signing deals with the spokes, is self-inflicted peripherality. They make small economies smaller than they need be.

Hysteresis in Location

A key lesson of the "new" economic geography (Fujita, Krugman and Venables 1999) is that the location of economic activity is marked by multiple equilibria. That is to say, there is not a unique constellation of economic concentrations towards which Asia is inevitably heading. There is true uncertainty about what the economic geography of Asia will look like in 50 years. Moreover, once a particular location gets a head start, it may be extremely difficult for other regions to catch up. The import of all this is that the temporary investment deterring effects of the current hub-and-spoke system may have consequences that last far beyond the termination of that system. In other words, bad policies - even when they are only temporary - may have very long-lived harmful consequences.

The importance of all this should be clear. Since hub-and-spoke bilateralism favors location in the 'hub', five or ten years of hub-and-spoke bilateralism will give Japanese locations a head start on other Asian locations. Thus, more new industry may end up in Japan than would be the case with a free trade area (i.e. FTAs among spokes as well). Given the logic of economic geography, circular causality will continue to favor regions that get a head start. The effect of a bad policy may be felt long after the policy is reversed.

7. SOME FACILITATING TACTICS

Asymmetric Liberalization Paths

Broadly speaking, small nations tend to gain more (as a percent of their GDP) from trade liberalization than to big nations. The reason is simply that gains from trade stem from an expansion of opportunities. Opportunities to arrange national production more efficiently and opportunities for national residents to arrange their consumption more efficiently. When a small nation opens to trade, it typically finds its opportunity set massively widened while the situation for a big country is less dramatic.

There is another size-linked asymmetry that is also important. When a small nation and a large nation integrate, there is a tendency for industry to migrate to the initially larger country. In trade theory this is the famous "home market effect" emphasized by Krugman (1980). The mechanism is quite similar to the one illustrated with my little numerical example on hub-and-spoke trade arrangements. The basic idea is that as trade becomes freer, it becomes more important, not less, to be located in the big market. This effect has been documented empirically by, for example, Davis and Weinstein (2002).

These effects might be taken as explaining or justifying the fact that small nations often fear that trade liberalization with larger, richer nations will erode their industrial bases. In practice, these concerns are recognized in free trade agreements and multilateral trade liberalizations since small nations are explicitly or implicitly allowed to maintain higher trade barriers. For example, the EU allowed Central European nations to phase out their tariffs on EU exports more slowly than the EU did on Central European exports. Likewise, the implementation of the US-Mexico FTA allowed Mexico to maintain higher tariffs during the transition to free trade. This was not an explicit element of the agreement, but rather a result of initial conditions. The US-Mexico FTA entails staged tariffs cuts with each stage reducing tariff levels by a specified percentage. Although these percentage cuts are the same for the US and Mexico, Mexican duties remain higher than US duties until duty-free trade is reach because Mexican tariffs on US exports were initially four times higher (on average) than US tariffs against Mexican exports.

The spirit of such asymmetry (large rich nations maintaining lower barriers than poor small nations) can also be found quite explicitly in the Generalized System of Preference, the Lomé Convention, and the Caribbean Basin Initiative, *inter alios*. Even multilateral trade negotiations, such as the Uruguay and Tokyo Rounds implicitly embrace asymmetry since the formula-approach to tariff cutting adopted in these rounds implies *de facto* asymmetry. The formula approach stipulates that negotiating nations will lower their tariff averages by an agreed percentage, e.g. by 30%. Since poor nations typically have much higher levels of protection on manufactured goods than do rich nations (see Table 2), an equal percentage cut allows the poor nations to maintain higher levels of protection before and after the liberalization.

Given that the Asian economies vary quite widely in size, it would seem natural that such asymmetric liberalization schemes were considered.

Redressing Hub-and-Spoke: Multilateralize the FTAs

This sort of phenomenon has been going on for a very long time. While the spokes generally do nothing about it, there have been exceptions. Perhaps the most important being the now nearly defunct European Free Trade Association formed in 1960 in reaction to the formation of the European Economic Community (as it was called then). Here is the story.

During the 1950s, many Western European leaders wanted to press ahead with closer regional integration as a means of forever leaving inter-European wars behind them. Some nations wanted this to be a loose free trade area; others wanted it to evolve into a full-blown political union. The latter eventually went ahead and signed the Treaty of Rome. This established what is now the European Union. The other Western European democracies reacted by forming their own club – the European Free Trade Association, which initially included Great Britain. But instead of relying on bilateralism, they formed one big free trade area for industrial goods. More importantly, when they did decide to liberalize trade with the EU (EEC at the time), they did so together so as to avoid the marginalizing effects of hub-and-spoke bilateralism.

The story of NAFTA has a similar ending. NAFTA was the idea of Canada, not the US or Mexico. Canada did not want to be one spoke around the US's hub, so it asked for and was granted a FTA with Mexico. And, if Chile joins NAFTA, it too will avoid the pitfalls of bilateralism.

Given the logic of hub-and-spoke marginalization and the examples of NAFTA and EFTA, it would seem wise to soon consider an association of free trade agreements in Asia that would build on bilateral FTAs with Japan.

Admittedly, this will be difficult. ASEAN members are politically and economically quite heterogeneous, and intra-AFTA trade is not overwhelming. Additionally, ASEAN members vary greatly in the composition of their exports (industrial versus agriculture goods, for instance) and in their current levels of protection. Consequently, going to zero tariffs on substantially all goods will entail very asymmetric - and therefore politically difficult - 'concessions' in terms of both tariff-cutting and 'winning and losing' sectors. Finally, it is probable that several ASEAN countries just could not accept the restriction that tariffs go to zero, as Article 24 of the GATT demands. Some of these nations just do not believe that free trade on the import side can be consistent with their development strategies.

8. Concluding Remarks

The 1997 Financial Crisis in East Asia was a traumatic event for policy makers used to decades of double-digit growth. As happens so often in contexts ranging from school exams to army training, the shared adversity in 1997 seems to have created human bonds among East Asian policy makers that were hereto inexistent. It also seems to have created a renewed awareness of the geographic reality of East Asia. These factors and many more have lead to a wave of free trade agreements being announced, or at least envisaged. In this paper I argue that East Asia regionalism has not really taken off yet, but an FTA between Japan and any other major country in the region may well trigger a domino effect that could result in the formation of a real East Asian trade bloc. On the whole, I think such a bloc would foster multilateral liberalization.

REFERENCES

Baldwin, R. and A. Venables. 1995. "Regional economic integration." In G. Grossman and R. Rogoff eds. *Handbook of international economics.* Amsterdam: North Holland.

Baldwin, R. E. 1997. "The causes of regionalism." *The World Economy*, Vol. 20, No, 7, pp. 865-888.

________. 1994. *Towards an integrated Europe*. London: CEPR.

________. 1993. "A domino theory of regionalism." NBER WP 4465. Published as: Baldwin, R. E. (1995), "The domino theory of regionalism." In Baldwin, Haaparanta and Kiander eds. *Expanding membership of the European Union.* Cambridge: Cambridge University Press.

Baldwin, R. E. and R. E. Baldwin. 1996. "Alternative approaches to the political economy of endogenous trade liberalization." *European Economic Review*, 40, pp: 7775-782.

Bhagwati, J and A. Krueger. 1995. *The dangerous drift to preferential trade agreements*. Washington D.C.: American Enterprise Institute.

Davis, D. and D. Weinstein. 2002. "Market access, economic geography and comparative advantage: An empirical assessment." *Journal of International Economics.*

Fujita, M., Krugman P. and A. Venables. 1999. *The Spatial Economy: Cities, Regions and International Trade*. Cambridge : MIT Press.

Krugman, P. 1980. "Scale economies, product differentiation, and the pattern of trade." *American Economic Review* 70, pp: 950-959.

Summers, L. 1991. "Regionalism and the world trading system." In L. Summers ed. *Policy implications of trade and currency zones.* Federal Reserve Bank of Kansas City.

CHAPTER 10

EU'S STRATEGY TOWARDS EAST ASIAN INTEGRATION AND REGIONALISM

SUNG-HOON PARK

1. INTRODUCTION

East Asia has long been immune to the ever-increasing worldwide tendency towards regionalism. In fact, with the greatest majority of WTO member countries on average maintaining 1.2 regional trading agreements (RTAs), such as free trade areas (FTAs) and customs unions (CUs), three major East Asian countries – China, Japan and Korea – do not have any RTAs in force yet. This prompted Scollay (2001) and Park (2001) to call this region "empty box" and "white spot" in the geography of regionalism, respectively. However, East Asia has recently, and especially since the 1997 Asian Financial Crisis, become very much keen to its own regional integration projects. Currently, more than twenty RTA initiatives, in which East Asian countries are involved, are under discussion and partly under serious negotiation. With this increasing possibility for East Asian trade blocs – in one form or another – to be established in a foreseeable future, major trading nations have become alerted. The United States, a country that maintains the strongest economic and political ties with the majority of countries in the region, and the European Union, a group of European developed countries that had several colonies in East Asia, seemingly have been competing to increase their profile and presence in the region.

The European Union, in particular, has been pursuing the so-called 'New Asia Strategy (NAS)' since 1994, thereby trying to catch up the predominant position of the US. More recently, the launch of ASEM in 1996 as the first official summit meeting between Asia and Europe, and upgrading of the NAS in 2001 have marked an important turning point in EU's external economic relations with East Asia. Especially, the ASEM process on one hand and the Asian financial crisis on the other seem to have contributed to increasing awareness in East Asia of positive impacts of regional dialogues and integration projects.

This paper aims at discussing the strategy of the European Union towards this relatively new phenomenon. The remainder of the paper is structured as follows. Section II discusses the status and importance of East Asia in the hierarchy of EU's external economic relations, and Section III overviews the main contents of EU's

C. Y. Ahn et al (eds.), *East Asian Economic Regionalism*, 175-191.

NAS concept. Section IV sketches, then, the current economic exchanges between the EU and East Asia, focusing on trade and investment, in order to show why the EU has been keenly interested in main changes taking place in East Asia. These first three sections will serve as a background discussion for the following sections. Section V then provides an updated overview of what with regards to economic integration and regionalism is under way in East Asia. Section VI elaborates on the strategy of the EU towards increasing regionalist tendency in East Asia. Section VII summarizes the preceding discussions and draws main conclusions.

2. EAST ASIA IN THE HIERARCHY OF EU'S EXTERNAL ECONOMIC RELATIONS

2.1. Characteristics and Hierarchy of EU's External Economic Relations

The external economic relations, and especially the common commercial policy (CCP), of the European Union can be characterized by several features, of which the following two seem by far the most important ones: (1) the sole competence of the European Commission, and (2) an extensive use of Article XXIV of GATT in approaching non-member countries. As for the sole competence of the European Commission, it is widely recognized that the progress of European integration from FTA-like three Communities established during the 1950s[1] over the Customs Union in the 1960s and finally to the Common Market in the 1980s prompted the European Union to adopt the CCP, which in turn became the European Commission. Also, the Article XXIV of GATT sets requirement for any Customs Union to adopt the Common External Tariff (CET) system.[2] With regards to EU's extensive use of the GATT Article XXIV, it is noticeable that the EU has been implementing a complex system of preferential trading arrangements for a long time.

The preferential trading arrangements that the EU is involved in are plenty and complex in the reality, as is shown in Figure 1. Figure 1 clearly shows that currently the European Union attaches to the Central and Eastern European Countries (CEECs), which are in the process of accession to the EU since the beginning of the 1990s, highest priority in its external trade relations. The Europe Agreements with the CEECs and the following official negotiation with them for their accession to the EU constituted the procedural and legal basis for the EU to treat these countries most favorably among its trading partners. A second-most favorable trading partner for the EU member states are the member countries of European Free Trade Association (EFTA) member countries, which entered into a common market agreement with the EU effective in 1993.[3] With the countries in the African,

[1] The three Communities – the European Coal and Steel Community (ECSC), the European Atomic Energy Community (EURATOM), and the European Economic Community (EEC) – were established based on Treaty of Paris and Treaty of Rome that went into force in 1953 and 1957, respectively. See Nicoll and William (2001) and Pelkmans (1997).

[2] The corresponding provision of the GATT Article XXIV, Par. 8(a)(i) reads "...substantially the same duties and other regulations of commerce are applied by each of the members of the union to the trade of territories not included in the union."

[3] The common market between the EU and EFTA is called the European Economic Area (EEA). Most of

Caribbean and Pacific region that were former colonies of EU member states, and Mediterranean countries, as well as remaining developing countries enjoying specific preferences in acceding the EU markets,[4] the OECD countries not included in any other special agreements with the EU are ranked as "normal traders" with the EU in the sense that for them the MFN tariff rates are applied. The EU also maintains discriminating trade regime for products originating from selected state-trading countries, such as Cuba and North Korea.

Figure 1. Preferential Trading Arrangements of the EU: A Pyramid Analysis

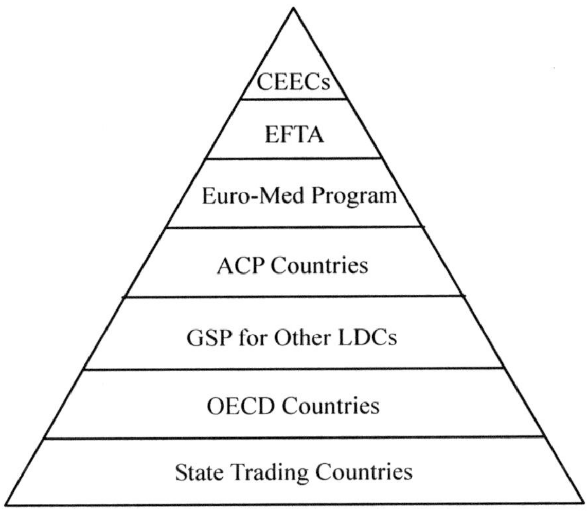

Note: Modified and updated based on a diagram provided in Pelkmans (1997)

2.2. *The Status of Asian Countries in EU's Preferential Trading Regime*

A brief overview of Figure 1 documents in a succinct manner that no Asian country, unless they are beneficiaries of the GSP scheme of the EU that are generally provided to developing countries, is enjoying any substantial preferences in trading with the EU member states. Also, Asian countries such as Japan and Korea that are member countries of the OECD have normal trading relations with the EU. In fact, the wide-ranging and complex system of EU's preferential trading regime results in a very small number of countries that are not enjoying any preferences in trading with the EU: among the member countries of the WTO only the US, Canada, New Zealand, Australia, Korea and Japan belong to this unprivileged group.[5]

the EFTA countries, except Switzerland and Norway, ratified the EEA agreement. In this respect, the EFTA lost its relevance in the world trading system considerably.

[4] These three groups of countries are provided preferential access to the EU markets based on Lome convention, Euromed Program, and GSP scheme, respectively. For a more detailed discussion, see McDonald & Dearden (1994), especially Ch. 1.

[5] It is to be noted that in 1996 Korea "graduated" from the GSP scheme of the EU, which the country had

Coming back to the status of Asian countries in the preferential trading regime of the European Union, one distinguished feature deserves our attention in the context of this conference, which Figure 1 and recent EU strategies reveal: the EU appears to prefer inter-regional rather than inter-national relations in doing trade with other countries and regions. This can be explained – in addition to EU's revealed preferences provided to ACP and Mediterranean countries – by the increasing number of FTA agreements that the EU has been negotiating with other regions: the EU agreed with MERCOSUR upon establishing an FTA by 2005, the EU had also been pondering on establishing an FTA with North America in the name of TAFTA (Transatlantic Free Trade Area) before the idea was discarded and replaced by the Transatlantic Economic Partnership (TEP) initiative launched in 1998.

That East Asia shows a relatively low profile in this wide-ranged and complex system of EU's preferential trading regime maybe due to the predominance of the US in the economic and political, as well as security relations of the Asian countries. This, in turn, served as a background of the initiative to launch an official link between the two parties, thus filling the "missing link" between Europe and Asia in an increasingly tri-polar world economy. The Asia-Europe Meeting (ASEM), which was inaugurated in 1996 in the form of summit meeting between the EU and 10 Asian countries (ASEAN + China, Japan and Korea), might be regarded as a main achievement of this effort.

3. MAIN ELEMENTS OF EU'S NEW ASIA STRATEGY

In the analysis of EU's approach towards East Asia in general and East Asian regionalism in particular, a detailed discussion of the New Asia Strategy (NAS) of the EU appears to be enormously important. The NAS, which was adopted in 1994 and revised and upgraded in 2001, was developed in the midst of deepening European integration and prolonged UR negotiations. In some sense, with the NAS, the EU had been preparing for the governance of world economy after these two major events.

The original NAS strategy identifies the Asian region as a group of some of the most dynamic countries that have the potential to lead the 21st century world economic growth and development. Dividing the Asian countries into three subgroups – Northeast Asia, Southeast Asia and South Asia – the strategy paper issued by the European Commission elaborates on ways and modalities to promote the presence of European firms and influence in Asia.[6] Especially, the NAS strategy focuses on the East Asian sub-group – comprising of Southeast and Northeast Asia – as major cooperation partner for the EU. In this regard, it is noteworthy that before and after the adoption of the NAS the European Union had adopted several strategy papers for relations with individual East Asian countries. Table 1 provides an overview of EU's NAS and other individual country strategy papers and their main contents.

long been a beneficiary of.

[6] The follow-up NAS concept paper of the EU, which was adopted in 2001, includes Australasia (Australia and New Zealand) as an additional sub-region of East Asia. See European Commission (2001).

Table 1. Main Contents of NAS and Country Strategy Papers adopted by the EU during 1993 – 1996[7]

Date of Issue	Country/ Region	Main Contents
August 1993	Korea1)	- Welcomes democratization and market opening - Expects to promote bilateral economic relations that are not matching the economic powers of the two countries - Wants to establish equal partnership
July 1994	Asia2)	- Wants to participate in the market expansion in Asia that has the potential to become the growth-center of the world economy - Specifies differentiated strategy towards three sub-groups (East, southeast and South Asia) in the region - Wants to promote the presence of EU firms and products
March 1995	Japan3)	- Wants to maintain and strengthen the existing economic and political dialogue channels - Making efforts to dismantle barriers to market access - Continuing Trade Assessment Mechanism and Cooperating in Respecting the WTO Rules
July 1995	China4)	- Strengthening the support for China in transition - Supporting the Chinese accession to the WTO - Promoting EU firms market and investment access to China
June 1996	ASEAN5)	- Taking part in the dynamism of ASEAN economies - Enhancing the direct investment into ASEAN countries - Upgrading the bilateral relationship

Note: 1) European Commission (1993).
2) European Commission (1994).
3) European Commission (1995a).
4) European Commission (1995b).
5) European Commission (1996a).

It is in this context important to note the timing of this series of EU's strategy papers towards the new relationship with Asia: until the beginning of the 1990s, the EU did not have enough energy and resources to design and implement a new-generation external economic strategy due to the strong involvement in internal integration and external trade policy programs. Internally, the EU finally completed the 1992 Program to officially launch a Single European Market, allowing goods, services and various factors of production including capital and labor to move freely within the EU territory. And externally, the EU had been in clinch with the US and then GATT contracting parties to negotiate the liberalization package in the Uruguay Round of multilateral trade liberalization under the auspices of GATT, which took place in 1986-1993. With these programs completed in the beginning of 1990s, the EU started taking a proactive stance in its external economic relations, leading eventually to a stronger-than-ever attention to the Asian region.

In reality, East Asia had been attracting increasing interest from the international

[7] Translated from Park (1998).

community, especially since the mid 1980s. Around that time, four East Asian countries – Korea, Singapore, Taiwan and Hong Kong – had emerged as newly industrialized countries (NICs), which enabled them to be called as Asian Tigers (Dragons). Also, many Southeast Asian countries began liberalizing their trade and investment regime, which led to increasing influx of FDI into the region, which in turn contributed to a dynamic economic growth. In addition, the region also experienced major policy changes in the economy that possesses the biggest population – China. The open-door policy and economic reform in China, as well, contributed to enhancing the overall strategic value of the whole region. In summary, the East Asian region had been regarded as "miracle economies", as the World Bank noted in its study of growth potential of the East Asian countries.[8] All these recent developments prompted major trading nations to take a more proactive approach in their bilateral and inter-regional relations with East Asia as a whole, on the one hand, and individual countries in the region, on the other. The adoption by the EU of the NAS was one example of this new development in the 1990s.

It is also noteworthy that the EU in its NAS strategy paper acknowledges the unique and predominant role of the United States in the area of regional security in East Asia. Thus, the EU's new approach towards East Asia can be interpreted as a stronger focus on the economic relationship rather than political and security cooperation. This might be the reason why the European Union – in almost all official documents on EU-East Asia relations – put the political agenda as the first-mentioned and therefore the most immediate area of cooperation.[9]

4. MAIN FEATURES OF RECENT EU-EAST ASIA ECONOMIC RELATIONS

Even though East Asia has not been treated preferentially by the EU, as discussed above in detail, it goes without saying that the region has been an important trading partner for most of the European Union member states. East Asia, with Japan, China and Korea being major regional economic powers, has long been "engine of world economic growth", and most observers believe it will continue in the 21st century despite a temporary backlash due to 1997 Asian Financial Crisis. A careful analysis of recent EU-East Asia trade (Table 2) and investment relations (Table 3) reveals several interesting characteristics.

First, as Table 2 shows, Asia as a whole, including Australasia,[10] has accounted for about one fourth of EU exports to non-EU countries in 1995, of which a lion's share of EU's exports to Asia has been directed to East Asian countries (sub-divided into Northeast and Southeast Asia). It is noteworthy that in the same year, the EU exports to Asia exceeded the EU exports to NAFTA member countries. In fact, it

[8] World Bank (1993).

[9] European Commission (2001), for example, identifies "... strengthening the EU's political and economic presence across the region, and raising this to a level commensurate with the growing global weight of an enlarged EU" as core objectives in its relationship with Asia.

[10] The EU recently uses the term 'Australasia' to group Australia and New Zealand as part of Asia, and devotes a special chapter in its upgraded new Asia strategy (NAS). For more details, see Chapter III of the paper.

was observed that the Asia has become a more weighted trading partner for the EU since the beginning of 1990s. A sharp decrease in Asia's share in EU's export destination, which is manifested in Table 1, is mainly due to the Asian Financial Crisis and unexpectedly strong economic performance of the US. A remarkable economic performance by China in recent and coming few years, as well as relatively rapid recovery from the crisis in Korea and other crisis-affected Southeast Asian countries are expected to bring this figure back to the trend path observed since the beginning of 1990s.

Table 2. Regional Distribution of EU's Exports (1995/2000)

Region	Share in EU Exports in 1995 (%)	Share in EU Exports in 2000 (%)	Trade Balance in 2000 (Million Euro)
Asia	25.9	*21.1*	*-121,509*
(NEA)	(15.0)	(13.0)	(-96,402)
(ASEAN)	(6.5)	(4.3)	(-29,255)
(South Asia)	(2.2)	(1.9)	(-2,579)
(Australasia)	(2.1)	(1.9)	(6,727)
Europe excluding EU	29.4	30.9	6,671
(Candidate Countries)	(12.3)	(16.1)	(33,403)
(EEA+Switzerland)	(12.2)	(10.5)	(-8,081)
(Others)	(4.9)	(4.3)	(-18,651)
NAFTA	20.6	28.4	43,105
(US)	(18.0)	(24.7)	(34,000)
(Others)	(2.6)	(3.7)	(9,105)
Others	24.1	19.6	-15,394
Total	100.0	100.0	-86,937

Source: EUROSTAT, compacted and rearranged from European Commission (2001).

Second, Asian countries, and East Asian countries in particular are some few trading partners of the EU that could manage to show trade surplus vis-à-vis the EU. In 2000, the EU registered a trade deficit of some 120 billion Euros in trade with Asia, whereas it showed trade surpluses vis-à-vis NAFTA and other European countries. This had and is expected to have some implications for the future EU trade policy towards East Asia, possibly leading to more TBR (trade barriers regulation) cases.[11]

In investment exchanges, Table 3 suggests that Asia is not as strongly represented as in trade relations with the EU. Asia's share in EU's FDI in 1999, 6.8%, does not represent the 'real' importance of the region as EU's investment partner. In fact, the sharp decrease of this figure compared to 1996, can be interpreted as a consequence of 1997 Asian Financial Crisis, considering the fact that the European Commission (2001) reported a continuously increasing share of Asia in EU's FDI statistics.[12] It

[11] The recent shipbuilding dispute between the EU and Korea, for which a WTO panel is established, can be quoted as an example.

[12] The European Commission (2001) reported the corresponding figure for 1995 to be 16.3%, which is substantially higher than the figure in 1999. This figure has reached its peak in 1996, to decrease strongly over the years to 9.8% (1997), 1.6% (1998) and then to 6.8% (1999).

seems that the EU companies during the reported period have been concentrating their investment projects to the NAFTA member countries, considering the weakened absorption capacity of Asian countries and strengthened economic activities in NAFTA region due to then flourishing new economy. In summary, the interests of European companies in the Asian region as their investment destination, which witnessed a strong surge in the beginning of 1990s and resulted in the conceptualization of the EU's New Asia Strategy in 1994, did in fact experience a watershed due to the Asian Financial Crisis.

Table 3. Regional Distribution of EU's Foreign Direct Investment (1996/1999)

Region	Share in 1996 (%)	Share in 1999 (%)
Asia	*21.1*	*6.8*
(NEA)	(9.6)	(6.0)
(ASEAN)	(5.8)	(-0.6)
(Others)	(5.7)	(1.4)
Europe excluding EU	18.7	7.5
(Candidate Countries)	(8.9)	(5.1)
(Others)	(9.8)	(2.4)
NAFTA	39.6	67.5
(US)	(37.4)	(65.6)
(Others)	(2.2)	(1.9)
Others	20.6	18.2
Total	100.0	100.0

Source: EUROSTAT, compacted and rearranged from European Commission (2001).

However, several surveys, including UNCTAD/ICC (1998), suggested that the foreign direct investment into Asia will rebound after a temporary decline, and European investors were relatively more optimistic with the future of Asian economies than other foreign investors. This indicates that the European FDI into Asia would have recovered from the bottom that had been shown during 1998-1999.

Summarizing the discussion in this section, we can draw a temporary conclusion that despite a temporary slowdown of economic exchanges between the EU and East Asia, the latter is expected to remain an important trade and investment partner for the EU. One important consequence of this assessment is that the EU will be keenly interested in and therefore be alerted to important economic and political changes taking place in Asia. An increasing regionalist tendency in East Asia, therefore, is expected to attract the interests of EU companies and policy makers.

5. EAST ASIA'S INCREASING INTERESTS IN ITS OWN REGIONALISM

5.1. Overview of East Asian Trade Integration

The dynamics of export-led development in the East Asian economies and their increasing role in world trade have been extensively studied so far. One of the main conclusions of these analyses is that the East Asian countries' strengthened integration into the world economy was a success factor for their rapid economic development.[13] In pursuing their economic development, the East Asian countries strongly relied upon developed countries' markets in Europe and North America, leading to a relatively weak regional economic integration. As stated before, there are until now no substantial RIAs covering the whole area of East Asia. Thus, the region was long believed to be a model of market-driven economic integration, contrary to the institutionalized or policy-induced ones like the EU or NAFTA. Nevertheless, especially since the mid-1980s there seems to have been several forces that contributed to strengthening economic integration in the region: liberalization of trade and investment regime of many Southeast Asian countries; increasing Japanese FDI into Southeast Asia; strengthening regional economic involvement of Asian NIEs (Newly Industrialized Countries); emergence of China as a new industrial location for many firms originating from the region, etc. As a result, East Asian economic integration, although not institutionalized, has been progressing continuously and reached a relatively high level: Park (2001) reported the intra-regional trade share of East Asia in 2000 to be 41.5%. Also the economic interdependence of the region appears to be at a reasonably high level, compared to such institutionalized RTAs (Regional trading agreements) as the EU, NAFTA and MERCOSUR.[14]

One distinguished feature of the current East Asian economic integration is the fact that Southeast and Northeast Asian countries are very important mutual trade partners: the intra-regional trade share for Southeast and Northeast Asia is around 20% respectively, whereas the same figure for East Asia as a whole reaches the above-mentioned level of 41.5%, implying that the two East Asian sub-regions trade very intensively with each other. In this context, Park (2001) acknowledges the prominent role that such Northeast Asian major economic powers as Japan, China and Korea have been playing in both East Asian economic integration and recent surge in regionalist tendency in the region.

5.2. Regional Integration and Cooperation Arrangements involving East Asia

AFTA and APEC, and since recently ASEM are major regional integration and cooperation arrangements that are currently in operation in East Asia. AFTA started originally as ASEAN, which had long been a security cooperation body in Southeast Asia, and have begun only recently to pursue economic integration programs. It comprises currently 10 member countries located in Southeast Asia, and envisages launching a full-fledged free trade area by 2003. In contrast, APEC was launched in 1989, and consists currently not only of East Asian countries, but also of countries in Pacific-basin, such as the US, Canada, New Zealand and Australia, as well as some

[13] See, for example, World Bank (1993).

[14] Park (2001) defines the intra-regional trade share as share of intra-regional trade in total trade of the countries in the region, and the economic interdependence as the share of intra-regional exports (and/or imports) in the GDP of each country and in the aggregate GDP of the group as a whole. For more details, see Park (2001).

countries in Central and Latin America. APEC adopted an ambitious goal of establishing "free trade in the region" at the latest by 2020. It has, however, had enormous difficulties to achieving this goal. There seems to be a long way to go for APEC to become a regional integration arrangement, such as FTA or Customs Union. The Asia-Europe Meeting, which inaugurated in 1996, has not only economic, but also political and cultural cooperation in its cooperation agenda, and is far from the stage of economic integration. Compared to other regions, especially Europe and the Americas, regional integration arrangements in East Asia with AFTA, which is the only regional setting in East Asia pursuing economic integration, are relatively new and smaller-scaled.

Despite this rather discouraging feature of East Asia in terms of regionalism, it is not to be neglected that the region has been receiving increasing spotlight from the European and North American countries, especially since the beginning of the 1990s. First, when the US designated 17 countries in 1994 as big emerging markets (BEMs) in the world economy, with which the US companies and government would have to strengthen economic ties, 12 of them were Asian countries. Also, the European Union launched an ambitious New Asia Strategy in 1994, with the view of strengthening economic, political and cultural ties with primarily East Asian countries. Even though this enthusiasm has been weakened due to the 1997 Asian Financial Crisis, the potential of East Asia to become the locomotive of world economic growth in the 21st century appears still valid. One of the consequences of this increasing interest of the developed world in the East Asian region is the increasing complexity of economic cooperation and integration networks, as was discussed by the European Commission (2000).

A notable new development that deserves close scrutiny is the increasing interest of East Asian economies in regionalism. Scollay (2001) reported that currently more than 25 regional trading agreements (RTAs) are under discussion and/or negotiation in the Asia-Pacific. Of these more than 25 new proposals, approximately 20 involve East Asian countries. At the center of this increasing East Asian integration/cooperation network stand the Northeast Asian countries, as can be seen from Table 4.

First, as stated in the previous sections, Northeast Asian economies have been playing the role of locomotive in the East Asian economic growth and development, providing markets and investment capitals to the other part of the region. Second, countries in Northeast Asia have been "white spots (empty boxes)" in the current geography of increasing regionalism. And, as they have very recently been pursuing several regional integration agreements with their trading partners within and outside the region, their position in regionalism might change in the coming years. Third, in the inter-regional and inter-continental settings like APEC and ASEM, the NEA countries have been detecting deficiencies in the coordination of their interests and positions, leading to an increasing interest among themselves in intensified regional cooperation and integration. Fourth, the 1997 Asian Financial Crisis awakened their long-sleeping consciousness for regional identity, which partly influenced them to more intensively consider regional integration arrangements.
These developments inevitably led to the establishment of official consultation and research process of NEA-wide regionalism and/or East Asian regionalism, which has recently aired under the heading of "ASEAN + 3", as Bergsten (2001) identifies

and the recent Brunei "ASEAN + 3 Summit Meeting" signifies. It is also noteworthy that China recently announced her readiness to enter into an FTA agreement with ASEAN countries. The question to be answered in this context is whether and how the long-lasting barriers to regionalism in East Asia can be overcome.

Table 4. Inventory of Regional Trading Agreements under Negotiation and/or Discussion Involving East Asian Countries (as of December 2002)

Regional Characteristic	Involved Countries	Form of RTAs	Current Status
Individual NEA Countries + outside East Asia	Korea-Australia	FTA	Study announced
	Japan-Mexico	FTA	Study released July 2000
	Korea-Mexico	FTA	Discussion reported
	Japan-Canada	FTA	Studies commissioned
	Korea-Chile	FTA	Agreement signed
	Japan-Chile	FTA	Study reported
NEA-internal	Korea-Japan	FTA	Study completed
	Korea-Japan-China	FTA	Studies being done
NEA + SEA (individual/collective)	ASEAN + 3	FTA	Study to be done
	Singapore-Japan	FTA	Agreement signed
	Singapore-Korea	FTA	Discussion reported
	China-ASEAN	FTA	Negotiations to begin
	Japan-ASEAN	FTA	Study reported
SEA-related	Singapore-US	FTA	Talks began
	Singapore-Canada	FTA	Talks announced
	Singapore-Chile	FTA	Exploratory talks announced
	Singapore-New Zealand	FTA	Study completed
	P5 (US/AUS/Chile/NZ/SING)	FTA	Informal discussion
	New Zealand-Hong Kong	FTA	Talks began
	AFTA-CER	FTA	High-level task force established

Source: Rearranged from Scollay (2001). Recited and updated from Park (2001)

Whether or not the countries in East Asia will be successful in launching their own regionalism covering the whole East Asian region will primarily depend on their capacity to resolve and eliminate such barriers as political and security rivalry between China, Japan and Korea, historical legacy from the Japanese colonial ruling during the Second World War, cultural and religious diversities between Northeast and Southeast Asian countries as well as among the individual countries in the region, etc.[15]

[15] For a more detailed discussion, see Park (2001).

6. THE APPROACH OF THE EU TOWARDS EAST ASIAN ECONOMIC INTEGRATION AND REGIONALISM

6.1. EU's Basic Strategy towards Regionalism

The EU enjoys the longest history of post-war regional economic integration. Also, EU's experiences with deepening regional integration – beginning from the three economic communities in the 1950s and customs union in the 1960s over the common market in the 1990s, and finally to the adoption and circulation of the single currency in 1999 and 2002 – do not have any comparable precedence in the history of world economy. In addition to her experience with regionalism, the EU also maintains a diverse and complex relationship with other regional integration arrangements and countries. As the EU has been in the process of enlarging its economic territory to central and eastern European countries for quite awhile, the EU has been most frequently resorting to the GATT Article XXIV, which is one of the three basic rules governing regionalism in the multilateral trading system. With regionalism, which in principle violates the non-discrimination principle of the multilateral trading system, having potential conflicts with the latter, the basic approach of the EU can be regarded as "ambiguous". On the one hand, the EU has continued its integration agenda for the last forty and more years, leading sometimes to strong criticisms from its major trading partners. This led the EU to take a relatively defensive position with regards to GATT Article XXIV. On the other hand, the EU also has to defend its interest in the midst of increasing regionalism in other parts of the world. In the context of economic integration, main issues of concern are trade diversion, which in pure economic sense should be minimized but in the reality is tolerated in the spirit of the GATT Article XXIV. In this respect, the EU increasingly takes an offensive position.[16]

As the most progressed form of regionalism that most frequently resorts to GATT Article XXIV, the EU intends to use the FTA agreements with potential partners as a tool to convey "a clear political message... with regarding its importance for the Union...."[17]. Also, the EU appears to acknowledge that conclusion of FTAs requires shorter-term and longer-term economic effects,[18] and strategic considerations of a political nature.[19] In addition, the EU recently proclaims that it favors open regionalism,[20] which the EU interprets the FTAs being consistent with the WTO rules.[21]

In short, the EU's basic strategy towards regionalism appears to show the

[16] See, for example, Nagarajan (1998).

[17] Cited from European Commission (1996b).

[18] These short- and long-term effects of FTAs are extensively discussed by, inter alia, Robson (1997) and empirically assessed by Cheong et al. (2002) at the example of Korea-Japan bilateral FTA.

[19] European Commission (1996b).

[20] For instance, the European Commission (1996b) asserts that the EU has consistently favored open regionalism. Also, in the context of the ASEM Summits, the Chairman's Declarations assure the preference of the both parties of open regionalism.

[21] See European Commission (1996), p. 2.

following characteristics. First, as is discussed many times in this paper, the EU has been extensively utilizing regionalism – such as FTAs and customs union – in its external economic relations. This is manifested in the statistics on regionalism compiled by the WTO (2000). Therefore, the apparently strong regionalist tendency in the world economy since the mid 1980s seems to have been strongly influenced by regionalism in which the EU is involved. Second, the EU has been approaching regionalism with an ambivalent strategic concept. On the one hand, the EU resorts extensively to GATT Article XXIV, in order to deepen and enlarge its own regionalism. On the other hand, the EU wants to strengthen the monitoring and investigating activities of GATT/WTO, with the final view to making other regionalism consistent to the WTO rules. In this respect, the EU has been searching for and criticized several cases – such as NAFTA – through which the interests of EU economies have been negatively affected.[22]

6.2. EU's Approach towards East Asian Regionalism

With the basic strategy of the EU towards regionalism being ambivalent, as analyzed in the preceding section, there seems to be no clear-cut "EU approach" towards East Asian regionalism. As far as the author is informed, there exist no official documents of the EU regarding East Asian regionalism. However, there are several academic and semi-academic discussion papers through which we can discuss the issue in some detail. The following three issues appear to be especially important in understanding the strategy of the European Union towards East Asian regionalism.

A first issue to be elaborated is how the Europeans see the future of East Asia in general, and East Asian integration in particular. For example, Galtung (2001) presented two possible and preferred forms of East Asian future: the EAC (East-Asian Community) and the OSCAP (Organization for Security and Cooperation in Asia/Pacific). His idea seems to be that East Asia can develop into either a fairly economic integration body as was the case in Europe, evolving from FTA via Common Market to the final stage of economic community, or an organization that focuses more on peace and security with a conflict resolution mechanism. In reality, these two scenarios are currently under discussion and serious review.[23] However, as of today no concrete conclusions are visible. No matter which path East Asian countries would ultimately take, Galtung's projection seems to point to the feasibility and necessity that East Asia develop into a community or an integrated organization with centralized power to resolve potential conflicts within the region. If one or another scenario becomes realized, it definitely will enhance the possibility to upgrade the bilateral EU-East Asia relationship to an inter-regional one. However, Galtung, in the same paper, suggests that the East

[22] Nagarajan (1998), for instance, criticizes trade diversion effects due to NAFTA, and sends a message that the corresponding WTO rules be made more stringent to avoid such impacts.

[23] The official establishment of "ASEAN+3" as a summit meeting, and elaboration of security issues as an agenda of APEC can serve as examples. See, for example, Song (2001).

Asian countries might face 'unfortunate mechanism' at work, which will make the integration project difficult: the reluctant United States. Therefore, to devise a mechanism to weaken the US resistance will be instrumental in both of these two alternatives. In contrast to Galtung, Markku (2001) acknowledged higher feasibility of developing Northeast Asian regionalism – both economic and political. He, in particular, regards big (strategic) cultural differences between Northeast and Southeast Asia, common historical background and complementary economies as main shaping factors for the Northeast Asian regionalism.

A second issue to be clarified in this context is whether the EU in approaching East Asia prefers to maintain an inter-regional or inter-national relationship. In the light of the launch of ASEM, this question was discussed in some circles. With the main function of ASEM being to fill the "missing link" between the two regions – East Asia and Europe – some Asian scholars analyzed that the ASEM basically has to promote inter-regional cooperation scheme.[24] In contrast, European scholars, noting the wide gap in the stage, coverage and scope of economic integration between the two, tend to see ASEM in the current structure as a basically inter-national cooperation framework.[25] A recent speech by Chris Patten, the EU Commissioner for external relations, provides also an influential EU view on this issue: "It is absurd to think of a single relationship between EU and a region as diverse as Asia". Though this is not the official position of the EU, a remarkable gap in the ways of seeing the Asia-Europe relations can be identified. Despite this gap between the Asian and European perspective of future bilateral relationship, it seems clear that with increasing possibility of East Asian regionalism as discussed by Galtung (2001) and Markku (2001), the possibility of establishing an inter-regional Asia-Europe relationship increases. This might prompt and help the EU to adopt a single relationship with Asia.

In case East Asian countries succeed in establishing an EAC-like regional integration arrangement, be it for the whole East Asian region or Northeast Asian sub-region, a third fundamental issue arises as to which level the bilateral economic relationship could be evolved to. The Asia-Europe Vision Group (1999), for instance, recommends in its official report the establishment of an FTA for ASEM member countries by 2025. Even though this recommendation did not receive positive response from the official track of ASEM, it is worth some more elaboration. First, the timing is well-placed, in the sense that by 2025 APEC would have completed its agenda to establish "free trade in the region" as stipulated in the Bogor Declaration and the worldwide trade barriers would be lowered substantially, which have led developing members of ASEM – especially East Asian ones – to higher readiness to accept liberalization within the inter-regional context. Second, the idea also takes into consideration the ever-intensifying institutional arrangements among the three big economic centers of the world economy: North America, Europe and Asia. The

[24] See, for example, Park (1996).

[25] For example, Köllner (2000) clearly favors the Asia-Europe relations as an inter-national process. Also, Brittan (1996) seems to implicitly support this view by saying that the ASEM process should not become a bureaucratic process.

proposed Asia-Europe FTA would possibly be followed by the much discussed TEP-TAFTA (Transatlantic Economic Partnership – Transatlantic Free Trade Area) and/or APEC-wide FTA, which links Asia and North America. Another possibility is that the discussion of Asia-Europe FTA would strengthen those already existing ties between Asia and North America (APEC) and between Europe and North America (TEP-TAFTA). No matter which path the bilateral Asia-Europe relationship will take in the future, an establishment of East Asian economic community will enhance the possibility and feasibility of promoting inter-regional relationship between Asia and Europe. Maybe this option is what the European Union prefers to pursue in approaching the East Asian region in the long run.

7. CONCLUDING REMARKS

This paper discussed the current status, challenges and opportunities of East Asian economic integration and regionalism, and analyzed the EU's strategy towards this relatively new phenomenon. Based on a detailed discussion of both 1994 and 2001 version of the New Asia Strategy, which the EU adopted officially, and of implications drawn from several papers written by influential European scholars and policy makers, the paper draws following conclusions.

First, especially since the 1997 Asian Financial Crisis, East Asian countries have become keen to establishing their own regionalism. This conclusion is to be supported by the increasing number of official discussions and negotiations on FTA agreements, in which East Asian countries are involved.

Second, to the emergence of this relatively new regionalist tendency in the region the EU seems to have contributed to a substantial extent, especially through the framework of the ASEM process, as the European Commission (2000) so claims.

Third, considering the deepest economic integration that the EU has accomplished over the last four decades, the EU seems to prefer basically inter-regional relationship rather than inter-country relationship when approaching other regions and countries. The inter-regional relationship between Asia and Europe on an advanced level, however, has to wait some time until East Asian countries have had successfully launched their own regional integration arrangements.

Fourth, in light of this basic strategy of the EU and despite the fact that as of today no official documents are available to judge EU's strategy towards East Asia correctly, the visible strategic choice of the EU discussed above – to promote the grouping and inter-relationship among the East Asian countries – can be interpreted that the EU basically wants to establish an inter-regional relationship, rather than inter-country relationship with East Asia.

Fifth, even though inter-regional relationship between Asia and Europe shall be promoted, the EU does not appear to have developed a clear vision in which direction – economic integration or security cooperation – the East Asian integration should go. There are dividing European views on the future shape of East Asian regionalism. As of today, the East Asian counterpart is no better in this regard.

REFERENCES

Asia-Europe Vision Group. 1999. "For a Better Tomorrow: Asia-Europe Partnership in the 21st Century." Report of the AEVG to ASEM leaders.

Brittan, Sir L. 1996. "Asia-Europe Cooperation to Open World Markets." An address delivered at the European Institute for Asian Studies, Brussels, November 28.

Cheong, I. *et al.* 2002. "A Dynamic Analysis of a Korea-Japan Free Trade Area: Simulations with the G-Cubed Asia-Pacific Model." KIEP Working Paper 02-09.

European Commission. 1993. "Relations Between the European Union and the Republic of Korea." Communication from the Commission to the Council. Brussels.

______. 1994. "Towards a New Asia Strategy." Communication from the Commission to the Council, COM(94)314 final. Brussels.

______. 1995a. "Europe and Japan: The Next Steps." Communication from the Commission to the Council, COM(95)73 final, Brussels.

______. 1995b. "A Long-term Policy for China-Europe Relations." Communication from the Commission, COM(95)279 final, Brussels.

______. 1996a. "New Dynamic in EU-ASEAN Relations." Communication from the Commission to the Council, the European Parliament and the Economic and Social Committee, Final Text, Brussels.

______. 1996b. "Free Trade Areas: An Appraisal." Communication from the Commission to the Council, Brussels.

______. 2000. "Perspectives and Priorities for the ASEM Process into the New Decade." Commission Working Document, COM(2000)241 final. (April).

______. 2001. "Europe and Asia: A Strategic Framework for Enhanced Partnerships." Communication from the Commission, COM(2001)469 final. (September).

Galtung, J. 2001. "East Asian Integration and the West European Model." In Pape, W. ed. *Models of Integration in Asia and Europe: Generating Public Space for Our Common Future.* Forward Studies Unit, European Commission.

Köllner, P. 2000. "Comparison of ASEM and APEC Process: Setting Agenda for ASEM in the 21st Century." A paper presented at the international conference on "Asia-Europe in a Global Economy" Co-hosted by the Korea Economic Association, the EU Studies Association of Korea, and the Korea-German Economic Association, on September 1-2, 2000, in Seoul, Korea.

Markku, H. 2001. "The Case of Northeast Asia." In Pape, W. ed. *Models of Integration in Asia and Europe: Generating Public Space for Our Common Future.* Forward Studies Unit, European Commission.

McDonald, F. & S. Dearden. 1994. *European Economic Integration.* Longman, 2nd edition.

Nagarajan, N. 1998. "Regionalism and the WTO: New Rules for the Game?" European Commission, Economic Papers No. 128, June.

Nicoll, Sir W. and T. C. Salmon. 2001. *Understanding the European Union.* Longman.

Park, S. 1996. "Economic Implications of the Asia-Europe Meeting (ASEM)." A paper presented at the international conference on "Towards a New Partnership Between Asia and Europe: Implications and Prospects of the Asia-Europe Meeting." Hosted by KIEP on February 9, 1996 in Seoul, Korea.

______. 1999. "Perspective of Long-term Economic Relations between Asia and Europe and the Strategy of Korea." *Korea Journal of EU Studies*, Vol. 4, No. 1, pp. 42-71. (in Korean)

______. 2001. "East Asian Economic Integration and Regionalism: Finding a Balance between Regionalism and Multilateralism." *Korea Review of International Studies*, Vol. 4, No. 1.

Patten, C. 2002. "The Relationship between the EU and Asia – One or Many?" A speech held at Chatham House on September 6, 2002.

Pelkmans, J. 1997. "European Integration: Methods and Economic Analysis." Netherlands Open University.

Scollay, R. 2001. "New Regional Trading Arrangements in the Asia-Pacific Region." A paper presented at the 2001 APEC Study Center Consortium Conference on "APEC: Heading Towards New Century and Bright Future." Held on May 18-20, 2001, in Tianjin, China.

Schott, Jeffrey J. 2004. "Free Trade Agreements: Boon or Bane of the World Trading System?" in *Free Trade Agreements: US Strategies and Priorities.* Jeffrey J. Schott. Institute for International Economics, Washington D.C., p. 6.

Song, X. 2001. "From Open Regionalism to Institutional Stability?" In: Wolfgang Pape ed. *Models of Integration in Asia and Europe: Generating Public Space for Our Common Future.* Forward Studies Unit, European Commission.

UNCTAD/ICC. 1998. "The financial crisis in ASIA and Foreign Direct Investment." Full report. Mimeograph.

The World Bank. 1993. "The East Asian Miracle: Economic Growth and Public Policy." Oxford University Press.

The World Trade Organization. 2000. "Mapping of Regional Trade Agreements." Committee on Regional Trade Agreements, WT/REG/W/41. October

NAME INDEX

Printed in the United States
87314LV00003B/230/A

9 780387 243306